D0368665

BAKHTIN

BAKHTIN

Essays and Dialogues on His Work

Edited by Gary Saul Morson

The University of Chicago Press
CHICAGO AND LONDON

The articles in this volume originally appeared in the following issues of *Critical Inquiry*:
Summer 1981, vol. 7, no. 4; September 1982, vol. 9, no. 1; December 1983, vol. 10, no.
2; and June 1985, vol. 11, no. 4.

The University of Chicago Press, Chicago 60637
The University of Chicago Press, Ltd., London

Library of Congress Cataloging in Publication Data
Main entry under title:

Bakhtin, essays and dialogues on his work.

    Articles in this volume originally appeared in
Critical inquiry, summer 1981, v. 7, no. 4; Sept. 1982,
v. 9, no. 1; Dec. 1983, v. 10, no. 2; and June 1985,
v. 11, no. 4.
    Bibliography: p.
    Includes index.
    1. Bakhtin, M. M. (Mikhail Mikhaïlovich), 1895–1975—
Addresses, essays, lectures.   2. Philology—Addresses,
essays, lectures.   I. Morson, Gary Saul, 1948-
P85.B22B35 1986   801'.95'0924   85-24624
ISBN 0-226-54132-0
ISBN 0-226-54133-9 (pbk.)

Contents

Preface: Perhaps Bakhtin

Je m'en vais chercher un grand peut-être. . . .
—RABELAIS, *alleged last words*

The "great perhaps": Rabelais' words evoke the central value of Mikhail Bakhtin's life and work—openness, the potential for *surprise*. In commenting about language or literature, history or psychology, Bakhtin continually sought and found unexpected ways to show that people never utter a final word, only a penultimate one. The opportunity always remains for appending a qualification that may lead to yet another unanticipated dialogue. Humanity is defined by its "unfinalizedness" [*nezaveršennost'*]. Whether existence is wholly determined or partially free, whether knowledge is possible or impossible, we retain the capacity to surprise ourselves and others. No knowledge is more valuable than an awareness of that capacity, and freedom can have no richer meaning.

Perhaps this underlying value suggests the reason for Bakhtin's current and surprising popularity. Only a decade or so ago, Bakhtin was but an obscure Russian critic, known (by a few) as the author of an overstated if brilliant book on Dostoevsky and a still more idiosyncratic study of Rabelais. It has now become evident that he was either partial author, or at least a key source of ideas, for several other important works, published under other names and (also until recently) largely forgotten: V. N. Vološinov's *Marxism and the Philosophy of Language* and *Freudianism: A Critique* and P. N. Medvedev's *The Formal Method in Literary Scholarship*, as well as several essays. In 1975, shortly before Bakhtin's death, a collection of over a half-century of Bakhtin's writings appeared in the Soviet Union. In 1981, Michael Holquist and Caryl Emerson published their translation of four of the essays on the novel from that collection.[1] That book, *The Dialogic Imagination*, has begun to appear in footnotes almost as often and inevitably as works by Northrop Frye, Roman Jakobson, or Jacques Derrida once did (or still do). In 1979, another collection of Bakhtin's writings, also spanning his entire intellectual life, came out in Russian. This volume, too, is currently being translated, and two excerpts from it are offered in the present volume.[2]

These newly available works produced revised impressions of Bakhtin's studies of Dostoevsky and Rabelais. *Problems of Dostoevsky's Poetics* was reread as a general contribution to theories of language and the novel and was consequently retranslated with these broader themes in mind; *Rabelais and His World* has also been reissued with an introductory essay by a theorist immersed in contemporary debate.[3]

So intense is the appetite for Bakhtin that defenders of Vološinov's sole authorship of the works published under that name have accused Bakhtinists of biographical imperialism.[4] Both Slavists and non-Slavists have (perhaps inevitably) produced samples of a new critical genre, which we may call "Bakhtin vs. Derrida." We have also seen or may soon expect instances of several other genres—Bakhtin and Marxism, Bakhtin and Freudianism—and articles with titles like "The Poetry of Dialogue and the Dialogue of Poetry," "Heteroglossia and Class Conflict," "Dialogue and Difference," and "Polyphony [or Dialogue, or Carnivalization, or Authorial 'Surplus'] in the works of [fill in the author's name]."

This reception of Bakhtin differs quite markedly from the American reception of earlier Russian theorists. As a rule, Russian scholars who have anticipated American critical debates have been translated at the point when they had little to add and when they could be credited only with a superfluous priority. Early Formalism from the 1910s and 1920s, with its insistence on the autonomy of literary works and literary studies, first became reasonably widely known in America in the 1950s, when New Criticism had long since propounded similar ideas.[5] Later Formalism, with its emphasis on literary history, on the role of the reader, on social institutions, and on the self-conscious development of criticism, came briefly to the fore only in the early 1970s, when its dynamic structuralist model was also no longer a radical innovation. By contrast, Bakhtin enters current debate at a time when post-structuralism has prepared the way but has in no sense exhausted or rediscovered all of his most remarkable insights. This more favorable reception bears a special irony because Bakhtin, unlike the self-demonstrative Formalists, was, if anything, something of a recluse and cared little for the notoriety and excitement of ongoing controversy.

Perhaps the sudden and dramatic interest in Bakhtin arises from his emphasis on debate as open, fruitful, and existentially meaningful at a time when our theoretical writings have become increasingly closed, repetitive, and "professional." As Bakhtin observed toward the end of his life, "[in modern criticism] there is no understanding of evaluative non-predetermination, unexpectedness, as it were, 'surprisingness'" (*E*, p. 370). We have jolted from scientist theories explaining (or explaining away) interpretation to radically relativist ones, skeptical even of skepticism itself. Bakhtin, by contrast, tended to view such opposite positions as equally "finalized," equally closed to surprise, and equally hostile to true dialogue. Genuine dialogue always presupposes that something, but not everything, can be known. "It should be noted," Bakhtin wrote in the Dostoevsky book, "that both relativism and dogmatism equally exclude all argumentation, all authentic dialogue, by making it either unnecessary (relativism) or impossible (dogmatism)" (*P*, p. 69).

Bakhtin's many concepts, neologisms, and theories often contradict each other (and at times themselves), but they share one concern: "surprisingness." "Dialogue," as Ken Hirschkop points out in his essay here, is not only a description of how language does function, but (in a different use of the same word) is also a program for how it should function. Bakhtin offers an ethical imperative for linguistic and all other social behavior: one should address others with a presumption that they are capable of responding meaningfully, responsibly, and, above all, *unexpectedly*. Both dogmatism and relativism, Soviet authoritarianism and what one recent critic has called "the ineffable ennui of hermeneutic narcissism" preclude such a response and so are, in the root sense of the word, irresponsible.[6]

Like dialogue, "carnival" (in Bakhtin's extended sense) serves to expose all dogmatic norms to parody, without, however, replacing them with pure antinomianism. So, too, the "word with a loophole" evokes the potential for the new in all utterances:

A loophole is the retention for oneself of the possibility for altering the ultimate, final meaning of one's own words. . . . This potential other meaning, that is, the loophole left open, accompanies the word like a shadow. Judged by its meaning alone, the word with a loophole should be an ultimate word and it does present itself as such, but in fact it is only the penultimate word and places after itself only a conditional, not a final period. [*P*, p. 233]

Perhaps because of the Soviet milieu in which they were composed, most of Bakhtin's writings stress resistance to dogma and certainty, but he was also aware that radical antidogmatism, whether in the form of epistemic anarchism or of selfhood conceived as "pure function," can be no less threatening. To speak only in loophole words, to write only "under erasure," also makes all formulations predictable, as the fate of Bakhtin's favorite literary example, Dostoevsky's underground man, illustrates.[7] As Shigalyov states in *The Possessed*, "I am perplexed by my own data and my conclusion is a direct contradiction of the original idea with which I start. Starting from unlimited freedom, I arrive at unlimited despotism. I will add, however, that there can be no solution to the social problem but mine."[8]

At the end of his longest discussion of perpetually elusive utterances, Bakhtin (or Vološinov) complains that, in some social arenas, loophole language has "completely overshadowed and relativized an utterance's ideational core." This state of affairs, which has of course progressed even farther among us, raises not only epistemic but profound ethical problems. *Marxism and the Philosophy of Language* thus ends quite differently from *Rabelais and His World*. Rather than celebrate rituals affirming the "joyful relativity" of all things, the author calls for the resurrection of "the word that really means and takes responsibility for what it says."[9]

Two of the contributors to the present volume subject Bakhtin's own description of carnival to just such criticism. In his essay on the "abject hero," Michael André Bernstein offers a "darker reading" of carnival laughter and loophole language.

> I want to begin my own questioning . . . [by] locating not so much a counter-tradition as a negative and bitter strand at the core of the Saturnalia itself. . . . what emerges is the image of a carnivalization of values during which it is no longer a question of breaking down ossified hierarchies and stale judgments but rather of being denied *any* vantage point from which a value can still be affirmed. [P. 100]

The tradition Bernstein traces culminates with Céline, which may serve to warn us that a *swarm* of gadflies may lead to the pestilence of extreme right (and extreme left) obscurantism. Then meaningful dialogue ends; and where there is no dialogue, all is permitted.

In a quite different tone and spirit, Wayne Booth makes a similar point. Discovering a morally objectionable antifeminism in Rabelais, he questions Bakhtin's celebration of Rabelaisian laughter: There are times when we should not laugh, when we should rather interrogate our own laughter, however much it may seek to parody the bar to which it is summoned. Booth's essay proceeds dialogically, as both literature and theory become an occasion for a special kind of ethical self- (and other-) examination. In short, this critique of Bakhtin is itself exemplary of one sort of "dialogic" criticism that Bakhtin favored. In his earliest publication, a two-page credo entitled "Art and Responsibility," Bakhtin asked:

> What is it that guarantees the internal connection among the elements of personality? Only the unity of responsibility. For what I have experienced and understood in art, I must answer with my life, so that everything experienced and understood does not remain inert within it. . . . Art and life are not one, but must become united in me, in the unity of my responsibility. [*E*, pp. 6–7]

The same kind of ethical responsibility (or "answerability," as the word may also be translated) applies to authors as well as readers. And as Holquist develops this point, Bakhtin reminds us that we are all always authors, every time we speak *or* listen, write or read. There is not, must not be, any ethical loophole from the responsibility of dialogue.

In fact, a strong ethical concern informs many of Bakhtin's most daring theses. In explaining the concept of "polyphony," for instance, Bakhtin attributes Dostoevsky's invention of that technique to his concern for representing others as "unfinalized," capable of surprise, and never "coincident" with themselves. For Bakhtin, the relation of "author and hero" (the title of another early study) raises the same moral problems as the relation of each of us to each other. If those problems are to be understood, Bakhtin believed, one must fundamentally reconceive these relations.

As the essays of Emerson, Susan Stewart, and Holquist demonstrate in different ways, perhaps Bakhtin's most radical contribution lies in his rethinking of traditional oppositions: of the individual to society, of self to other, of the specific utterance to the totality of language, and of particular actions to the world of norms and conventions. In his arguments with Freudianism, Marxism, and structuralism, he repeatedly maintained that each of these oppositions is fundamentally untenable, whether the individual is reduced to the social, or the social to the sum of individuals. His constant concern is to show that analytic categories have been mistaken for social facts and that, in fact, apparent opposites are made up of the same material: dialogic "words" (and actions) in the whole complex field of answerability. On the one hand, because thinking necessarily takes the form of socially defined conversations with imagined others, and because concepts of selfhood are themselves cultural products, the psyche is by its very nature social, a "borderline phenomenon." On the other hand, because the social exists only insofar as it is implemented in particular moments of particular people's lives, it is always also individual. In short, Bakhtin did not seek a middle way between traditional binary oppositions; he instead dissolved them—a method that, he believed, provided the only meaningful escape from an endless oscillation between dead abstractions.

The field of answerability is not divided in two, but neither is it whole. Neither culture, nor language, nor the self ever achieves anything like "systematicity" or unity, as the great philosophical systems have variously described them. Quotidian randomness and other "centrifugal" forces intervene. "Heteroglossia" insures the partial asystematicity of language; the inevitably multiple "chronotopes" of daily life insure the diversity of culture; and the often unpredictable dialogues that constitute the self and social interaction create the uniqueness of each utterance and each person. Wholeness and system are never given, only posited; if that were not so, freedom and "unfinalizability" would disappear. Here Bakhtin reflects his debt to the "accursed questions" and questioners of Russian literature: "If we concede that human life can be governed by reason," wrote that committed rationalist Leo Tolstoy, "the possibility of life is destroyed."[10] And as Tolstoy also knew, it is destroyed as well if no meaningful bases for responsibility are allowed. Between the inescapably futile quest to speak in absolute language and an inevitably impoverishing contentment with the everyday flux lies the potential of the most enriching and informative dialogue.

A critical and serious inquiry into Bakhtin's work is clearly in order. This volume contains an article in the form of a dialogue, a dialogue between two interpreters of Bakhtin's achievement, and essays that establish their own dialogic perspectives and methods for developing his ideas. It also includes extracts from two of Bakhtin's articles, presented in English for the first time. In "The Problem of Speech Genres," Bakhtin discusses some factors that stabilize dialogue enough to make it possible; in his "Notes" of 1970–1971, he enters into dialogue with the most interesting theories of modern literary studies, including his own. Taken as a whole, the volume is designed to offer a (dialogic) framework for examining his thought. Bakhtin's numerous and heterogeneous theories provide both new ways to consider fundamental theoretical issues and new methods to respond to particular works. Still more important, perhaps, they project a vision which is also a faith and a guiding assumption: *"nothing conclusive has yet taken place in the world, the ultimate word of the world and about the world has not yet been spoken, the world is open and free, everything is still in the future and will always be in the future"* (*P*, p. 166).[11]

Gary Saul Morson

1. See M. Baxtin, *Voprosy literatury i èstetiki: Issledovanija raznyx let,* ed. S. Lejbovič (Moscow, 1975); the translation of four of this volume's essays on the novel is *The Dialogic Imagination: Four Essays by M. M. Bakhtin,* ed. Michael Holquist, trans. Caryl Emerson and Holquist (Austin, Tex., 1981).

2. See M. M. Baxtin, *Èstetika slovesnogo tvorčestva,* ed. S. G. Bočarov (Moscow, 1979); all further references to this work, abbreviated *E,* will be included in the text and are my own translations. The two extracts presented here are from a forthcoming collection of Bakhtin's essays, *Speech Genres and Other Essays,* ed. Emerson and Holquist, trans. Vern McGee. I would like to thank the translator, the volume editors, and Suzanne Comer and Zora Molitor of the University of Texas Press for their help in securing permission to preprint these excerpts.

3. The first English translation of *Problems of Dostoevsky's Poetics* is by R. W. Rotsel (Ann Arbor, Mich., 1973); the new version is edited and translated by Emerson, Theory and History of Literature Series, vol. 8 (Minneapolis, 1984). All further references to the Emerson edition, abbreviated *P,* will be included in the text. The Emerson edition also includes in its appendices translations of some other Bakhtin texts, as well as an informative glossary, a theoretical preface by Emerson, and a significant introduction by Wayne Booth. I discuss this edition and a number of recent studies of Bakhtin in "The Baxtin Industry," forthcoming in *Slavic and East European Journal* (Spring 1986). Holquist wrote a new "Prologue" to *Rabelais and His World* (Bloomington, Ind., 1984), pp. xiii–xxiii. It should also be noted that the recent reissue of *The Formal Method in Literary Scholarship* (Cambridge, Mass., 1985) includes an excellent theoretical preface by Wlad Godzich.

4. I. R. Titunik has been arguing against Bakhtin's authorship of the "disputed texts" since his preface (written with Neal H. Bruss) to his translation of *Freudianism: A Marxist Critique* (New York, 1976). Most recently, Katerina Clark and Holquist, in *Mikhail Bakhtin* (Cambridge, Mass., 1984) have presented a detailed case for Bakhtin's sole authorship. Titunik replies in a review article forthcoming in *Slavic and East European Journal* (Spring 1986).

5. Victor Erlich's classic study, *Russian Formalism: History–Doctrine* (originally published in 1955) has recently gone into a third edition (New Haven, Conn., 1981) with a new preface by the author. Incidentally, in that preface, Erlich notes: "Were I writing today, I would undoubtedly pause before the achievement of Mikhail Bakhtin . . . " (p. 10).

6. As cited in my commentary to part 3 of *Literature and History: Theoretical Problems and Russian Case Studies,* ed. Gary Saul Morson (Stanford, 1986). Thomas M. Greene's comments, which I cite only in part, reply to criticisms that his paper "History and Anachronism" is itself anachronistic in its nonrelativist approach to texts. The criticisms and Greene's reply were originally made at a conference held at the University of Pennsylvania in 1983; the volume also contains papers by Holquist and by Clark on Bakhtin.

7. See Robert Louis Jackson, "Aristotelian Movement and Design in Part Two of *Notes from the Underground," The Art of Dostoevsky: Deliriums and Nocturnes* (Princeton, N.J., 1981), pp. 171–88. Disputing those (including those following Bakhtin) who have identified Dostoevsky's position too closely with that of the Underground Man, Jackson describes the iron logic that renders the very attempt to escape predictability and finalization utterly predictable.

8. Fyodor Dostoevsky, *The Possessed,* trans. Constance Garnett (New York, 1963), p. 409.

9. V. N. Vološinov, *Marxism and the Philosophy of Language,* trans. Ladislav Matejka and I. R. Titunik (New York, 1973), pp. 158, 159.

10. Leo Tolstoy, *War and Peace,* trans. Ann Dunnigan (New York, 1968), p. 1354 (first epilogue).

11. For a gloss on these lines, see the close of Emerson's preface to Bakhtin, *Problems of Dostoevsky's Poetics,* p. xxxix.

Who Speaks for Bakhtin?

Gary Saul Morson

> Born under all the changeful stars there are.
> —DIDEROT, citing Horace

> I do not know which one of us has written this page.
> —BORGES, "Borges and I"

We had met to write an introduction to a collection of essays on Mikhail Bakhtin's implications for contemporary literary theory. Our conversation, however, seemed to take a direction of its own. Although neither of us intended it, we soon found ourselves arguing about the most fundamental issue on which we differed: the possibility, to use her words, of "a science of literature."

The subject of this science, she explained, would not be texts but, rather, behavior with respect to texts—how they are created and interpreted, transmitted and used. "It would be the science that the Russian Formalists projected but never achieved; the science whose paradigms were first understood by that Formalist heresiarch, Mikhail Bakhtin." Her efforts to transform literary studies into a science always provoke my humanist biases. I involuntarily wince at her use of the word "behavior." She responds, "Behaviorists don't own the word, after all. You know very well I'm not a behaviorist," she adds, "but not out of humanist prejudices. Although they oversimplify human behavior [I would have said "human

---

The first epigraph of this introduction also cites the epigraph to part 4 of Michael André Bernstein's essay, printed below.

1

nature"], at least they do try to study it scientifically and [a faintly perceptible smile] 'responsibly.' " I wasn't sure whether the undue emphasis on her last word alluded to Bakhtin's actively responding listeners or, somewhat self-mockingly, to Pavlov's passively responding dogs.

Our joint editorial project had been, from the start, a complicated one. True, we are both Slavists and had read Bakhtin in Russian. We interpreted particular passages and concepts in his work in much the same way. We both regarded *Marxism and the Philosophy of Language* and *Discourse in the Novel* as his best books. And we both saw his two key themes as dialogue and the suspicion of system. We diverged, however, when we attempted to place Bakhtin in our own conceptual frameworks. Whereas I took his attack on the systematizers as a justification of the humanities, she, a Kuhnian, took it as a paradigm for a truly sophisticated and adequate *science* of culture. "That's the challenge and excitement of the human sciences," she would say, "to find better and better ways of describing behavior that is so often random and uncertain." To Dostoevsky's question, "Is it possible to perceive as an image that which has no image?" she responded, emphatically, yes. If anything, she disliked structuralism, positivism, and "scientific socialism" even more than I did, because, she would say, "scient*ism* gives science a bad name." Perversely, I often defended these -*isms* and even, occasionally, incorporated pieces of them into my own arguments. Her usual reply to these intellectual raids was that "eclecticism is the worst and most characteristic sin of the humanists."

The more we spoke, the more we discovered disagreement behind our agreements and envisaged different implications for the same—or were they the same?—ideas. "I suppose that's what Bakhtin meant when he wrote that agreement, not just disagreement, is a dialogic relationship," she reflected. "Agreement is never identity. It always presupposes or becomes the occasion for differences—which I guess may be one reason why it can be so profitable to agree." I could detect Kuhn's concept of a scientific consensus here but agreed anyway.

It turned out, in fact, that I had hidden disagreements with all the contributors to the collection. I had undertaken the project with the evidently quixotic hope that we could create, in imitation of Bakhtin's eccentric circle of linguists, Marxists, Christians, biologists, and literary theorists, a circle of our own. "You want to be a living allusion," she would say. By the end of that afternoon, however, neither she nor I were confident that we could—despite all the views we did share—ever sign

---

Gary Saul Morson, associate professor and chairman of Slavic languages at the University of Pennsylvania, is the author of *Boundaries of Genre: Dostoevsky's "Diary of a Writer" and the Traditions of Literary Utopia.*

both our names to the same introduction. "Not to be a Formalist," she interrupted, "perhaps it's a question of form . . ."

MOI: . . . You know, the most appropriate form for an article introducing Bakhtin would be a dialogue, since dialogue is his central concept.

ELLE: Of course, if you can speak of a center in a writer so eccentric. How would it begin?

MOI: Well, like *Notes from Underground*, on an ellipsis . . . That would illustrate his idea that all speech is a response to words that have been uttered before, that we never confront a linguistically virgin world, that each utterance is a response to other utterances and is formulated in expectation of a response to it—all that might be developed later on in the dialogue. *Moi* could explain it all to *Elle*.

ELLE: Well, but wouldn't it be more fitting to have *Elle* already know Bakhtin? Otherwise, what you would get is *Moi*'s "monologic" speech, practically treating *Elle* as someone incapable of making an intelligent response or forcing *Moi* to change and develop his own thoughts meaningfully in the process of uttering them. *Elle*—and Why must *Elle* be the one to be spoken *to*, if anyone is?—could dramatize the point that all understanding is active, not passive reception. Understanding, after all, is not a simple act of decoding, as in that well-known telegraphic model of communication—you know, the one that looks like this:

Code

Speaker ----------------→ Listener

Understanding is a much more complex process than that. It involves an implicit definition of context, selections, estimations of importance, the invocation of social rules signaled by contextual cues, and the preparation—at least in inner speech—of a response. I suppose that's why I keep wanting to interrupt you and why you, seeing my impatience, abbreviate, exaggerate, appeal to some unseen judge to arbitrate. In fact, you often seem to incorporate answers to objections you think I am *about to* make, to qualify statements before you make them, which distorts your syntax. And I wish you'd stop pacing about like that, as if to show me how patient you're being, and still being, and still being!—and *Why*, you seem to be saying, don't I let you get a word in edgewise?

MOI: You're saying that I speak in "double-voiced words," "words with a sidelong glance." I do, of course, but all discourse is that—because it's always shaped by the audience, whose potential reactions must be taken into account from the onset. You're saying that the arrow in that diagram should be drawn *both* ways. I guess that would be a distinction between Bakhtin and reader-reception theory, which only discusses the active role of the audience *after* an utterance is made. For Bakhtin, the audience shapes the utterance *as* it is being made—which I suppose is another way of saying that every utterance is, as Bakhtin puts it, a "two-sided act," "the product of the reciprocal relationship between the addresser and addressee," "territory shared."

ELLE: Or "a bridge" which "depends on" both sides. That's why we speak differently to different people. After all, we must speak in *some* particular speech genre, jargon, and tone, and we must make some choice of words, and style. Part of the meaning of what we say is the set of values implicit in the style and jargon we use. Our stylistic choices mark us as a particular sort of person, one who would use that word or style in that situation. The dictionary, and systematic linguistics, are deaf to the play of voices and insensitive to the cacophony of values.

I, for instance, would never have referred to a "linguistically *virgin* world." If you had thought about it, you probably wouldn't have used that word in speaking to me, either, given all the implications it has absorbed from its contexts of usage.

MOI: As I might have to your mother? Or a woman of that generation?

ELLE: Yes, but not in my presence. Or if you did, its meaning in *that* situation would include an allusion to *this* situation, an ironic playing with my beliefs and, perhaps, the prejudices and evaluations embedded in your own characteristic choice of words.

MOI: Well, . . . but there's always some set of allusions, both verbal and nonverbal, between any pair of speakers or between a writer and his anticipated readers. Otherwise, there could be no discourse. Every utterance is a "social enthymeme," analogous to a logical argument with unstated premises and an implicit specification of a context. You know, it occurs to me that a good deal of comedy depends on people identifying a context differently from their listeners—and their unseen judge—and betraying their values in the process.

ELLE: As you do when you speak of "virgin" words, "emasculated" theories, and "gentlemanly" behavior. Your words sound different when I quote them, don't they?

MOI: Yes, but that's because they're part of your sentence and so owe allegiance to two speech centers. You can never really quote *in* context. That's why Bakhtin was able to study the forms of direct discourse, indirect discourse, and quasi-direct discourse not just as grammatical and syntactic categories but as ways in which one speaker or writer can orient himself—all right, himself or herself—to the words of another. New forms arise as a result of changing attitudes toward authority, the semantic implications of forms of speech, and social situations that bring with them new speech genres.

ELLE: When I speak, we speak. In fact, everyone we have heard speaks, which implies that any real stylistics would have to be dialogic. Style never belongs solely to the speaker, but to at least two people . . .

MOI: Yes, but not to two people simply as two *particular* people but to two people as shaped by their experience as members of social groups. You know, in a real sense, we don't speak *the* English language, because there isn't *an* English language. Any language is really a set of languages. The people of different groups, ages, generations, and locales have their own dialects, each bearing the imprint of a collection of values and a distillation of experience. All of these languages compete for ascendancy. Their competition, enacted in the particularity of each utterance, generates the history of language. The idea that language is a system, so dear to the Saussurians and their Formalist-structuralist heirs, is a fiction: language is a constant struggle *among* systems and between systematic and unsystematic elements. Or, as Bakhtin says, between "centripetal" and "centrifugal" forces. Each culturally predominant group strives to legislate *its* dialect as *the* language, whereas it is, in reality, only one dialect among many, albeit the one enjoying the greatest social prestige. That turns other dialects into implicit forms of cultural opposition. **The unity of a language is not given but posited—and reposited, over and over again.**

ELLE: But maybe language is systematic at least in the mind of each speaker, even if the speaker can't articulate the rules of the system? And even if the systematization is somewhat different for each speaker?

MOI: Not really, because we don't learn our native language in that way. It's not as if a language is handed down, ready-made: instead, we simply enter upon the stream of communication. In fact, we learn to speak by learning to participate in particular kinds of basic, everyday speech genres—say, to our mothers. Only when a particular function is to be served or a need arises do we systematize. Given our internal economy, it is usually too costly in time and effort to systematize every linguistic fact we learn.

ELLE: But you know, linguists like Chomsky would not deny that the actual behavior of speakers may differ from the rules of the system. He would simply say that linguistics is a study of system, you know, the exchange between an ideal speaker and ideal listener, in a situation free from the distortions of particular needs, interests, and shifts of attention. Surely, Bakhtin could not possibly deny that in some sense such a shared system or set of rules, and accepted definitions of words, exist.

MOI: I think he would say that the systematic aspect of language studied by Saussure and Chomsky is necessary but never sufficient for speaking and understanding. Speech always takes place between particular people, in a particular situation, for particular reasons. The particularities shape the creation of each utterance. Bakhtin's linguistics would be a metalinguistics from the point of view of most linguists. That is, it is essentially a study of utterances *in context* and *in dialogue*. Meaning—in the sense of dictionary meaning—means nothing; it only has the potential for meaning. When linguists analyze model sentences as if they were utterances, they are implicitly smuggling into their analysis information from an *assumed* context. The key distinction is between sentence and utterance. Sentences and words are repeatable, but utterances never are, which means that each utterance contains both what is repeatable and what is unrepeatable.

ELLE: What is repeatable and what is unrepeatable. According to Bakhtin, speech is always a way of controlling people's behavior or directing their thinking. Referential models of language are false to the core. Reference is incidental to language; language *is* what it does. That's why Bakhtin never chooses as examples of utterances those old linguistic chestnuts, "The cat is on the mat" or "The carpenter hit the nail with the hammer." Instead, he chooses utterances like "Well" or "Ah!" pronounced with a particular intonation that presumes, and partially creates, a context for the interaction of the speaker and listener. Speech is *inter*locution. Understanding is active, is responsive, is a process. That process of understanding includes the listener's identification of the speaker's apparent and concealed motives and of the responses that the speaker invites and hopes to forestall. The interaction among speaker, listener, and context constitutes a "field of answerability," which *is* the meaning of the utterance. For Bakhtin, to interpret utterances as a sequence of signs pointing to things is to mistake the nature of human speech.

Trotsky once observed that the Formalists were followers of John the Evangelist because "they believe that in the beginning was the Word. But we Marxists believe that in the beginning was the Deed; the word follows as its phonetic shadow." Bakhtin answers, "the word *is* a deed" or, rather, a doing.

MOI: You know, it occurs to me that a lot of that sounds like speech-act theory—we *do* things with words.

ELLE: Well, that's what I like about Susan Stewart's article: it points out the differences between Bakhtin and both speech-act theory and sociolinguistics. For instance, Bakhtin stresses the *un*systematic nature of language and of everyday speech situations. He doesn't just expand the grammar of language to produce an equally systematic (and false) grammar of situation and usage. Language is, for him, much more open to history and social conflict. The world clusters and unclusters. In fact, each word is open to conflicting pronunciations, intonations, and allusions and so may be an arena of social conflict and a sensitive barometer of social change.

MOI: If you take Bakhtin at his word, it would appear that the usual distinction between pragmatics, on the one hand, and semantics and syntactics, on the other, is misleading—at best, an occasionally useful abstraction. For Bakhtin, *everything* is "pragmatics," and semantic and syntactic codes are really "context in *rigor mortis.*" Above all, he seems to be calling for a wholistic study of language, one which would necessarily have as its starting point not what it *is*, in any structuralist sense, but what it *does*. For Bakhtin, being is event, is action, which means that it is purposeful, uncertain, and, in short, historical.

ELLE: Yes, and the main objection Bakhtin makes to the Saussurian model is not that it does not allow for history—he knew that it did—but that it can't explain history *in the same terms* that it explains language at any given moment. He would have had little more patience with Formalist models of linguistic change—you know, like Jakobson's— models which explain linguistic history as a series of corrections of systemic imbalances. According to Jakobson, these corrections produce still newer imbalances, which, in turn, lead to further corrections. Jakobson's formulation, "the history of a system is also a system," may be partially true, but it enormously overstates the systematicness of language and so misses the real point: the principal engine of linguistic change is the conflict of values implicit in the varieties of speech. Change bespeaks "*heteroglossia,*" the unsystematic conflict of tongues. There is no algorithm of history.

MOI: I agree and disagree. For me, the *main* significance of Bakhtin's linguistic theories is their implications *outside of* linguistics. They also imply a rethinking of all the social sciences and humanities. You know, Bakhtin says at one point in *Marxism and the Philosophy of Language* that Saussure's disjunction of *langue* and *parole* is really a restatement of the opposition of society and the individual. That sociological dualism is no more tenable than the philosophical one of mind and body. Most of the social sciences have been plagued, before Bakhtin and since, with a recurring problem: Which is the fundamental unit, the individual or the group? Whichever you choose, you tend to resolve the other into it. One choice leads to an enormous underestimation of the role of individual action, as with most Marxists; the other, to an insufficient appreciation of the manifold social factors which really make us who we are. Bakhtin's idea was to find a *new* minimal unit of social analysis (much the way that linguists found the phoneme) from which both the social and individual, the macro- and micro-, the systematic and the un- systematic could be derived.

ELLE: That sounds a lot like Vygotsky, Luria, and their school of Soviet psychology. In that case, "minimal unit" refers to a unit of analysis that retains all the basic properties of the whole and which cannot be subdivided further without losing those properties. It's a sort of social molecule. The double-voiced word, the dialogic utterance, would be such a unit and could form the basis for the general science of culture and for its constituent disciplines.

MOI: Don't you think he goes too far?

ELLE: Perhaps. Maybe what he should have said is that a closely analogous unit would be found in each discipline. On the other hand, maybe he was right as he said it.

MOI: His idea seems to be that the individual consciousness is social through and through, the psyche existing on a sort of borderline between self and others. On the other hand, ideology—by which he seems to mean the whole domain of shareable mental life—is also individual, bearing the imprint of each person who uses it, thinks it, speaks it, and changes it by dialogic words.

ELLE: You know I'm a confirmed Vygotskyite myself, so *I* would emphasize the fundamental way those ideas lead to a rethinking of psychology. If I can paraphrase it in my own terms . . .

MOI: . . . that is, state it in your own "innerly persuasive words," which sound to me a lot like the ones Vygotsky addressed to *his* audience . . .

ELLE: . . . *I* would stress the concept of inner speech, which both Bakhtin and Vygotsky use, their alternative to the Freudian model. They conceive of thought as dialogues conducted with imagined addressees who may be more or less fully defined, but who are always drawn from voices one has already heard.

We *are* the voices that inhabit us. They conduct an unceasing dialogue, in which each of them intones values and recalls contexts. Spoken words are the "islands" that emerge from that inner stream. You know, Vygotsky developed the idea of inner speech in his critique of Piaget's early theories. He demonstrated experimentally that children engage in inner speech *after* they have learned outer speech and that inner speech is the internalization of outer dialogue. You give yourself shape, psychic identity through the verbal community to which you belong, and in which you have learned your "words." "The psyche is an extraterritorial part of the organism."

MOI: "There is no such thing as privacy," because we include our others.

ELLE: "The search for my own word is really the search for a word that is not my own."

MOI: All of that sounds like one of those typically Russian critiques of Western individualism. For Bakhtin, the creation of a self is the selection of one innerly persuasive voice from among the many voices you have learned, and that voice keeps changing every time it says something. His idea is that many of the phenomena that the Freudian model was formulated to explain—slips of the tongue, for instance—can be explained as well or better by his model, which does not indulge in the creation of elusive and mythic entities like the id, the ego, and the superego. For Bakhtin, Freud resorts too quickly to the biological and too little to the social. By contrast, in Bakhtin's model, specifically social, historical, and linguistic elements form the core of personality, and so he avoids some of the improper cross-cultural claims Freud or Freudians sometimes tend to make. Also, Bakhtin was sensitive very early to the ways in which the particular dialogic situation of the psychoanalytic sessions shapes what is said. But, that's not what I wanted to say . . .

ELLE: You're not yourself today. Except in one respect: you keep doing what you always do when you talk about Bakhtin. For you, the phrases "it is true that" and "Bakhtin says" are equivalent. You're trying to make him into another guru of the humanists, another one of those successive heroes whom literature professors cultivate, another Derrida. . . . I hear you spelling his name "Bakhtin*e*."

MOI: Well, there *is* one Frenchman I think of in connection with Bakhtin— Jean-Paul Sartre. I can imagine writing one of those "threshold dialogues" Bakhtin talks about so often. You know, a conversation at the gates of the other world between Bakhtin and Sartre, all arranged by some Boswell. I haven't figured out yet what language they'd speak. It would emerge in the course of the dialogue that throughout their careers they were concerned with essentially the same problems, which they worked out in different terms because they belonged to different intellectual traditions. And so they would agree but disagree. Bakhtin arrived at more successful formulations because he had the benefit of the tradition of Formalist linguistics and literary theory, especially in its later, sociological phase.

ELLE: I think you should have them *search* for a common language— have them paraphrase and quote each other ironically, mix French and Russian, combine philosophical, literary, and scientific discourse, juxtapose the serious with the comic, marry the exalted to the Rabelaisian. . . . You could enact a lot of Bakhtin's ideas without having to spell them out and, in the process, produce an example of one of his favorite literary genres, the Menippean satire. Your Boswell could be Menippus. You might also use as an epigraph a quotation that has already been used as an epigraph by one of their favorite writers. That quotation would then become a kind of palimpsest, whose uppermost layer would anticipate its own overlaying, as words anticipate their response.

What would they talk about?

MOI: About how to understand the relation of the general to the particular, social systems to individual experience, and the given world to particular decisions. I'm thinking, for example, of the later Sartre, his *Search for a Method* and his biography of Flaubert. Sartre objects to a mechanical, vulgar Marxism, and Bakhtin to what might be called a "vulgar Formalism." Both *-isms* attempt to derive everything particular from overarching general laws. This sort of thinking produces dualisms like the split between *langue* and *parole* and leads to the idea that there can be a science only of *langue*. In *Search for a Method*, Sartre attacks what he calls "lazy Marxism," which endlessly rediscovers what it already knows. When it stumbles upon facts that don't conform to the laws of historical materialism, it describes them as the product of mere chance. And so, Sartre says, the real experience of men is dissolved in a bath of sulfuric acid. The "lived" is not studied but thrown over to the irrational, unutilizable, non-signifying . . .

ELLE: It occurs to me that Bakhtin's criticism of early Formalism may in fact *be* a disguised criticism of Soviet Marxism. That criticism is certainly truer of Soviet Marxists than of later Formalists like Tynjanov, who were quite sensitive to the role of the particular. Because of the censorship, Bakhtin had to write allegorically, in what the Russians called "Aesopian language." It occurs to me *now* that the prevalence of Aesopian language throughout Russian history may be one reason why so many Russian theorists, including Bakhtin, understood that meaning cannot be described as "locked in" in a text. Since they were aware that any text can be made to mean so many different things, they viewed meaning as the product of the reciprocal relationship between texts and readers.

MOI: Sartre would no doubt emphasize *particular* writers and *particular* readers. That's why he administers a dose of existentialism to traditional Marxism. He describes in Marxist terms the situations *given* to men and in existentialist terms the ways men *make* themselves. "Valery was a petit-bourgeois intellectual, no doubt about it. But not every petit-bourgeois intellectual is Valery." Sartre's "method"—

ELLE:—which is not very methodical . . .

MOI: . . . Sartre's "progressive-regressive method" . . .

ELLE: ?

MOI: Stop being so silent, just be quiet. Sartre's method [pause with a sidelong glance] is a way of analyzing the relationship of the general to the particular. He sees concrete experience as a function of, but not wholly determined by, general conditions and laws. He looks for "mediations"—for example, in the experience of childhood. He sees each family as a particular refraction of a given set of social and historical circumstances. He describes how a selfhood is fashioned from a person's sense of his immediate world, his perception of space and time, and his imagination of the past and of possible futures.

ELLE: But don't you see why that solution is not as good as Bakhtin's and Vygotsky's? Sartre begins, as so many do, with a fundamental opposition between general and particular, objective and subjective, and *then* seeks mediations. That's why he winds up with all those paradoxical formulations, such as "the subjective surpassing of objectivity toward objectivity." According to Sartre, his project, "stretched between the objective conditions of the environment and the objective structures of the field of possibles, represents in itself the moving unit of subjectivity and objectivity"! Things like that. He calls all that the dialectic of the subjective and the objective. There's all the difference in the world, however, between Bakhtin's dialogue and Sartre's dialectic. Bakhtin doesn't have to worry about mediations, because the minimal unit *he* chooses, the utterance (including its presence in inner speech), is already what Sartre would call mediate. Instead of *arriving at* a synthesis, he *begins* with a unit that is already both "subjective" and "objective," a unit, moreover, that is immediately available for scientific study.

MOI: But can the social world *be* studied scientifically? You agree that it contains purposes, decisions, and uncertainty. What sort of science can you shape from all that?

ELLE: Like most humanists, you have a seventeenth-century view of science and think it requires purely mechanical laws and admits only what Aristotle called "efficient causes." But even the physical sciences study the random and use teleological explanations: "the disorder of the universe tends to a maximum" implies both. And a number of potential human sciences, like decision theory and general systems, often begin by describing humans as purposeful beings and discuss how people or social groups respond to situations of uncertainty. Your picture of science is a caricature. Bakhtin's was not.

MOI: You view him as a scientist occasionally inspired by Christianity, and I, as a Christian who conducted raids on science. He was not so scientifically minded as you think. You'll probably say that in *Marxism and the Philosophy of Language* he defines the humanities as ideological *sciences*. But in his later writings, like that volume published in Russian in '79, for instance, he describes the "methodology of the humanities" quite differently. He contrasts the monologic approach of the sciences with the dialogic approach of the humanities. The scientist observes the data of the world from outside. The true humanist engages the texts directly in dialogue. The humanist takes his own act of observing as part of the field of observation. Geertz has recently made similar points. Don't you see a contradiction between Bakhtin's earlier and later views of the humanities?

ELLE: No, I don't. I see Bakhtin describing two different kinds of activity, each with a specific function—two approaches to the same material, both valuable for different reasons. On the one hand, one can do what he *usually* did: study culture scientifically, "monologically." One can even study *dialogue* monologically, and look for regularities, patterns, and determinants of social change. One would try to be accurate. For Bakhtin, that would include an awareness of the historicity of science itself and of the many social factors that shape scientific theories, including his own. He knew that the structure of scientific revolution is dialogic.

But one doesn't always have to be a scientist. Bakhtin also envisaged another kind of activity in which there would be no question of accuracy. One would enter into dialogue with texts, open oneself to anachronisms and contemporary issues, and make the entire process an occasion for discovering ourselves and our world. Attempts at accuracy would not only lead to improper claims but also impoverish the dialogue. If literary criticism were practiced this way, it would become less hidebound and more vital. We would argue more openly about the value of canonical texts, realizing that our evaluations are always renegotiated and ever renegotiable: value is always value for someone.

Bakhtin would probably have approved of Wayne Booth's article, the one in which Booth takes Bakhtin to task dialogically for an apparent insensitivity to feminist issues. Booth uses that dialogue to reflect on his own values. Bakhtin would also have liked Sandra Gilbert's feminist critique of Milton, and Michael André Bernstein's meditations on Celine and Pound. Instead of downplaying or apologizing for those writers' reprehensible political views, Bernstein makes them the occasion for reflecting on his own values. Instead of leading to false apologetics, difference provokes exploration.

However, we must be careful not to confuse these dialogic approaches with scientific method.

MOI: If we do confuse them, we will either monologize dialogue or tend to offer historically limited judgments as eternal verities.

ELLE: Which is what official culture *always* does, and what real laughter, "carnival laughter," mocks. You could read all of Bakhtin as an extended, dialogic footnote to Heraclitus and to his various reincarnations: Menippus, Cervantes, Sterne, Gogol, Diderot, and, especially, Rabelais . . .

MOI: . . . whom he sees not as a satirist castigating particular vices or institutions, like the clergy, but as a sort of carnival king, laughing at all claims of eternity or certainty. That's the spirit of medieval carnival, the spirit of relativism. Medieval carnival wasn't, strictly speaking, an art form, because everyone participated: "carnival knows no footlights" and allows no outside vantage point. Therefore, it is unlike modern satire, in which the satirist usually excludes himself from the laughter. Modern satire is "reduced laughter," a "laughter that does not laugh."

Carnival travesties: it crowns and uncrowns, inverts rank and exchanges roles, makes sense from nonsense and nonsense of sense. Its logic is "the logic of the turnabout," of "the inside-out." It is the systematic parody of systems and points to the arbitrariness of all norms and rules.

ELLE: Carnival expresses the "gay relativity" of all things and so fears no judgment. The work of Rabelais "is the most fearless book in the world." Fearless also, because it knows no death. Carnival and Rabelais merge the individual body into the collective body of the people. Death is not final and burial brings forth new life from the womb of the earth. The result is a "grotesque realism," in which the individual body is no longer a unit or a complete entity. Its essential organs are the apertures and orifices. Its essential processes are shitting, pissing, sweating, vomiting, and ejaculating, all those things you can occasionally say but can't print or refer to in official spheres. "Time plays and laughs! Dominion belongs to the child."

MOI: Amen. Or, as you would say, Q.E.D. But does Bakhtin see carnival as a conservative or as a revolutionary force? Since it is securely framed off from everyday life, it can serve the function of isolating that sense of relativity in a safe place: now, and only now, may you laugh fearlessly . . .

ELLE: But it is *potentially* revolutionary, because no frame is ever secure. In fact, Bakhtin sees the immense significance of Rabelais and the Renaissance as the eruption of folk laughter into official culture. Seriousness and folly enter into an open dialogue, which changes both sides, as real dialogue does.

MOI: And that dialogue leads to the creation of the novel, the "carnivalized" genre, which embodies the spirit of relativism and, especially, of parody. That's the point Bakhtin makes in his essay, "Epic and Novel," which might more accurately be called "The Novel and Every Other Genre." He argues that the novel is unlike other genres because they have a canon, but the novel, in its essential spirit, is anti-canonic. It is not a genre but the anti-genre and recognizes the arbitrariness and conventionality of all forms and norms, including its own. It is aware of its own historicity, its immediate participation in the social flux. Whereas mock-epic is quite a different thing from epic, the history of the novel includes parodies of the novel. In fact, parodies of the novel, like those of Sterne, Pushkin, and Dostoevsky, are for Bakhtin the quintessence—better still, the "quintephemera"—of "novelness." Novelness is the ever changing incarnation of the Heraclitian spirit. In the novel, each truth is someone's truth, reflects someone's experience, and serves someone's interests. As one critic of Bakhtin and the novel wrote, it subjects all thoughts and actions to an "irony of origins." The epic knows; the novel asks how we know. It takes the speech genres of everyday life and the written genres of high culture, incorporates them into its all-dialogizing context, and re-accentuates them . . .

ELLE: Then a stylistics of the novel must be a very different thing from the stylistics of other genres. Its style is the orchestration of styles, and so can only be understood from a metalinguistic standpoint. The novel is the genre most sensitive to dialogue. It surveys the linguistic landscape, takes the utterances, forms of speech and writing of a passing social world (of a "polyglot," "heteroglot" world), and uses language as an index to history. In fact, Bakhtin even says at one point that characters exist in novels so that words may be spoken. However closely the narrator may resemble the author, even *his* language "knows itself" as but one language among many, one language reflecting one particular set of social values among many . . .

MOI: I suppose that's why Dostoevsky is Bakhtin's favorite writer. He takes the novel's "polyphonic" tendency to an extreme.

ELLE: As he also takes to an extreme the novel's characteristic way of representing personality. Personality in the novel, like the genre itself, is always unfinished, incomplete, and incompletely integrated. It is always changing itself in the act of expressing itself. "In the novel, man is never coincident with himself."

MOI: As opposed to personality in the epic, which is finished and sure from the outset.

ELLE: I wonder. I can think of counterexamples, like Satan in *Paradise Lost*. Bakhtin seems to be speaking of some sort of generalized spirit of "epicness," conceived in opposition to novelness. That's also true of his observation that the events of epic take place in an "absolute past," a time qualitatively different from the time in which the epic is heard or read. The time of epics is the age of "firsts" and "bests"; in novelistic time, people are always remaking values.

MOI: Another way Bakhtin makes that point is in terms of the "time-space," the "chronotope" in which the novelistic character lives. In the novel's chronotope, the social world defines and shapes from within the possibility of action, the succession of thoughts, and the world of choices. The chronotope of the novel is unlike that of, say, the Greek romance, in which time is "abstract" and place a mere background. In the romance, circumstances may aid or hinder the hero but never change him. Character is given, as it also is in the chronotope of Plutarch's *Lives*. People simply live *out* their destinies, manifesting their unchanging essential qualities. Time forges nothing new.

I find it interesting that a number of contemporary physicists and chemists have begun to suspect that time may be chronotopic in Bakhtin's sense. For instance, Ilya Prigogine's *From Being to Becoming* explores a number of scientific implications of temporal irreversibility and asymmetry—of varying and changing fields of temporality—of time's being, as he puts it, not just a parameter but an operator.

ELLE: If that's what Bakhtin meant—and Holquist's work suggests that he might well have—he may have been either prophetic or playful, but he was also vague. Something like Gregory Bateson at his most brilliant and most exasperating. He seems to have entertained so

many reconceptualizations of so many disciplines—reconceptualizations that he left others to fill in—that he is bound to appear a
forerunner of whatever might happen. I wish he had been less far-
reaching but more careful in his claims and exposition. For instance,
one thing I *don't* like about his chronotope essay is that he doesn't
make the chronotope of his own history explicit. How does he see
cultural and literary change happening? He seems to assume that
real time is novel time, the time of *War and Peace* and *Anna Karenina*.
In Bakhtin's narrative, as in the novel, history and biography penetrate
each other, like, well, like war and peace. For him, real time is
extensive. Particular moments are not filled with things decisive.
Real time is time without a "nick of." Bakhtin loves duration. The
novel, the long Russian novel, is not just his subject, it is his hero.
His problem is that he novelizes the history of the novel, and it is
an implicitly *Russian* history of the novel. Indeed, his theories are
suspiciously Slavophile, for two reasons: first, because any celebration
of the novel implicitly celebrates Russian literature, whose greatest
works are, after all, novels; and second, because to focus attention
on generically self-conscious novels is implicitly to praise Russian
novels, most of which were written in deliberate violation of European
novelistic conventions. His favorite European novels are the ones
that most resemble, and most influenced, Russian novels: *Don Quixote*,
Gargantua and Pantagruel, *Tristram Shandy*, *Tom Jones*, *Pamela*, and
Don Juan. He notably does not discuss the works of Jane Austen,
George Eliot, and Henry James. Bakhtin should have called his
book *The Great Anti-Tradition*. For him "novel" is not a descriptive
term but, to use his words, "a valorized-temporal category"—a sort
of Platonic ideal of the anti-Platonic, Heraclitian spirit. Bakhtin's
tacit Slavophilism may be one reason why his current Soviet executors
are members of the extreme right wing, non-Marxist, religious,
Russian nationalist faction of the Soviet intelligentsia.

Moi: I think they overstate their case. I see him as religious but not
specifically Orthodox. Every reader seems to make his own Bakhtin.
He has been claimed by structuralists, post-structuralists, and Marxists
like Raymond Williams. This confusion is understandable, given
Bakhtin's peculiar, elusive, even weird biography and style, not to
mention his breadth of interests. He knew and made contributions
not only to linguistics and literary theory but also to psychology,
anthropology, the sociology of knowledge, theology, philosophy,
even biology—and so it is not surprising that each discipline would
have its own Bakhtin. Besides, there also seem to be French "Bakh-
tines," American "Bakhtins," and, of course, Russian "Baxtiny." Even
these national Bakhtins are hybrids: the French were introduced
to him by Bulgarians, Todorov and Kristeva, and the Americans
by professors of Russian literature and epigones of French criticism.

His texts are also mediated in many other ways, most obviously by his translators. Stressing the text's Marxist element, Titunik has rendered a title *Freudianism: A Marxist Critique* that in Russian is simply *Freudianism: A Critical Essay*. And then there is the problem of Bakhtin's executors, who provide, select, and edit his unpublished manuscripts for publication. From what point of view? Because of Soviet publishing conditions, Bakhtin published many of his works a half-century after he wrote them. They contain additions inconsistent with original points, comments that seem to take "sidelong glances" at the censor, and obscurities that invite all sorts of "Aesopian" readings.

ELLE: Not to mention the problem of who wrote what. Because of Stalinist dangers, some of his work was published under the signatures of V. N. Vološinov and P. N. Medvedev—and since there really *were* a Vološinov and a Medvedev, it is hard to tell just how much of each text is theirs and how much is Bakhtin's.

MOI: I like Holquist's explanation of that problem, based on his extensive work in the USSR—

ELLE:—with how much provided by those executors?

MOI: Hard to tell. He believes that Bakhtin "ventriloquized" those texts, that is, wrote them in the language his friends Vološinov and Medvedev *would* have used *if* they had written them. Of course, this creates all sorts of dialogic ironies he must have appreciated: for example, at the end of Vološinov's book on language, where the author pleads for a Communist resurrection of "confident and categorical language" of "a word that really means and takes responsibility for what it says."

ELLE: All of that in a book largely written by someone else, and someone else who, it appears, believed something quite different.

MOI: The master of the genre of silence. Here we have a man who was exiled to Central Asia, lost a leg, and yet wrote in ecstatic terms of "the lower bodily stratum"; who used one of his own manuscripts for cigarette paper; who had enough experience of "the people" not to put too much faith in them, and yet produced some of those silly, naive passages in the Rabelais book.

ELLE: But if the sign of Bakhtin is so elusive, how can you know who has him right, if anyone? I imagine him sitting up there, wryly listening to our dialogue or, perhaps, in some grimy room, seeding his texts with ironies, allegories, and "double-voiced words," laughing us into a labyrinth. You know, in one of those notebook jottings that appear in the '79 volume, he writes that he will prepare a collection of his essays in a way that shows the *developing* of his ideas, with all their "internal unfinishedness." He writes of his habit of using a panoply of terms and discourses to dramatize the problem of varying dialogic perspectives. At least some of his obscurities must be deliberate.

MOI: Yes, but he also says that some of them are not. He is aware that sometimes he is genuinely inconsistent, and that he ought not to mislead himself into making a virtue of a deficiency. *That* may be his greatest virtue.

How do *you* read the sign of Bakhtin?

ELLE: The way Richards read the sign of Coleridge. He saw a lot of inconsistencies in Coleridge, but he wanted to present an image of him that would contribute to contemporary theoretical debates. He knew his image of Coleridge might not resemble Coleridge's image of himself. Even if *Marxism and the Philosophy of Language* does ventriloquize and partially misrepresent Bakhtin's intentions, that fact is irrelevant to me. It is still the strongest book on language I know. The question we should ask is whether the text's statements are true or false, not whether there is some concealed allegory. I am interested in his speech, not his silences.

MOI: *You* want to approach him monologically, as a "scientist," and *I*, dialogically, as a humanist. Or maybe it's the other way around . . . ?

In any case, in *your* approach, the author disappears.

ELLE: But Bakhtin would say that the author is *never* really present. "It is just as impossible to forge an identity between myself, my own 'I,' and that 'I' that is the subject of my stories as it is to lift myself up by my own hair." It occurs to me that maybe the central idea that Bakhtin was always developing, and wanted to *show* developing, was a theory of authorship and of related concepts such as expression and intention. He *could* be viewed as the most profound of intentionalists. He saw intention and authorship as much more complex than people usually take them to be. He spent his whole life examining and enriching these neglected or impoverished concepts. From his first essay, "Art and Responsibility," to his last notes, he was concerned with the nature of expressing and with the relation of inner thought to outer speech. He questioned the extent to which we can be present in our own utterances and investigated our strategies for appropriating languages we have not made in contexts we have not chosen. He saw that we cannot *be* ourselves, we must *cite* ourselves.

MOI: I accept your summary but not your implicit scientific framework. For me, what is most valuable in Bakhtin comes from his religious and philosophical concerns. His idea of "word" is a rethinking of *logos*, his concept of dialogue recalls Buber, and his sense of elusive selfhood parallels Sartre's. He sounds especially like Sartre when he says that the search for myself is for "the not-I in me." I do not own myself, others participate in me, make me, have rights to me. So much of the drama of everyday life and of world literature can be seen as a working out of this truth. Besides, we cannot really express ourselves fully, because we are always talking to someone, in some situation, a fact which makes every statement, in all senses, "partial." We never just speak as "a speaker" but as some *sort* of speaker, in some sort of role, using some sort of genre: as poet, journalist, father, mother, petitioner, interrogated prisoner.

ELLE: Shades of Soviet conditions in that last example, especially when he says that the process of interrogation changes the one interrogated . . .

MOI: We are never fully ourselves in our utterances. What we make or say is always somewhat alien to us, never wholly ours, as we ourselves are not wholly ours. No one, not even the author himself, ever sees more than a "secondary image" of an author. The "primary author" stands behind that image and is its creator. If you try to construct the primary image of an author, you have really created another secondary image of which *you* yourself are the primary author. We are *outside* ourselves, and that "outsidedness," "extralocality," creates the tragedy of expression.

ELLE: I see no tragedy, and I don't like your philosophical and theological explication of Bakhtin's ideas. I don't see the impossibility of full expression of self as resulting from anything grand, mystical, or existential. It's merely the inevitable consequence of the dynamics of speaking and writing, of communicating with others. Vygotsky's development of this idea, in an empirical and scientific framework, is the clearest and most convincing. He explains that a lot happens between thought and expression, between inner speech and outer speech. That's another inadequacy of the telegraphic model of communication. Putting a thought into words is not like putting words into Morse code. Once you have words, there is only one way to put them into code, that is, there is a clear algorithm of encoding. There is *no* algorithm of expression. Inner speech may be transformed into outer speech in a variety of ways, with many different results. Consider: when you speak to someone very close to you, you can abbreviate enormously, speak in fragments, and assume enormous amounts of context, as lovers sometimes seem to speak a private language incomprehensible to others. In inner speech, you can abbreviate still more. If someone could eavesdrop on the psyche, he might understand little or nothing of what was going on. Now, when you have to say a thought to someone else, you must *supply* grammatical and logical links, imply context, make all sorts of choices which are not given in the initial thought. In the act of making these choices, in the *process* of expression, something must be added. The thought becomes different from what it was, which means expressing may be a form of learning. The study of speaking and, more generally, of creating would require the specification and description of how all this happens.

MOI: What you say suggests the need for a general theory of the creative process, which would explain how speakers shape their utterances and how writers compose their works. Such a theory would describe the creative process as one of genuine work, of making, not just as the process of transcribing an already given idea.

ELLE: We must rethink the whole of literary studies. What we need is not just a separate theory of creativity, placed alongside a theory of reception and a theory of the text, but, rather, a general theory which would describe creation, text, and reception, the whole field of answerability, *in the same terms*. This theory would also describe how the field of answerability changes over time . . .

MOI: There you go again, stressing the gay relativity and historical openness of things, the river of utterance into which you can't step twice. Time without privilege. But me, I see all of Bakhtin as a *dissatisfied* Heraclitus, one longing to be a Plato. Especially in his last notes, written with all the poetic thickness of possible but unfulfillable projects, I hear a deep nostalgia in the wise old man's voice. He asks, yet again, to what extent is a purely monologic, serious word possible? Can there be a word in which only the speaker—and the whole of the speaker—speaks? Or must we be content with genres of silence? I suspect an allusion here to Gogol's dying words—"A ladder! A ladder!"—to that step out of history, to that apocalyptic time when "there shall be time no longer," when we can talk, each of us entirely present in what we say, directly to God. His epitaph should have been drawn from those last notes: "Christ as truth. I ask him."

ELLE: . . . What could they, Bakhtin and Christ, possibly talk about?

MOI:

ELLE: That's plagiarism.

*   *   *

MOI: Well, have you read the transcript of our dialogue?

ELLE: Yes, but I didn't like it. Our speeches are too long for real dialogue, and we use words nobody ever says. Whoever *says* "albeit"? People don't talk that way.

MOI: But we *did* talk that way. You know Mark Twain's "Jumping Frog" story? He *writes* in the form of conversation. We academics, on the other hand, *speak* as if we were writing aloud.

ELLE: . . . And as if we were mimicking Diderot, which we were.

MOI: Well, it was hopeless from the start. We knew all along that the readers of *Critical Inquiry* would be listening in.

What bothers *me* is that *you* have all the best lines. I never quite say what I want to. I never really express myself. I never say what I think . . .

ELLE: Do you ever?

The Outer Word and Inner Speech: Bakhtin, Vygotsky, and the Internalization of Language

Caryl Emerson

> Language is no longer linked to the knowing of things, but to men's freedom.
>
> —MICHEL FOUCAULT, *The Order of Things*

In this statement from *The Order of Things*, Michel Foucault speaks of the nineteenth-century revolution in linguistics that, in effect, rediscovered language and made it the object of systematic study in its own right. Language, no longer seen as a transparent medium, was granted "its own particular density . . . and laws of its own."[1] Yet it is not self-evident how we are made more free by understanding that words are not just a repository of knowledge. The density of language is a troublesome postulate. That postulate, according to Foucault, raises difficult epistemological problems and presents theorists with a choice:

> The critical elevation of language, which was a compensation for its subsidence within the object, implied that it had been brought nearer both to an act of knowing, pure of all words, and to the unconscious element in our discourse. It had to be either made transparent to the forms of knowledge, or thrust down into the contents of the unconscious. [*OT*, p. 299]

The debate on the status of language has been enormous and subtle, but it would seem that these two poles described by Foucault remain constantly in effect. Language is, on the one hand, a transparent medium from which to deduce a metalanguage and on which to build statistical and mechanical models, or language is, on the other hand, a product of the individual psyche and ultimately subject to psychic transformation, to what Foucault calls "dim mechanisms, faceless determinations, a whole landscape of shadow" (*OT,* p. 326).

In the twentieth century, these two poles were reevaluated in the light of Ferdinand de Saussure's celebrated binary oppositions: synchrony/diachrony, syntagmatic/paradigmatic, *langue/parole.* Language had moved from the realm of naming to the realm of relationships—a truly revolutionary shift. But as is so often the case with intellectual revolutions, success tended to institutionalize and finalize the new terminology. One of the most productive (and most quickly canonized) distinctions was that between *langue* and *parole,* between the social-collective institution of language (the code) and the individual act of combination and actualization (the message). Not surprisingly, such an unbridged opposition was not congenial to Marxist dialecticians, and in the Soviet Union of the 1920s Saussure's dichotomy stimulated vigorous debate. Literary scholars, philosophers of language, and developmental psychologists all questioned that opposition in their separate disciplines and were concerned to explain the integration of individual with society in a more benevolent way. It became a central issue in clinical psychology, especially in the branch dealing with language acquisition. And it was a lifelong preoccupation for those members of the Bakhtin circle who were especially interested in language: Mikhail Bakhtin, Valentin Vološinov, and Pavel Medvedev. These various groups, it should be emphasized, worked in and with the terminological frameworks of their time, including an experimental and open-ended Marxism that stressed process, change, and the interaction between organism and environment. Among the most eloquent contributions to the debate were two books that appeared under Vološinov's name: *Freudianism: A Marxist Critique* (1927) and *Marxism and the Philosophy of Language* (1929).[2] Each in its own way reassessed the two Saussurian poles and attempted a synthesis. The nature of that synthesis, and the light it casts on the interplay between language and consciousness, is the focal point of this essay.

Members of the Bakhtin circle objected in particular to one fundamental aspect of the *langue/parole* schema, namely, its opposition of the social to the individual. Instead of opposition, they spoke of interaction—and warned the while against understanding this interaction in a mechanical and narrowly rational (by which they meant formulaic) way. As Bakhtin defined the problem:

Caryl Emerson, assistant professor of Russian literature at Cornell University, has translated (with Michael Holquist) *The Dialogic Imagination,* a collection of Mikhail Bakhtin's essays, and edited and translated Bakhtin's *Problems of Dostoevsky's Poetics* (1984). She is currently at work on a study of Boris Godunov in Russian cultural history.

The idea of the *conventionality, the arbitrariness of language,* is a typical one for rationalism as a whole, and no less typical is the *comparison of language to the system of mathematical signs.* What interests the mathematically minded rationalists is not the relationship of the sign to the actual reality it reflects nor to the individual who is its originator, but the *relationship of sign to sign within a closed system* already accepted and authorized. In other words, they are interested only in the *inner logic of the system of signs itself,* taken, as in algebra, completely independently of the ideological meanings that give the signs their content. [*MPL,* pp. 57–58]

This insensitivity to "ideological meanings," Bakhtin suggests, is the ultimate danger behind the fascination with the arbitrary nature of the sign. The corrective, in his view, is a proper understanding of the concept of *ideologija.* Its English cognate "ideology" is in some respects unfortunate, for our word suggests something inflexible and propagandistic, something po-litically unfree. For Bakhtin and his colleagues, it meant simply an "idea system" determined socially, something that *means.* In this sense of the term, all sign systems are ideological, and all ideologies possess semiotic value (see *MPL,* pp. 9–10). But in contrast to Saussure's claim that a verbal sign is ultimately a mental construct—that the acoustic image and the concept are both contained in an arbitrary closed system—the members of the Bakhtin circle posited four *social* factors that make the understanding of speech and writing possible.

First, they assumed that the sign and its effects occur in outer ex-perience. "[In the] chain of ideological creativity and understanding . . . nowhere is there a break in the chain, nowhere does the chain plunge into inner being, nonmaterial in nature and unembodied in signs" (*MPL,* p. 11). Each ideological product is meaningful not in the soul but in the objectively accessible ideological material.

Second, this outer experience, if it is to register significance, must in some way be organized socially. Signs "can arise only on *interindividual territory.*" But this territory "cannot be called 'natural' in the direct sense of the word: signs do not arise between any two members of the species *Homo sapiens.* It is essential that the two individuals . . . compose a group (a social unit); only then can the medium of signs take shape between them" (*MPL,* p. 12). A social unit is therefore an indispensable aspect of semiotic activity—and for this reason the study of ideologies cannot be grounded in individual psychology. Far from positing a Saussurian tension between society and the individual, Bakhtin posits an individual who actively creates the society in which his discourse occurs. The whole tradition opposing individual to society is misguided: an individual person is simply one biological specimen in a group (see *MPL,* p. 34).

Third, the ideologies that are generated by the material reality of language must be studied *inter*-systemically, not as independent and isolated phenomena. That is, ideology always exists as a relation between (or among) speakers and listeners and, by extension, between or among social groups. According to Bakhtin, each social group—each class, profession, generation, religion, region—has its own characteristic way of speaking, its own dialect. Each dialect reflects and embodies a set of values and a sense of shared experience. Because no two individuals ever entirely coincide in their experience or belong to precisely the same set of social groups, every act of understanding involves an act of translation and a negotiation of values. It is essentially a phenomenon of interrelation and interaction.[3]

Fourth and last, Bakhtin profoundly redefined the Word itself and attempted to infuse it with its original Greek sense of *logos* ("discourse"). For Bakhtin, words cannot be conceived apart from the voices who speak them; thus, every word raises the question of authority. Fully half of *Marxism and the Philosophy of Language* is devoted to an investigation of "indirect" and "quasi-direct" discourse, multileveled speech acts in which more than one voice participates. For Bakhtin, words come not out of dictionaries but out of concrete dialogic situations. He saw the distinction between dialogic words—that is, utterances—and dictionary words as one between *theme* and *meaning:*

> Theme is the *upper, actual limit of linguistic significance;* in essence, only theme means something definite. Meaning is the *lower limit* of linguistic significance. Meaning, in essence, means nothing; it only possesses potentiality—the possibility of having a meaning within a concrete theme. [*MPL,* p. 101]

Words in discourse always recall earlier contexts of usage, otherwise they could not mean at all. It follows that *every* utterance, covertly or overtly, is an act of indirect discourse.

These, then, are the amendments the Bakhtin circle would attach to Saussure: the sign is external, organized socially, concretely historical, and, as the Word, inseparably linked with voice and authority. These four dialectical alterations work a great change in the original distinction between *langue* and *parole.* Bakhtin deals with this dichotomy (in somewhat expanded form) in his discussion of the twin sins of "abstract objectivism" and "individualistic subjectivism" (see *MPL,* pp. 47–63). Abstract objectivism can be seen as the Cartesian extreme, language taken as a code independent of its interpreters. This is an excess to which the Neogrammarians were prone, the myth that language makes poets. Individualistic subjectivism, on the other hand, is the Humboldtian extreme, embodied for Bakhtin in the Vosslerites. They are faulted for grounding the message too exclusively in the individual psyche—thus giving rise to the myth that poets make language. Bakhtin himself does not deny the two poles. But he would synthesize them, and he claims that their opposition in real life, at any given moment, is a fiction. In the Bakhtinian model, every individual engages in two perpendicular activities. He forms lateral ("horizontal") relationships with other individuals in specific speech acts, and he simultaneously forms internal ("vertical") relationships between the outer world and his own psyche. These double activities are constant, and their interactions in fact *constitute* the psyche. The psyche is thus not an internal but a boundary phenomenon. Or to use Bakhtin's political metaphor, the psyche "enjoys extraterritorial status . . . [as] a social entity that penetrates inside the organism of the individual person" (*MPL*, p. 39).

This concept of the psyche is indeed radical. The assumption that the psyche is, at its base, a "social entity," a space to be filled with ideological signs, sets the Bakhtinian concept of consciousness at odds with much of Western thinking since Freud on the subject. In his remarkable descriptions of the transitions from "social intercourse" to "outer speech," and from "outer speech" to "inner speech" and to consciousness, Bakhtin fundamentally rethinks both the relation of consciousness to the world around it and the relation of the self to others. We read that a poet's style "is engendered from the style of his inner speech, which does not lend itself to control, and his inner speech is itself the product of his entire social life."[4] And in *Marxism and the Philosophy of Language* we read:

> Although the reality of the word, as is true of any sign, resides between individuals, a word, at the same time, is produced by the individual organism's own means without recourse to any equipment or any other kind of extracorporeal material. This has determined the role of [the] word as *the semiotic material of inner life—of consciousness* (inner speech). [*MPL*, p. 14]

When so firmly tied to outer experience, this tripartite equation of inner life = inner speech = consciousness is quite audacious. "People do not 'accept' their native language," Bakhtin insists; "it is in their native language that they first reach awareness" (*MPL*, p. 81). Individuation of the personality is the process of a consciousness working over the "ideological themes" that penetrate it "and there take on the semblance of individual accents" (*MPL*, p. 22). Indeed, a clear distinction between inner and outer speech is impossible, because the very act of introspection is modeled on external social discourse: it is self-observation, communion with the self, "the understanding of one's own inner sign" (*MPL*, p. 36). Thus, the problem of origins in personality is in fact no problem at all, and there is likewise no problem of self-expression:

> *Not only can experience be outwardly expressed through the agency of the sign* . . . but also, aside from this outward expression (for others), *experience exists even for the person undergoing it only in the material of signs*. Outside that material there is no experience as such. In this sense *any experience is expressible*, i.e., is potential expression. . . .

Thus there is no leap involved between inner experience and its expression, no crossing over from one qualitative realm of reality to another. [*MPL,* p. 28]

Individual consciousness is a socio-ideological fact. If you cannot talk about an experience, at least to yourself, you did not have it.

A person's experiences exist "encoded in his inner speech" (*MPL,* p. 118). Thus the word, Bakhtin affirms, "constitutes the foundation, the skeleton of inner life. Were it to be deprived of the word, the psyche would shrink to an extreme degree" (*MPL,* p. 29). Purely private, speechless, isolated experience—the realm of the mystic, the visionary—is essentially impossible *as experience.* It can only be viewed as erratic, as something bordering on the pathological. Experience that "lacks a socially grounded and stable audience" cannot "take firm root and will not receive differentiated and full-fledged expression" (*MPL,* p. 92).

Bakhtin would say, therefore, that we evolve the mechanisms to express that which our environment makes available for us to experience. At any given time the fit between self and society may not be perfect, indeed cannot be perfect, but the mechanisms are always present to engage self and society in dialogue. In such a model of reality, there is no room for—and perhaps no conceptual possibility of—an independent unconscious.

Bakhtin develops this argument in his polemical work *Freudianism: A Marxist Critique.* For Bakhtin, the teachings of Freud represent a debasing of that already discredited extreme, individualistic subjectivism. As Western culture declines and its social fabric disintegrates, Freud's star rises. Bakhtin opens his "critical sketch" (see p. 37 n. 2) on this comment, and it is no accident: Freudianism is analyzed here not as a viable scientific theory but as a social symptom. Psychoanalysis saves bourgeois man by taking him out of history, by explaining him to himself not as a concrete social entity but as an "abstract biological organism." According to Bakhtin, Freud would have us everywhere seek the answers within; we forget the social crisis and "take refuge in the organic warmth of the animal side of life" (*Fr,* p. 11). The "ideological motif of Freudianism" is an emphasis on *sex* and *age,* common motifs, Bakhtin claims, in eras of crisis and decline, when nature (especially "human nature," in the form of biological drives) is seen as all-powerful and history is seen as impotent (*Fr,* p. 11).

It need hardly be pointed out that Bakhtin is very selective in his reading of Freud. Nowhere does he engage Freud's most provocative works, the great sociopsychological essays of the war years and the 1920s. In those works Bakhtin would have found a more complex opponent and, at times, an uncomfortable ally. But it was precisely the early clinical Freud, and his pioneering assumptions and methods of psychoanalysis, that posed a challenge to the Bakhtinian model for perceiving and assimilating reality. Those assumptions and methods had to be confronted. In Bakhtin's model, phenomena originate in the external material world, as do the means to express them. The "unconscious," that is, the part of ourselves that is outside our control and awareness, is best comprehended as merely that portion of the conscious not yet articulate—an "unofficial conscious," if you will, or perhaps a struggle among various motives and voices within the conscious (*Fr,* pp. 76, 85). According to Bakhtin, Freud's projection of autonomous drives and nonnegotiable demands is mere "psychologization of the somatic" (*Fr,* p. 71). It follows that the forces of id and ego that emerge so colorfully during psychoanalysis are not repressed inner realities in the process of discharge but reflections of overt social dynamics, including those between doctor and patient (see *Fr,* p. 79). For Bakhtin, in short, the unconscious in the Freudian sense is a myth— and it functions in society as Roland Barthes has claimed all contemporary myths function: "Semiology has taught us that myth has the task of giving an historical intention a natural justification, and making contingency appear eternal."[5] This evasion of history and the social process is the real sin of the "mythical" unconscious. Eliminate time and society, and a structure cannot be modified. It can only be satisfied or repressed.

Bakhtin's model had to account for the phenomena Freud had observed but do it differently. An alternative system of explanation would have to provide, through experimental work and clinical documentation, specific answers to the key psychological question: How precisely does environment impress a personality, how do outer words become inner speech? One remarkable scholar committed to this project was Bakhtin's contemporary Lev Vygotsky—a man comparable to Bakhtin in productivity and interdisciplinary brilliance. Vygotsky's final work, *Thought and Language* (1934), supplemented by his essays of the 1930s, can be read as an important predecessor and perhaps even as clinical underpinning to Bakhtin's philosophy of language.[6] Soviet scholars such as Vyacheslav Ivanov have made this connection explicitly in discussions of Bakhtin's contribution to semiotics.[7]

It must be said at the outset that this interaction between Bakhtin and Vygotsky is somewhat hypothetical, although none the less intriguing for that. There is no direct evidence that Bakhtin and Vygotsky ever met, and Vygotsky makes no reference to Bakhtin in his work.[8] Interest in dialogic relations and the social context of speech was, of course, rather widespread in the 1920s; both men doubtless pulled upon and were pulled by many of the same social and scholarly currents. Where Bakhtin and Vygotsky intersect is not on the plane of their actual texts, that is, not in the reality of a cross-reference, but in the ultimate implications of their thought. It is this projected intersection that I will now discuss.

Vygotsky's initial inquiry was very similar to that of the Bakhtin circle. Could not the unsatisfactory stalemate between individualistic subjectivism and abstract objectivism—or, as Vygotsky casts the opposition, between idealist and behaviorist psychology—be resolved with a dynamic synthesis focusing on the concrete speech act itself? At both those extremes, the loser had been time: "Whether inclining toward pure naturalism or extreme idealism, all these theories have one trait in common—their antihistorical bias" (*TL,* p. 153). Time, Vygotsky argues, had long been misunderstood and misapplied in the psychological sciences. The development of the child had once been described in terms of botanical models (maturation, "kindergarten") and then in terms of zoological models (the performance of animals under laboratory conditions), but in Vygotsky's view it is precisely what can*not* be learned from plants and lower animals, namely, the uniquely human assimilation and production of language, that psychologists should examine.[9] Language is man's greatest tool; and so it should be seen precisely as a tool, that is, as a means for communicating with and extracting from the outside world. So viewed, language offers special problems to the psychologist. For if language is always a means of interaction with the world, it is perilous to study it in isolated environments or in traditional controlled experiments. Vygotsky replaced those conventional locales of science with much looser "task situations," which involved putting subjects in confrontation with real problems in a real social setting.[10] Vygotsky's distrust of the classic psychological experiment (what he derisively called the "stimulus-response framework") should in fact recall Bakhtin's distrust of the classic linguistic model, with its ideal speaker and ideal (or nonexistent) listener. Both were suspicious of modeling, for both insisted that only the concrete historical event could validate a human communication or lead to an act of learning.

Vygotsky created for himself a powerful clinical tool out of two convictions: that psychological events must be studied in history and that external society is the starting point of consciousness. The two are closely allied, for whatever we can perceive in outer reality, we can change, or try to change, through time. In ingenious experiments, Vygotsky extended (and then modified or rejected) the language-learning maps offered by Jean Piaget, William Stern, and Freud. His primary target was Piaget's "egocentric thought," a stage Piaget claimed is intermediate between autistic play and directed (that is, reality-oriented) thought. Piaget had assumed that a child's thought was originally autistic and became realistic only under social pressure; visible here is the direct impress of Freud's pleasure principle and reality principle. Vygotsky was unsympathetic to the idea that an individual is reluctant to adjust to its environment, that reality, work, and social intercourse are somehow not "pleasurable." In order to test the opposite assumption, Vygotsky conducted the experiments described in *Thought and Language*—and created his own scenario for language acquisition.

According to this scenario, the child's first efforts at perception result in an isolation of word meanings—but "meanings" only in the sense of verbal stimuli, functioning in context as signals rather than as proper signs.[11] A child cannot translate much of the speech he hears into his rudimentary "signal systems," because the ability to generalize comes slowly. Until the age of two years, language serves the human child much as a thirty-two-"word" vocabulary serves the chimpanzee throughout its life: words—or, better, vocalizations—are purely emotional; they coincide with gestures but exclude any simultaneous intellectual activity. The child passes out of this chimpanzoid stage when he begins to ask for the names of objects, and at this point one of the critical moments in human maturation occurs: "Thought becomes verbal and speech [becomes] rational" (*TL*, p. 44). Vygotsky could not define the precise mechanism linking overt to inner speech, but he assumed—and this, of course, is the crucial point—that this process followed the same course and obeyed the same laws as did other operations involving signs. External experiments could be devised to monitor and refine the seepage between levels.

To this end, Vygotsky isolated four stages of "internalization": the natural or pre-intellectual stage, the stage of naive psychology, the stage of egocentric speech, and the so-called ingrowth stage. The third stage, egocentric speech, was the most conducive to analysis in task situations. Uncomfortable with Piaget's conclusion that this speech is fantasy-talk and generated asocially, Vygotsky ran a series of experiments designed to socialize and complicate the child's environment at precisely the age when the child "talked to himself." He demonstrated that a child talks twice as much when presented with obstacles (see *TL*, pp. 16–17) and that this externalized "conversation with oneself," commenting on and predicting the results of an action, is in fact the natural dynamic of problem solving (see "TS," pp. 24–26).[12] Furthermore, this talk turned out to be extremely sensitive to social factors. Piaget had observed similar phenomena: that egocentric speech occurs only in a social context, that the child assumes he is being understood by others, and that such speech is not whispered or abbreviated but spoken as an utterance, that is, as public speech in a specific environment. Vygotsky accepted this data but then devised experiments to detach it from Piaget's conclusions.

When Vygotsky varied the social factors—by isolating the child, placing him with deaf-mutes, putting him to play in a room filled with deafening music—it was found that egocentric speech dropped drastically, to one-fifth its previous rate (see *TL*, pp. 136–37). Vygotsky concluded that egocentric speech was not, as Piaget had suggested, a compromise between primary autism and reluctant socialization but rather the direct outgrowth (or, better, ingrowth) of speech which had been from the start socially and environmentally oriented. Piaget was correct when he observed that private and socialized speech did indeed intersect at this stage. Development, however, was proceeding not along the lines of Piaget's scenario but in the opposite direction. The child was not externalizing his internal thoughts but internalizing his external verbal interactions. That was why egocentric speech is relatively accessible in three-year-olds but quite inscrutable in seven-year-olds: the older the child, the more thoroughly has his thought become inner speech (see *TL*, p. 134). "Development in thinking," Vygotsky concludes, "is not from the individual to the socialized, but from the social to the individual" (*TL*, p. 20).

Like Bakhtin, Vygotsky offers us a restructuring of the Saussurian dichotomy. In Vygotsky's model of language acquisition, a child's first speech is social; words evoke specific responses and must be reinforced by adults. Only gradually does language assume the role of a "second signal system," that is, become for the child an indirect way of affecting his environment. When it does, his speech differentiates into two separate though interlocking systems: one continues to adjust to the external world and emerges as adult social speech; the other system begins to "internalize" and becomes by degrees a personal language, greatly abbreviated and predicative (see "TS," pp. 27–28). In this inner speech, the *sense* of a word—a "dynamic, fluid, complex whole"—takes predominance over a word's *meaning*.[13]

When internalization begins, egocentric speech drops off. The child becomes, as it were, his own best interlocutor. Crucial to this process, however, is the presence of a challenging verbal and physical environment. The descriptive "monologue" of which egocentric speech is composed can be internalized creatively only if questioned and challenged by outside voices. In this way alone is intelligence possible, "intelligence" defined not as an "accumulation of already mastered skills" but as a "dialogue with one's own future and an address to the external world." It should come as no surprise that Vygotsky was unsympathetic to the standard intelligence test, which measured (in a competitive and isolated context) prior achievement and punished children for "cheating." A true test of intelligence, Vygotsky argued, was one that posited problems beyond the capacity of the child to solve and then made help available. How a child seeks help, how he utilizes his environment, how he asks questions of others—all these constitute the child's "zone of proximal development," where all true learning occurs (*TL*, p. 103). Intelligence is a *social* category.[14]

Speech and behavior interact dynamically in a child's development. First, speech accompanies action, then precedes it, finally displaces it— that is, speech assumes the planning function so essential for the higher mental processes (see "TS," pp. 27–28). Just as children outgrow the need to count on their fingers or memorize by means of mnemonic devices, so do they outgrow the need to vocalize their activities. This final stage of speech development, the ingrowth stage, coincides with the appearance of logical memory, hypothesis-formation, and other mature mental processes.

Vygotsky does not, however, claim a one-to-one fit between thought and speech. There is speech without thought, as in chimpanzees and infants; there is also thought without speech. The two areas overlap in "verbal thought," and this is coincident with language (see *TL*, pp. 47–48). Since we can share only what we articulate and communicate, it is this linguistic dimension alone that has historical validity. In this respect, Vygotsky seems somewhat more modest than Bakhtin, who suggests more strongly that experience can be given absolute expression—inwardly to oneself, outwardly to others—through the word.

For Vygotsky, the Word is a powerful amalgam: part sign, part tool, it is *the* significant humanizing event.[15] One makes a self through the words one has learned, fashions one's own voice and inner speech by a selective appropriation of the voices of others. It would obviously be of great interest to know how this process of self-fashioning takes place. Here we can turn to Bakhtin, to an essay from the 1930s and thus contemporary with Vygotsky's last writings.[16] In this essay Bakhtin mentions two ways of assimilating the words of others. Each plays its own part in shaping the process of inner speech, and each has a ready analogue in the way schoolchildren are asked to learn texts. One may "recite by heart" or "retell it in one's own words." In reciting, the language of others is authoritative: it is distanced, taboo, and there can be no play with the framing context. One cannot even entertain the possibility of doubting it; so one cannot enter into dialogue with it. To change a word in a recitation is to make a mistake. The power of this kind of language, however, has its corresponding cost: once discredited, it becomes a relic, a dead thing. Retelling in one's own words, on the other hand, is a more flexible and responsive process. It is the only way we can *originate* anything verbally. In retelling, Bakhtin argues, one arrives at "internally persuasive" discourse—which, in his view, is as close as anything can come to being totally our own. The struggle within us between these two modes of discourse, the authoritative and the internally persuasive, is what we recognize as intellectual and moral growth.

Both Bakhtin and Vygotsky, as we have seen, responded directly or indirectly to the challenge of Freud. Both attempted to account for their data without resorting to postulating an unconscious in the Freudian sense. By way of contrast, it is instructive here to recall Jacques Lacan—who, among others, has been a beneficiary of Bakhtin's "semiotic rein-terpretation" of Freud.[17] Lacan's case is intriguing, for he retains the unconscious while at the same time submitting Freudian psychoanalysis to rigorous criticism along the lines of Bakhtin. By focusing attention on the dialogic word, he encourages a rereading of Freud in which the social element (the dynamics between doctor and patient) is crucial. As Lacan opens his essay "The Empty Word and the Full Word":

Whether it sees itself as an instrument of healing, of formation, or of exploration in depth, psychoanalysis has only a single intermediary: the patient's Word. . . . And every word calls for a reply.

I shall show that there is no word without a reply, even if it meets no more than silence, provided that it has an auditor: this is the heart of its function in psychoanalysis.[18]

The word is conceived as a tool not only of the external world but also of an autonomous internal world as well. And what emerges, it would seem, is a reinterpretation of the role of dialogue in the painful maturational processes of the child. For Vygotsky, the child's realization of his separateness from society is not a crisis; after all, his environment provides both the form and the content of his personality. From the start, dialogue reinforces the child's grasp on reality, as evidenced by the predominantly social and extraverted nature of his earliest egocentric speech. For Lacan, on the contrary, dialogue seems to function as *the* alienating experience, the *stade du miroir* phase of a child's development. The unconscious becomes the seat of all those problems that Bakhtin had externalized: the origin of personality, the possibilities of self-expression. The *je-moi* opposition in the mirror gives rise to that permanent hunger for "a locus where there is constituted the *je* which speaks as well as he who has it speak."[19] And consequently, the Word takes on an entirely different coloration: it is no longer merely an ideological sign but a potent tool for repressing knowledge of that gap, the face in the mirror, the Other. Lacan's celebrated inversion of Saussure's algorithm, with the line between signifier and signified representing repression, created a powerful but ominous new role for language. The child is released from his alienating image only through discovering himself as Subject, which occurs with language; but this language will inevitably come to him from the Other. Thus speech is based on the idea of lack, and dialogue, on the idea of difference.

Here the contrast with the Bakhtin circle is especially fruitful, for dialogue between inner and outer speech is central to both approaches. In each case, the gap between inner and outer can be a cause of pain: in Lacan it is the pain of desire, in Bakhtin, the pain of inarticulateness.[20] But Bakhtin defines "the *strife*, the *chaos*, the *adversity* of our psychical life" as conflicts of motives *within* the conscious sphere (albeit an expanded conscious sphere) and thus retains for the Word an objective role in a historically concrete context (*Fr*, p. 75). He does not deny the reality of internal conflicts, but he does socialize them, thus exposing their mechanisms to the light of day. If enough individuals experience the same gap, it is re-socialized: there develops a political underground, and the potential for revolution (see *Fr*, pp. 89–90).

Thus we see that alienation, if it is to survive at all, must be externalized—at which point it can become the basis for collective rebellion, or for a new dynamic community. One can never, it seems, be existentially alone. In fact, the very concept of solitude is a fiction—or, rather, it is a paradox. When in 1961 Bakhtin returned to his 1929 study of Dostoevsky (then scheduled for republication), he jotted down an eloquent series of thoughts on this question of solitude:

> No Nirvana is possible for a *single* consciousness. A single consciousness is a contradiction in terms. Consciousness is essentially multiple.
> I am conscious of myself and become myself only while revealing myself for another, through another, and with the help of another. . . .
> Separation, dissociation, and enclosure within the self as the main reason for the loss of one's self. Not that which takes place within, but that which takes place on the *boundary* between one's own and someone else's consciousness, on the *threshold*. . . . Thus does Dostoevsky confront all decadent and idealistic (individualistic) culture, the culture of essential and inescapable solitude. He asserts the impossibility of solitude, the illusory nature of solitude. The very being of man (both external and internal) is the *deepest communion*. *To be* means *to communicate*. . . . To be means to be for another, and through the other, for oneself.[21]

This passage is in part the product of that deep meditation on Christianity that occupied Bakhtin all his life.[22] But it is also an integral part of his philosophy of language. In a world beset with the existential image of no exit, this insistence on community, on true social-ism, gives the Bakhtin circle an aura of almost old-fashioned coziness in an insecure age.[23]

In the Russian model, inner speech is thus a benevolent quantity, a "unique form of collaboration with oneself."[24] Lacan, as we have seen, also depends on the Word to discharge the negative potential of the gap between self and society. But as part of the Freudian model, this word is only with great difficulty available for "collaboration." It is potentially neurotic, the proof of that permanent gap between objectification and identification. It can be mediated only through that structure whose presumed presence makes it possible to pose (and solve) the problem at all: the unconscious. In Lacan, language is a means of expressing the inexpressible. For Bakhtin and Vygotsky, there is, in essence, no inexpressible. In Lacan's world, therefore, the Word is a tool of psychoanalysis. For Bakhtin and Vygotsky, it is a tool of pedagogy.

* * *

The gap between self and society has been, of course, a theme not only of modern linguistics but also of the modern study of literary genres. We may recall that Georg Lukács defines the epic as a genre embodying the absence of such a gap, as the product of "integrated civilisations" where there "is not yet any interiority, for there is not yet any exterior, any 'otherness' for the soul."[25] Invoking a rather primitive Marxism, Lukács also defines the novel as the opposite extreme: for him, the novel is the product of a fragmented world, a world in which the interior not only exists but is also maximally at odds with the exterior. It would appear that Lukács needed to posit a time when there was no gap between self and society so that he might better describe by contrast the world in which, he thought, we now live.

Two decades after Lukács, Bakhtin addressed the issue of epic and novel in an essay that borrowed some of Lukács' terminology but reversed almost entirely its ethical charge.[26] For Bakhtin, the healthy individual *in life* is the one who can surmount—not deny—the gap, who can break down the barriers between inner and outer; likewise, the healthy *artistic genre* is the one that guarantees a *non*-coincidence between hero and environment. The gap so lamented by Lukács is seen, in Bakhtin's "Epic and Novel," as the beginning of dialogue, of temporal development, and of consciousness. The fullest realization of all three is the novel. For Bakhtin, then, the novel-epic distinction, though historically instantiated, is really trans-historical, a relationship between different *perceived qualities of time*—or, as he would say, "chronotopes"—whenever in history they might occur. When he describes the epic narrative as taking place in an "absolute past" and novel time as truly novel, he is really drawing an ontological distinction. He is speaking of temporal types that are always potential: whenever we talk about a world that does not know time, we are "epicking."

And whenever we talk about a world that fully experiences time, we are "noveling." The novel is alienated from epic wholeness. What results in Bakhtin's construct, however, is not loneliness but freedom. Specifically, characters in novels experience the freedom to be more than their roles in given stories. The epic hero, by contrast, is inseparable from his plot; there is only one way his life could be lived.

> Neither an epic nor a tragic hero could ever step out in his own character during a pause in the plot or during an intermission: he has no face for it, no gesture, no language. In this is his strength and his limitation. The epic and tragic hero is the hero who, by his very nature, must perish. ["EN," p. 36]

Novelistic heroes, on the other hand, are like medieval fools on stage: their roles are temporary, their masks are not their selves. "These are heroes of free improvisation and not heroes of tradition, heroes of a life process that is imperishable and forever renewing itself, forever contemporary—these are not heroes of an absolute past" ("EN," p. 36). A novelistic hero always has a "surplus of humanness" that is not embodied in his biography: thus "there always remains in him unrealized potential and unrealized demands. . . . There always remains a need for the future, and a place for this future must be found. All existing clothes are always too tight, and thus comical, on a man" ("EN," p. 37). When we think away his roles, there is something left: that remainder, that non-coincidence of self and social categories, that capacity to change into different clothes, is freedom.

Novelists rejoice in subjects that are homeless, that is, free to develop. Novels also grant freedom for the *author* to develop, which is to say, freedom for the author to play with his own image on the plane of his own work. The reader (or, for that matter, the creator) of the *Iliad* cannot imagine himself chatting with Hector on the walls of Troy; epic heroes need neither audience nor author. But the writer of novels has an implicated voice. He can enter and manipulate, fuse or distribute his voice among characters. Or he can—and this requires an extra measure of commitment to freedom—grant autonomy to his characters; he can create not just objects but full-fledged *subjects*. This was the "Copernican revolution" that Bakhtin had, in 1929, attributed to Dostoevsky. In Dostoevsky's novels, the author is no longer the creator around whom characters are forced to revolve but is, so to speak, himself but a planet among planets. By the end of his life, Bakhtin had come to see this freedom as characteristic of all true novels. Or to put the point another way, he had come to see the force of "novelness" as the guarantee of freedom.

* * *

These, then, are the ways an awareness of the gap between inner and outer might function in both life and literature: as an index of individual consciousness, as a measure of our escape from fixed plots and roles, as a prerequisite for discourse itself. What now remains is for us to return to Foucault's statement that language, de-privileged, is an instrument of man's freedom. In light of this discussion, we can understand this freedom two ways, both valid and both linked to the persistent dichotomy between *langue* and *parole*, between the code and the message.

One way of understanding this freedom can be found in a passage from *The Order of Things* which argues that literature as such could emerge only when language was deprived of privilege and thus made self-conscious (see *OT*, pp. 299–300). This being so, the purpose of literature could be seen as the preserving, and perhaps even the widening, of this self-consciousness. Through the artistic word we learn who we are. And that knowledge could be harnessed to utilitarian purposes, including, for example, the purpose Freud in "The Relation of the Poet to Day-Dreaming" attributes to literature. In that essay, Freud discusses poetry as a sort of fantasy-play for adults and suggests that our appetite for art has at its base the desire to discharge guilt for such indulgence in play: "The true enjoyment of literature proceeds from the release of tensions in our minds."[27] Literature thus serves as a psychic safety valve, much as, in the Aristotelian view, catharsis serves as a social safety valve. In his role as psychoanalyst, Lacan would probably agree with Freud. If the acoustic image is defined as the repressor of the concept, then human neuroses can be released through, and only through, their identification in the Word. Words have a purpose and a function: they are a code, they can pin down. Definition implies release, and therefore freedom.

In contrast, we might consider Freud's essay as Vygotsky treats it in "Art and Psychoanalysis," a chapter from his early work *The Psychology of Art*. In opposing what he considers a reduction of art, Vygotsky argues that Freud left largely unexplained the effects of the artwork on the audience. Moreover, Vygotsky contends, "such an interpretation of art reduces its social role; art begins to appear as an antidote whose task it is to save mankind from vice, but which has no positive tasks or purposes for man's psyche."[28] Vygotsky began his career as a teacher of literature. The affinities among language, literature, and psychology were never far from his mind, and in studying all three he raised the same question: How might man be kept from closing in on his self? One answer he gives is that we learn, through the word, who we are *not*, who we might yet become. It is precisely this positive task—not identification but liberation— that is taken up by Foucault and by such philosophers of language as Paul de Man. In the modern era, Foucault writes in *The Order of Things*,

> the name ceases to be the reward of language; it becomes instead its enigmatic raw material.

> This proper being of language is what the nineteenth century was to call the Word (*le Verbe*), as opposed to the Classical "verb", whose function is to pin language, discreetly but continuously, to the being of representation. And the discourse that contains this being and frees it for its own sake is literature. [*OT*, pp. 118, 119]

The same sentiments are echoed by de Man:

> Here, . . . consciousness does not result from the absence of something, but consists of the presence of a nothingness. Poetic language names this void with ever-renewed understanding and . . . it never tires of naming it again. This persistent naming is what we call literature.[29]

The eternal and inevitable inadequacy of all names permits new meanings to happen and new messages to be created. This permission— or intermission—is Bakhtin's novelistic gap, which not even the author can (nor should wish to) bridge. And it is the lack, the absence at the center, that keeps the outer word and our inner speech in permanent dialogue, out of that danger Bakhtin saw of collapse into single consciousness, which would be non-existence. Inside that gap, it is always worthwhile to try naming it again.

1. Michel Foucault, *The Order of Things: An Archaeology of the Human Sciences* (New York, 1973), p. 296; all further references to this work, abbreviated *OT,* will be included parenthetically in the text.

2. See V. N. Vološinov, *Freudianism: A Marxist Critique,* ed. in collaboration with Neal H. Bruss, trans. I. R. Titunik (New York, 1976); all further references to this work, abbreviated *Fr,* will be included parenthetically in the text. The title has been translated in an unnecessarily misleading way; the Russian is simply *Frejdizm: kritičeskij očerk* [Freudianism: a critical sketch]. And see Vološinov, *Marxism and the Philosophy of Language,* trans. Ladislav Matejka and Titunik, Studies in Language, vol. 1 (New York, 1973); all further references to this work, abbreviated *MPL,* will be included parenthetically in the text. Vološinov's authorship of these two texts is disputed: there is evidence that Mikhail Bakhtin wrote them both, or substantial portions of both. The collaboration between the two men was, at any rate, very close. In the text of this article, I refer to Bakhtin as the author of both works.

3. For a clear and provocative discussion of this aspect of Bakhtin's work, see Gary Saul Morson, "The Heresiarch of *Meta,*" *PTL* 3 (Oct. 1979): 407–27. In a note written near the end of his life, Bakhtin emphasized the necessity of difference in any act of understanding: "Understanding cannot be understood as emotional empathy, or as the placing of oneself in another's place (the loss of one's own place). This is required only for the peripheral aspects of understanding. Understanding cannot be understood as translation from someone else's language into one's own language" ("Iz zapisei 1970–1971 godov," *Èstetika slovesnogo tvorčestva* [Moscow, 1979], p. 346; my translation). Even understanding, itself, is a threshold phenomenon.

The Tartu school of Soviet semioticians has been very creative with Bakhtinian concepts, which it recognizes as complementary to its own work. For an extension of Bakhtin's insights into the micro-dynamics of the psyche, see Iu. M. Lotman, "On the Reduction and Unfolding of Sign Systems (The Problem of 'Freudianism and Semiotic Culturology')," in *Semiotics and Structuralism: Readings from the Soviet Union,* ed. Henryk Baran (White Plains, N.Y., 1976), pp. 301–9. For an extension of Bakhtin's insights into the macro-dynamics of history, see B. A. Uspenskii, "Historia sub Specie Semioticae," in *Semiotics and Structuralism,* pp. 64–75.

4. Vološinov, "Discourse in Life and Discourse in Art (Concerning Sociological Poetics)," appendix 1, *Fr,* p. 114.

5. Roland Barthes, "Myth Today," *Mythologies,* trans. Annette Lavers (New York, 1972), p. 142.

6. See L. S. Vygotsky, *Thought and Language,* ed. and trans. Eugenia Hanfmann and Gertrude Vakar (Cambridge, Mass., 1962); all further references to this work, abbreviated *TL,* will be included parenthetically in the text. A more precise translation of the work's title, *Myšlenie i reč',* would be "Thinking and Speech": the thinking is specifically a process and not a product, and the language is *uttered.*

An edited selection of Vygotsky's essays has been published in English, with two excellent explanatory essays, as Vygotsky, *Mind in Society: The Development of Higher Psychological Processes,* ed. Michael Cole et al. (Cambridge, Mass., 1978).

7. See Viach. Vs. Ivanov, "The Significance of M. M. Bakhtin's Ideas on Sign, Utterance, and Dialogue for Modern Semiotics (1)," in *Semiotics and Structuralism,* pp. 310–67. I should point out, however, that Ivanov makes very wide claims for Bakhtin's influence; in certain of his cases, parallel development would be a more reasonable hypothesis.

8. For this information I am grateful to James V. Wertsch of Chicago's Center for Psychosocial Studies, who read this manuscript and made a number of very astute and helpful suggestions. It is his conviction that Vygotsky's ideas about dialogue are less influenced

by Bakhtin than by the formalist linguist Lev Yakubinsky, whose 1923 essay "On Dialogic Speech" Vygotsky does cite (see L. P. Iakubinskij [Lev Yakubinsky], "O dialogičeskoi reči," in *Russkaja reč'*, ed. L. V. Ščerba [Petrograd, 1923]). In this essay, Yakubinsky advises those who study "practical language" to investigate first the seminal distinction between monologic and dialogic speech (or, better, dialogic processes). Dialogue, he claims, is the prior and more natural form, while monologue requires an artificial structure. Yakubinsky also argues (as Bakhtin does) that dialogue does not depend solely on words: shared context, intonation, visual stimuli are all also powerful carriers of a message.

There are certainly areas of overlap in the thinking of Bakhtin, Yakubinsky, and Vygotsky on the question of dialogic speech. But Yakubinsky's treatment remains rather naive. For a comprehensive discussion of the Vygotsky-Yakubinsky connection, see chapter 4, "The Semiotic Mediation of Human Activity," from Wertsch's forthcoming study, *Cognitive Developmental Theory: A Vygotskian Approach*. I thank its author for generously sharing with me a draft of this chapter.

9. See Vygotsky, "Tool and Symbol in Child Development," *Mind in Society*, pp. 19–20; all further references to this work, abbreviated "TS," will be included parenthetically in the text.

10. See Vygotsky, "Problems of Method," *Mind in Society*, pp. 58–69.

11. "Signals" and "signal systems" are basic concepts in the Russian school of psychology. The school traces its fundamental assumptions and terminology to Ivan Pavlov and, in particular, to two physiological laws which were worked out for lower animals and then extended to man. The first law provides that all learning is conditional (*uslovnyj*, usually mistranslated into English as "conditioned," as in the phrase "uslovnyj refleks"). In a human context, this means that learning is basically not intuitive but environmental. The second law posits a "second signal system," a derivation and extension of classical conditioning. According to Pavlov, speech introduces a new principle into nervous activity: the ability to abstract and generalize signals from the environment. Whereas animals develop at most a "primary signal system" that links concrete stimuli and visual relationships, speech provides man with a second level of links, by which we inhibit direct impulses and project ourselves in time and space. Through language, man knows time. We can control the strength of stimuli on our senses and thereby modify the rule of force by which all organisms are bound. Thus man assumes conscious control over his behavior when the word becomes, in Pavlov's terms, a "signal of signals." For a helpful discussion, see Alexander R. Luria, *The Role of Speech in the Regulation of Normal and Abnormal Behavior*, ed. J. Tizard (New York, 1961), pp. 20–42. See also Stephen Toulmin's summary in his excellent review of Vygotsky's work: "The Mozart of Psychology," *New York Review of Books*, 28 Sept. 1978, pp. 51–57.

The distinction between sign and signal is not, of course, exclusively Pavlovian. Vygotsky also incorporated the Husserlian distinction between *meaning* and *objective reference* (the latter term Vygotsky rendered as "the indicatory function of speech"). Although these categories are similar to Charles Sanders Peirce's symbolic sign and indexical sign, there is no evidence that Vygotsky got them from Peirce. I am grateful to James Wertsch for bringing the above to my attention.

12. Vygotsky proceeds to enumerate the advantages of the speaking child over the ape in the area of problem solving: the speaking child is more independent of his immediate field of vision, more capable of planning, and has greater control over his actions. Speaking children "acquire the capacity to be both the subjects and objects of their own behavior" ("TS," p. 26).

13. Vygotsky, *TL*, p. 146. Vygotsky further states:

> The sense of a word . . . is the sum of all the psychological events aroused in our consciousness by the word. . . . Meaning is only one of the zones of sense, the most stable and precise zone. A word acquires its sense from the context in which it appears; in different contexts, it changes its sense. Meaning remains stable throughout the changes of sense. The dictionary meaning of a word is no more than a stone in

the edifice of sense, no more than a potentiality that finds diversified realization in speech. [Ibid.]

Vygotsky's distinction here between *meaning* and *sense* has a nice parallel in Bakhtin's distinction between *meaning* and *theme* cited earlier in this essay (see p. 248). Again, I thank James Wertsch, for pointing out this parallel.

14.   See Vygotsky, "Interaction between Learning and Development," *Mind in Society,* pp. 84–86. The American educator John Holt seems to have something similar in mind when he writes, with wonderful simplicity: "The true test of intelligence is not how much we know how to do, but how we behave when we don't know what to do" (*How Children Fail* [New York, 1964], p. 205).

15.   Vygotsky's distinction between tool and symbol has a parallel in the bifurcating functions of speech. Both tool and symbol involve mediated activity, but tools are externally oriented, aids to mastering nature, whereas signs are internally oriented, ultimately aids to mastering oneself. See his "Internalization of Higher Psychological Functions," *Mind in Society,* p. 55.

16.   See Bakhtin, "Discourse in the Novel," *The Dialogic Imagination: Four Essays,* ed. Michael Holquist, trans. Caryl Emerson and Holquist, University of Texas Press Slavic Series, no. 1 (Austin, Tex., 1981), pp. 259–422, esp. pp. 341–42.

17.   See Ivanov, "The Significance of M. M. Bakhtin's Ideas," p. 314.

18.   Jacques Lacan, "The Empty Word and the Full Word," in *Speech and Language in Psychoanalysis,* ed. and trans. Anthony Wilden (Baltimore, 1981), p. 9.

19.   Lacan, from "La Chose freudienne" (1955), quoted in Wilden, "Lacan and the Discourse of the Other," in *Speech and Language in Psychoanalysis,* p. 266.

20.   On this, see Vološinov, *Fr,* p. 89: "The wider and deeper the breach between the official and the unofficial conscious, the more difficult it becomes for motives of inner speech to turn into outward speech "

21.   Bakhtin, "K pererabotke knigi o Dostoevskom" [Toward a reworking of the Dostoevsky book], *Estetika slovesnogo tvorčestva,* pp. 313, 311–12; my translation. The complete text of Bakhtin's 1961 notes for the Dostoevsky book is included as an appendix in my translation of Bakhtin, *Problems of Dostoevsky's Poetics,* Theory and History of Literature Series, vol. 8 (Minneapolis, 1984).

22.   In Leningrad of the 1920s, Bakhtin was well known as a *cerkovnik,* a devout Orthodox Christian; it was for his connections with the underground church that he was arrested in 1929. During these years he wrote a huge metaphysical work—only portions of which survive—on the meaning of Christian "responsibility," on "the Word become flesh," and on the implications of the Biblical injunction "In the Beginning was the Word." On this and other points of biography and doctrine, I am indebted to Katerina Clark and Michael Holquist, who have generously shared draft chapters of their *Mikhail Bakhtin.* See also Holquist, "The Politics of Representation," in *Allegory and Representation,* ed. Stephen J. Greenblatt, Selected Papers from the English Institute, 1979–80, n.s. 5 (Baltimore, 1981), pp. 163–83.

23.   For an American echo of the voices of Bakhtin and Vygotsky, see Toulmin, "The Inwardness of Mental Life," *Critical Inquiry* 6 (Autumn 1979): 1–16. Very much in their spirit, Toulmin argues that "inner" and "outer" are not on either side of a great divide but that "the moral and emotional ambiguities of our inner lives are simply the moral and emotional ambiguities of our open lives *internalized*" (p. 9).

24.   Vygotsky, quoted in Ivanov, "The Significance of M. M. Bakhtin's Ideas," p. 326.

25.   Georg Lukács, *The Theory of the Novel,* trans. Anna Bostock (Cambridge, Mass., 1971), pp. 29, 30.

26.   See Bakhtin, "Epic and Novel: Toward a Methodology for the Study of the Novel" (1941), *The Dialogic Imagination,* pp. 3–40; all further references to this work, abbreviated "EN," will be included parenthetically in the text. In this essay, Bakhtin posits three generic characteristics of the novel that free it from the strictures of epic: the novel is stylistically multi-languaged ("heteroglot"); it uses time in a way maximally open to the future; and it

creates a new zone for structuring images, a zone maximally close to the present. As a result, novelistic heroes are never exhausted by their plots; there is always some other way they might have acted and some other way of understanding their actions. Epics can prophesy; novels only predict.

27. Sigmund Freud, "The Relation of the Poet to Day-Dreaming," trans. I. F. Grant Duff, *On Creativity and the Unconscious: Papers on the Psychology of Art, Literature, Love, Religion,* comp. Benjamin Nelson (New York, 1958), p. 54.

28. Vygotsky, *The Psychology of Art* (Cambridge, Mass., 1971), p. 79.

29. Paul de Man, "Criticism and Crisis," *Blindness and Insight: Essays in the Rhetoric of Contemporary Criticism* (New York, 1971), p. 18.

Shouts on the Street: Bakhtin's Anti-Linguistics

Susan Stewart

During the period of the New Economic Policy, as Lenin sought, rather abashedly, to approach communism via a new form of "state capitalism," and as the concrete mode of peasant existence was being transformed into the abstractions of industrial labor, the contradictions between synchrony and diachrony, between "sincerity" and "irony," between insistences simultaneously upon meaning and "multivocality" were in full flower. The work of the Bakhtin school may be located within this milieu of contradiction. It is clear that Mikhail Bakhtin's project was not a linguistics but, to use his word, a "metalinguistics," an attempt to avoid an essentialist view of language and to see, within a social and historical frame, the creation and uses of both language and the term "language."[1] As Bakhtin wrote in *Problems of Dostoevsky's Poetics:*

> The point is not the mere presence of several linguistic styles, social dialects, etc., a presence which is measured by purely linguistic criteria; the point is the *dialogical angle* at which they (the styles, dialects, etc.) are juxtaposed and counterposed in the work. But that dialogic angle cannot be measured by means of purely linguistic criteria, because dialogic relationships, although they belong to the

Early concepts of this article were informed by participation in a National Endowment for the Humanities Summer Seminar on the Sociolinguistics of Literature, held at the University of Pennsylvania in the summer of 1980. I would like to thank in particular John F. Szwed, leader of the seminar, and the other participants for discussions on the parameters of a social theory of linguistics and literature, and the place of creolized forms within such a theory.

41

province of the *word,* fall outside the province of its purely linguistic study.

Dialogical relationships (including the dialogical relationships of the speaker to his own word) are a matter for metalinguistics.[2]

In short, only through metalinguistics could one account for the history and social life of language.

It is important to remember, however, that Bakhtin's meta-position is not so much a move toward transcendence as it is a battle stance, a polemical insistence upon situating theories of language within the constraints of their particular social and historical periods. M. A. K. Halliday has noted that some forms of speech, such as thieves' jargon and tinkers' argot, are shaped in direct opposition to the speech of the dominant class of their times; he calls these forms of speech "anti-languages."[3] Analogously, Bakhtin's linguistics is an *anti-linguistics,* a systematic questioning and inverting of the basic premises and arguments of traditional linguistic theory. It follows that recent attempts to "appropriate" Bakhtin's theories of language into the tradition he rejects are largely misguided. Erasing not only Bakhtin's sense of the radically *un*systematic nature of the linguistic world but also the conflicting, anarchic nature of his very texts, semioticians and structuralists have let him speak only by silencing him.

Bakhtin's Critique of "Language"

Nowhere does this problem of appropriation emerge more clearly than in examining Bakhtin's critique of language. Indeed, even using the term "language" skews the position that Bakhtin took toward verbal behavior. In *Marxism and the Philosophy of Language,* his critique of "abstract objectivist" theories is directed to the following points: that such theories stabilize language at the expense of its real mutability and the creativity of its users; that such theories assume language to be outside of contextualization and consequently outside of history; and that such theories tend to hypostatize their own categories.[4] Ferdinand de Saussure had written in the *Cours de linguistique générale:*

> In separating language from speaking we are at the same time separating: (1) what is social from what is individual; and (2) what is essential from what is accessory and more or less accidental.

Susan Stewart is associate professor of English at Temple University. She is the author of a book of poetry, *Yellow Stars and Ice* (1981), and two books of literary theory, *Nonsense: Aspects of Intertextuality in Folklore and Literature* (1979) and *On Longing: Narratives of the Miniature, the Gigantic, the Souvenir, and the Collection* (1984).

> Language is not a function of the speaker; it is a product that is passively assimilated by the individual. It never requires premeditation, and reflection enters in only for the purpose of classification. . . .
>
> Speaking, on the contrary, is an individual act. It is wilful and intellectual.[5]

No position could be more the antithesis of Bakhtin's. Saussure is interested in language as an abstract and ready-made system; Bakhtin is interested only in the dynamics of living speech. Where Saussure sees passive assimilation, Bakhtin sees a process of struggle and contradiction. And whereas Saussure dichotomizes the individual and the social, Bakhtin assumes that the individual is constituted by the social, that consciousness is a matter of dialogue and juxtaposition with a social Other.

In "Discourse in the Novel" Bakhtin writes: "A passive understanding of linguistic meaning is no understanding at all, it is only the abstract aspect of meaning."[6] For Bakhtin such an abstraction from the concrete utterance would be a dead end, reifying its own categories of the linguistic norm and producing a model with no capability of discussing linguistic—and thereby, for Bakhtin, social—change. If Bakhtin has until recently lacked his true inheritors, Saussure has not, and the major heirlooms of Saussurian linguistics—*langue* vs. *parole*, the arbitrary nature of the sign, and, more indirectly, the distinction between poetic and ordinary language—reappear in transformational grammar, in the old (and the new) stylistics, and even, surprisingly, in quasi-Marxist theories of language such as Julia Kristeva's.

The transformational grammarian's devoted outlining of abstract syntactical structures and the stylistician's almost magical rendering of phonetic and morphological structures into thematic structures stand in direct contrast to Bakhtin's object of study.[7] When Bakhtin discusses "problems of syntax," he has in mind the utterance as it occurs in context, in lived social time. Hence that object of study has rather fluid, generically determined boundaries, ranging from utterances consisting of a single word to utterances consisting of the entire text of a literary work. In *The Formal Method in Literary Scholarship,* he writes:

> It is the whole utterance as speech performance that is directed at the theme, not the separate word, sentence, or period. It is the whole utterance and its forms, which cannot be reduced to any linguistic forms, which control the theme. The theme of the work is the theme of the whole utterance as a definite sociohistorical act. Consequently, it is inseparable from the total situation of the utterance to the same extent that it is inseparable from linguistic elements.[8]

The critique of abstraction in Bakhtin's work is a profound and relentless one. At every point he proclaims that the model of pure linguistic form arose from neoclassical philosophies and from the study of dead languages, that only in its living reality, shaped and articulated by social evaluation, does the word exist. He insists upon contextualizing even the notion of abstraction itself, suggesting that the tradition of normative linguistics from Aristotle and Saint Augustine through the Indo-Europeanists served the needs of sociopolitical and cultural centralization. These "centripetal forces," he contends, can be perceived only against the backdrop of the very "heteroglossia" they sought to deny (*DI*, p. 271). We see a rejection in his work not only of a distinction between "language" and "speech" but also of a distinction between synchrony and diachrony. Bakhtin traces these dichotomies to Cartesian rationalism and Leibniz's conception of a universal grammar (see *MPL*, p. 57). Because it denies the actual creativity of language use, Bakhtin rejects the systematizing impulse of such linguistic thought: "Formal, systematic thought about language is incompatible with living, historical understanding of language. From the system's point of view, history always seems merely a series of accidental [*sic*] transgressions" (*MPL*, p. 78).[9]

Not only does such systematization lead to a denial of history—it also results in a vision of speech as a series of "accidental transgressions," a vision we find most prevalent in Noam Chomsky's distinction between competence and performance. There is perhaps no clearer description of linguistic alienation than Chomsky's position on this point: "Any interesting generative grammar will be dealing, for the most part, with mental processes that are far beyond the level of actual or even potential consciousness; furthermore, it is quite apparent that a speaker's reports and viewpoints about his behavior and competence may be in error."[10] The social and political consequences of such an abstract linguistics are brought out in Bakhtin's own observations on the concept of error: "Only in abnormal and special cases do we apply the criterion of correctness to an utterance (for instance, in language instruction). Normally, the criterion of linguistic correctness is submerged by a purely ideological [i.e., thematic] criterion" (*MPL*, p. 70). Rather than assume a transcendent grammar to which actual speech performance can be only imperfectly compared, Bakhtin looks at the social articulation and uses of diversity. The consequences of the Cartesian position become clearer when we look at its current application in state policy. In such domains as the exclusion of bi- (and multi-) lingual education, language requirements attached to immigration restrictions, tensions between nonstandard and standard "dialects" (these terms themselves the necessary fictions by which a transcendent "standard" is created), and the language of state apparatuses in general, the Cartesian position functions to reinforce state institutions and to trivialize change and everyday linguistic creativity. To silence the diversity of the powerful "unsaids" of actual speech in favor of an opaque and universal form of language is to strip language of its ideological significance—a stripping that is itself strongly and univocally ideological.[11]

His careful attention to actual social behavior also prohibits Bakhtin from accepting any facile distinction between ordinary and poetic language.

Such distinctions tend to trivialize both everyday speech acts—by making them automatic or indistinguishable—and "poetic" utterances—by making them parasitic. Most important, theories of poetic language trivialize the activities of speakers by assuming an essentialist, rather than a social, definition of genre.[12] A critique of the concept of poetic language forms a major part of *The Formal Method:* "If the poetic construction had been placed in a complex, many-sided relationship with science, with rhetoric, with the fields of real practical life, instead of being declared the bare converse of a fabricated practical language, then formalism as we know it would not have existed" (*FM,* p. 98). In this study, Bakhtin not only objects to the formalist concept of the autonomy of poetic language but also, in a characteristic move, attempts to show the sources and purposes of this formalist position in futurist poetics.

Although we find in Bakhtin an early critic of the linguistics of abstract objectivism, we do not find a neat precursor of contemporary social theories of language. Whereas such studies as William Labov's on the social implications of sound-change vindicate Bakhtin's rejection of a purely "linguistic" conception of phonology, the majority of sociolinguistic studies tends, no less problematically, to emphasize context in a highly abstract way—that is, without a corresponding discussion of the location of the utterance in history and social life.[13] In other words, as the abstract objectivists tend to hypostatize grammar, the sociolinguists often tend to hypostatize rules for speech behavior. They do not seem to realize that such rules are not simply located *behind* the historical processes of social life but are also *emergent in* them. Hence there is a tendency to want to *name* the situation, to close off its boundaries, particularly in speech-act theory. Consider, for instance, John Searle's original formulation of his philosophy of speech acts: "The form this hypothesis will take is that the semantic structure of a language may be regarded as a conventional realization of a series of sets of underlying constitutive rules, and that speech acts are acts characteristically performed by uttering expressions in accordance with these sets of constitutive rules."[14]

Similarly, although the sociolinguistic study of styles of speaking goes beyond such a static concept of situation by contrasting the "referential" and "social" aspects of discourse, it does not present a model of the historical transformation of social values and ideologies. The emphasis on rule-governed behavior in current social studies of language again tends toward a focus on "form" at the expense of ideological strategy and a focus on "system" at the expense of social creativity. As a result, such studies search for a grammar of situation; and so, their Romantic humanism notwithstanding, they recapitulate many of the methodological pitfalls of the abstract objectivists.

Bakhtin's positions on verbal interaction thus overlap—but also go beyond—the aims of both sociolinguistics and speech-act theory. The difference is that his primary concern is not so much with how things *work* as with how things *change*. In contrast to Searle's atemporality,

Bakhtin presents a theory of the sequential order of change: "This is the order that the actual generative process of language follows: *social intercourse is generated* (stemming from the basis); *in it verbal communication and interaction are generated; and in the latter, forms of speech performances are generated; finally, this generative process is reflected in the change of language forms*" (*MPL*, p. 96). Like Searle and John Austin, Bakhtin is concerned with identifying what he calls the "little behavioral genres" of speech situations—question, exclamation, command, request, the light and casual causerie of the drawing room. But Bakhtin is even more interested in the relationships between those genres and their contexts in the rest of social life: "The behavioral genre fits everywhere into the channel of social intercourse assigned to it and functions as an ideological reflection of its type, structure, goal, and social composition," particularly as history changes the ideological functions of such contexts (*MPL*, p. 97). Searle specifies the "happiness conditions" of successful speech acts; Bakhtin is the master of what we might call "unhappiness conditions," those circumstances in which the utterance stands in tension or conflict with the utterances of others. For utterances are always preceded by alien utterances which face them in the form of an addressee or social Other and which surround them with an always significant silence. Whereas linguistic theory must be grateful to sociolinguistics for specifying the profound uses of silence, it must be grateful to Bakhtin for articulating the powerful force of the silenc*ed* in language use.[15]

Bakhtin's Critique of the "Sign"

Thus, Bakhtin presents us with a "generative" linguistics, but that linguistics is accounted for in a *social* sense. The "rules" it seeks are conventions of genre, conventions of voice, character, idea, temporality, and closure which will be modified by the ongoing transformations of social life. Because it emphasizes the social, it is directly opposed to those contemporary theories of language, such as Chomsky's, that ultimately locate transformation in biological evolutionary processes. And although Bakhtin presents an investigation of utterances in context, his concern with dialogue, with conflict, and, especially, with the cumulative forces of history acting upon each speech situation distinguishes his work from contemporary sociolinguistic theories. Finally, although many careful comparisons have been made between Bakhtin's semiotics and contemporary semiotic theory, Bakhtin's position on the sign differs from traditional semiotics in several crucial ways.[16]

The powerful critique of "language" offered in *Marxism and the Philosophy of Language* is supplemented throughout the rest of his works by an equally powerful critique of the concept of the sign. The Saussurian theory of the referent naively assumes a univocality of meaning, and

Charles Sanders Peirce's theory of iconicity assumes an actual physical referent to which the sign-vehicle corresponds. In contrast, Bakhtin clearly distinguishes between the mechanistic and pragmatic functions of signals and the cultural and "polyvocal" functions of signs: "The process of understanding is on no account to be confused with the process of recognition. These are thoroughly different processes. Only a sign can be understood; what is recognized is a signal" (*MPL*, p. 68). For Bakhtin, the material life of the sign does not arise out of the world of physical objects; rather, it arises out of the actual material practices of everyday social life. And, unlike Saussure, Bakhtin does not see the sign as a part of an abstract system resulting from the structure of psychological perception. Instead, he looks for the ontology of the sign in the "practical business of living speech." Here again we see Bakhtin's rebellion against system. The semiotic character of culture is the result of concrete and dynamic historical processes, processes of tension and conflict inseparable from the basis of social and economic life.

Bakhtin's critique of the univocal sign is perhaps most fully developed in his study of Dostoevsky and in his early essay, "Discourse in Life and Discourse in Art." In the works of Dostoevsky, Bakhtin both found and created the aesthetic correspondent to his theories of thought and language:

> The idea, as *seen* by Dostoevsky the artist, is not a subjective individual-psychological formulation with a "permanent residence" in a person's head; no, the idea is interindividual and intersubjective. The sphere of its existence is not the individual consciousness, but the dialogical intercourse *between* consciousnesses. The idea is a *living event* which is played out in the point where two or more consciousnesses meet dialogically. In this respect the idea resembles the *word*, with which it forms a dialogical unity. Like the word, the idea wants to be heard, understood, and "answered" by other voices from other positions. Like the word, the idea is by nature dialogical, the monolog being merely the conventional form of its expression which arose from the soil of the ideological monologism of modern times. [*PDP*, p. 72]

The idea and the word are here conceptualized as "arenas of conflict," and this conflict arises not simply, as sociolinguistics suggests, out of the tension between the referent and the physical context of utterances but rather from bringing all past experience with the word to bear upon the present situation. For example, Bakhtin sees the works of Dostoevsky as integrating the aphoristic thinking of the Enlightenment and Romanticism into locations of contrast and conflict. And those locations invite the social value judgments of readers who are themselves implicated in the text.

In "Discourse in Life and Discourse in Art," these aspects of polyvalence are worked into a sociological theory of literature. Bakhtin outlines the ways in which the relations between the author's, hero's (character's), and reader's voices intersect within the constraints of genre. "The inter-relationship of author and hero, never, after all, actually is an intimate relationship of two; all the while form makes provision for the third participant—the listener—who exerts crucial influence on all the other factors of the work" (*Fr*, p. 112). It is out of these contrasting and col-laborating positions that satire, parody, and irony arise as forms depicting conflicting social value judgments.

We might contrast this approach to literature with modern speech-act theories that assume, in Mary Louise Pratt's term, that literary works are "verbal displays." Such theories often neglect the specific effects that the literary work uses to create distancing and irony.[17] In other words, speech-act theories of literature often assume the same systematic and transparent univocality we find in speech-act theories of language. But Bakhtin's literary theory assumes that the problems of dialogue and multivocality that are found in face-to-face communication will be com-pounded by the specific effects used within the structure of the literary genre. Because the literary work relies on a common ideological purview of both author and reader and, at the same time, cannot rely upon an apparent "extraverbal" context, the work is a complex presentation of display *and* concealment, of the over- and under-articulated. This pre-sentation is further complicated by the history of generic conventions. Bakhtin writes: "We might say that *a poetic work is a powerful condenser of unarticulated social evaluations*—each word is saturated with them. *It is these social evaluations that organize form as their direct expression*" (*Fr*, p. 107).

Bakhtin's concerted opening up of the word may be characterized as having distinguishable, if interwoven, formal and semantic levels. We have seen how his position takes a stance against both abstract objectivism and Romanticism, but we also might consider the influence of Bakhtin's historical work on the development of his theory. In the introduction to *Rabelais and His World*, Bakhtin writes that the function of the "carnival-grotesque" is "to consecrate inventive freedom, to permit the combination of a variety of different elements and their rapprochement, to liberate from the prevailing point of view of the world, from conventions and established truths, from clichés, from all that is humdrum and universally accepted."[18] It is characteristic of Bakhtin that, in several ways, the carnival-grotesque serves as a model of the normal. For carnival contains both the conventional and the unexpected, the established and the creative. He also focuses on the transitional linguistic forms of the Hellenic period, the late Middle Ages, and the Renaissance—that is, on loci of change. Here and in his discussion of the prehistory of the novel, he is interested in how traditional forms are parodied, or "carnivalized," as part of the complex interaction of social forces within particular historical periods of upheaval and transformation (see *DI*, pp. 3–83). He consequently paid great attention to the creolized language of the marketplace and street while he formed an image of language as mediating between conventionality and creativity.

For Bakhtin, language is mutable, reversible, anti-hierarchical, contaminable, and powerfully regenerative. It is always meeting—has always been meeting—what is strange, foreign, other:

> Linguistics, itself the product of [the] foreign word, is far from any proper understanding of the role played by the foreign word in the history of language and linguistic consciousness. On the contrary, Indo-European studies have fashioned categories of understanding for the history of language of a kind that preclude proper evaluation of the role of [the] alien word. Meanwhile, that role, to all appearances, is enormous. [*MPL,* pp. 75–76]

At language's point of origin, Bakhtin assumes ambivalence, multivocality, conflict, incorporation, and transformation. Not the least profound implication of this position might be that the model which linguistics has assumed, whereby stable languages eventually become creolized, has been moving backward; instead, we might assume creolization at the point of origin and view stabilization of the linguistic system not as the normal but as the restricted case.

The Invention of "Ideology"

Semantically, Bakhtin's dialogic conception of the word can be seen not only as a contribution to linguistic theory but also as a contribution to the theory of ideology. For although Bakhtin continually erases the abstract concept of language, he just as continually reformulates the concept of ideology. Indeed, it might be more appropriate to place Bakhtin among theorists of ideology rather than among theorists of linguistics and semiotics. To understand the radicalism of Bakhtin's theory of ideology, we must first turn to his own outline of the subject.

Alongside the rejection of transcendence implicit in Bakhtin's critique of abstraction and system is a corresponding rejection of "individual" consciousness. His critique of Freud suffers from the naiveté of his rather knee-jerk reaction to Freud's early published writings; yet that critique substantially predicts Jacques Lacan's reformulation of Freudianism in light of linguistic theory, particularly the translation of the unconscious into a form of language. In place of the concept of the unconscious, which Bakhtin viewed as unanalyzable so long as it remained neither physiological nor verbal, Bakhtin advances the concept of inner speech: through inner speech, all consciousness is social in its formulation. Accordingly, Bakhtin sees inner speech and outer, articulated speech as having ideological status. Inner speech is no less subjected to social evaluation than outer speech, because of the intrinsically social history and nature of the word:

> The complex apparatus of verbal reactions functions in all its fundamental aspects also when the subject says nothing about his experiences but only undergoes them "in himself," since, if he is conscious of them, a process of *inner* ("covert") speech occurs (we do, after all, think and feel and desire with the help of words; without inner speech we would not become conscious of anything in ourselves). This process of inner speech is just as material as is outward speech. [*Fr,* p. 21]

To be sure, Bakhtin recognizes that "the formation of verbal connections (the establishment of connections among visual, motor, and other kinds of reactions over the course of interindividual communication, upon which the formation of verbal reactions depends) proceeds with special difficulty and delay in certain areas of life (for example, the sexual)," but he nevertheless does not explore in any depth the tensions between the unarticulated and articulated in those cases (*Fr,* p. 24). In his work, little distinction is made between the nature of inner and outer speech, and he sometimes describes inner speech as a mere practice ground for what will or may later be articulated. This theoretical lack might be attributed to Bakhtin's apparent adherence in *Freudianism: A Marxist Critique* to a rather mechanistic behavioral psychology. He does write, however, that both inner and outer speech form a type of behavioral ideology that "is in certain respects more sensitive, more responsive, more excitable and livelier than an ideology that has undergone formulation and become 'official' " (*Fr,* p. 88).

Thus we begin to receive an outline of constraints that could distinguish between the qualities of inner and outer speech. His sensitivity to those varying constraints was most likely responsible for a major contribution in his discussion of Freud: Bakhtin stresses the shaping power of the specific dialogic situation of the psychoanalytic interview. Going beyond Freud's own individual-centered notions of transference, Bakhtin explains that the interview situation is a highly complex one and must be understood in light of the social dynamic between doctor and patient, and not—or not only—in terms of the patient's individual psyche.[19]

Bakhtin's insistence upon the primary place of the social, the "already said," in the formation of consciousness is at the heart of his struggle against the "bourgeois ideology" of individualism. In *Marxism and the Philosophy of Language,* we see a critique of Herderian linguistics, with all its Romantic assumptions about the individual soul. In the work of Wilhelm von Humboldt, Karl Vossler, and their followers, Bakhtin points out that a reformulation of this bourgeois philosophy appears in the theory that laws of linguistic creativity are laws of individual psychology (see *MPL,* p. 48). Bakhtin argues that such a position strips language of its ideological content and neglects the intrinsically social nature of linguistic change. In his book *Freudianism,* he pursues his attack on the abstract concept of the individual by criticizing Freud's asocial and tautological notion of self-consciousness. Here Bakhtin writes:

> In becoming aware of myself, I attempt to look at myself, as it were, through the eyes of another person, another representative of my social group, my class. Thus, *self-consciousness,* in the final analysis, always leads us to *class consciousness,* the reflection and specification of which it is in all its fundamental and essential respects. Here we have the *objective roots* of even the most personal and intimate reactions. [*Fr,* p. 87]

According to Bakhtin, all social, antisocial, and warring impulses within consciousness are reflections of social, antisocial, and warring impulses within the mutually experienced world of lived reality. When a class is in decline, we may expect to see manifestations of its decay in the behavior of its individual members.

In *Freudianism* and the essay on discourse in life and art, the critique of individualism is mirrored within an aesthetic theory. Bakhtin criticizes theories of art that place the significance of the artwork within the psyche of either the creator or the contemplator: "We might say that such a thing is similar to the attempt to analyze the individual psyche of a proletarian in order thereby to disclose the objective production relations that determine his position in society" (*Fr,* p. 97). Instead, Bakhtin places the work in the interaction between these two positions and concludes that artistic value arises only in the dynamics of such social communication. Similarly, in *Problems of Dostoevsky's Poetics,* Bakhtin situates the subject within sociality and argues that identity is produced by speech, particularly through the contradictions of narrative. Using Dostoevsky as an example, Bakhtin observes that each of that novelist's heroes is *the man of an idea,* an idea that is itself a construct of contradiction and dialogue:

> Only the unfinalizable and inexhaustible "man in man" can become the man of an idea, whose image is combined with the image of a full-valued idea. This is the first condition of the representation of the idea in Dostoevsky.
>
> But this condition contains, as it were, its inverse as well. We can say that in Dostoevsky's works man overcomes his "thingness" (*veshchnost'*) and becomes "man in man" only by entering the pure and unfinalized sphere of the idea, i.e., only by becoming the selfless man of an idea. Such are all of Dostoevsky's leading characters, i.e. all of the participants in the great dialog. [*PDP,* p. 70]

Here we find a radical departure from traditional Marxist aesthetics, in fact, the inverse of Marx's position in *The German Ideology* where he writes: "We do not set out from what men say, imagine, conceive, nor from men as narrated, thought of, imagined, conceived, in order to arrive at men in the flesh. We set out from real, active men, and on the basis of their real life-process we demonstrate the development of the ideological reflexes and echoes of this life-process."[20] Rather than assume the "real" man at the point of beginning for ideology, Bakhtin would say that it is precisely within narrative, and within ideological structures, that the concept of the individual subject, of the "real" man is born. And the conclusion to *The Formal Method* makes clear that such ideological structures are themselves constituted by and through speech.

Bakhtin's concept of ideology differs significantly from the early reflectionist theories of Marx. In *Capital,* Marx writes:

> The religious world is but the reflex of the real world. And for a society based upon the production of commodities, in which the producers in general enter into social relations with one another by treating their products as commodities and values, whereby they reduce their individual private labour to the standard of homogeneous human labour—for such a society, Christianity with its *cultus* of abstract man, more especially in its bourgeois developments, Protestantism, Deism, etc., is the most fitting form of religion.[21]

Marx's theory is deferred and utopian in its outlook: ideology represents the false consciousness produced under class society; after the revolution of the proletariat, the slippage between this false consciousness and the real world will be healed and an actual relation to reality lived. This notion of ideology as false consciousness also lies behind Louis Althusser's distinction between ideology and science and Georg Lukács' attempt in *History and Class Consciousness* to identify truth with proximity to proletarian consciousness. Similarly, in Lucien Goldmann's distinction between a limited ideology and an embracing world view, we see a kind of "monologic" vision of ideology.

By contrast, Bakhtin asserts that ideology is manifested and created in the practical material activity of speech behavior: hence his notion of "behavioral ideology." As in his theory of linguistics, Bakhtin rejects the abstract concept in favor of the material and dynamic relation. The dialogic nature of the sign, its inner and outward form, allows the intersection of sign with sign, idea with idea, at the same time that it ensures continual upheaval and change in signifying practices as they occur in concrete historical contexts. Thus, ideology is not only the product of social life but is also both productive and reproductive of lived social relations. Furthermore, although in Bakhtin's theory of ideology the socioeconomic base is seen as determining, it is not a base that locks ideology into a static and transcendent form. Rather, ideology is seen as an arena of conflict: one's speech both reveals *and produces* one's position in class society, in such a way, moreover, as to set into dialogue the relations among classes. Consider this passage from Bakhtin's *Marxism:*

Existence reflected in sign is not merely reflected but *refracted*. How is this refraction of existence in the ideological sign determined? By an intersecting of differently oriented social interests within one and the same sign community, i.e., . . . with the community, which is the totality of users of the same set of signs for ideological communication. Thus various different classes will use one and the same language. As a result, differently oriented accents intersect in every ideological sign. Sign becomes an arena of class struggle. [*MPL*, p. 23]

Once he moves the materiality of language away from essence into the domain of practice, Bakhtin can present the cacophony of voices present in any utterance, can reject a notion of speech community based on phonology in favor of a much more useful one based on interest and on what might be termed "positionality," the place of the subject within the social structure, a place where subject and structure are mutually articulated.[22] What Bakhtin's theory of ideology offers is a model of ideological production. In this model, ideology is not assumed to be either a foggy lens or a mirroring cloud. It is, rather, assumed to be an ongoing product and producer of social practices. The semantic transition from reflection to refraction marks a movement from repetition to production.

Most radically, Bakhtin is unwilling to limit the place of ideology to a particular or narrow sphere of social life. Instead, he concludes that "all of these things [ideological phenomena] in their totality comprise the ideological environment, which forms a solid ring around man. And man's consciousness lives and develops in this environment. Human consciousness does not come into contact with existence directly, but through the medium of the surrounding ideological world" (*FM*, p. 14). This is a considerable departure from traditional Marxist positions, which either locate the real in the supposedly direct purview of science or in the deferred idealism of revolution.[23] In contrast, Bakhtin concludes that both science and ideology are products whose absolute "reality"—if it existed at all—could be apprehended only by a transcendent consciousness, a consciousness that would itself be, ironically, an ideological construct. Bakhtin's movement away from a reflectionist theory can perhaps be traced to his familiarity with the carnival mode, where refraction and inversion considerably complicate a traditional functionalist model.

To understand how ideological practice is performed, we cannot begin with a model of the utterance as the spontaneous production of an individual consciousness. Rather, the utterance must be seen as bearing within itself a complex and contradictory set of historical elements. In this sense, Bakhtin observes, *all* speech is reported speech, for all speech carries with it a history of use and interpretation by which it achieves both identity and difference. It is within this rather remarkable capacity for making present the past that speech acquires its social meaning. Hence for Bakhtin the proper study of ideology would begin with an examination of ideological form, with the study of genre, and not in any autonomous or transcendent sense of genre or form but in the sense that form presents a location of tension between the past and the present. Bakhtin begins by distinguishing ideological objects both from instruments of production (which are consumed by their function) and from consumer goods (which, in existing for individual use, are not available for social evaluation). The specificity of ideological objects lies in their "concrete material reality" and "social meaning" (*FM*, p. 12).

In *The Formal Method*, Bakhtin insists that literary form is unique in that it refracts the generating socioeconomic reality in ways particular to its own history and at the same time "reflects and refracts the reflections and refractions of other ideological spheres" (*FM*, p. 16). Thus, literature serves as a type of super superstructure, in part because of the levels of representation involved in literary production. Here we might contrast the various possibilities of slippage offered by this model to the currently fashionable notion, offered by newer Marxist critics, of the absences in ideological discourse.[24] Bakhtin offers a much more positivist outlook than this deconstructionist one, for he believes that the utterance will carry within it a set of articulate silences and that the common ideological purview of author and reader will work toward the discernment of patterns in the unsaid. Thus, his theory is not necessarily burdened with a nostalgia for full presence: here the contradictions, ambivalences, and silences of the text are seen as part of its essentially dialogic nature.

According to Bakhtin, the reason that literature is the most ideological of all ideological spheres may be discovered in the structure of genre. He criticizes the formalists for ending their theory with a consideration of genre; genre, he observes, should be the first topic of poetics. The importance of genre lies in its two major capacities: conceptualization and "finalization." A genre's conceptualization has both inward and outward focus: the artist does not merely represent reality; he or she must use existing means of representation in tension with the subject at hand. This process is analogous to the dual nature of the utterance, its orientation simultaneously toward its past contexts and its present context. "A particular aspect of reality can only be understood in connection with the particular means of representing it" (*FM*, p. 134). Genre's production of perception is not simply a matter of physical orientation; it is also a matter of ideology: "Every significant genre is a complex system of means and methods for the conscious control and finalization of reality" (*FM*, p. 133). According to Bakhtin, nonideological domains are "open work," not subject to an ultimate closure; but one goal of works of art is precisely to offer closure, a "finalization" that accounts for their ideological power and their capacity to produce consciousness. In the particular finalization of genre, we see a continual tension between tradition and situation.[25] As Terry Eagleton suggests in *Criticism and Ideology*, "A power-loom, for one thing, is not altered by its products . . . in the way that a literary convention is transformed by what it textually works."[26] Analogously, Bakhtin writes that "the goal of the artistic structure of every historical genre is to merge the distances of space and time with the contemporary by the force of all-penetrating social evaluation" (*FM*, p. 158). It is perhaps because of this purported goal that Bakhtin himself seemed to prefer the novel, which he viewed as a meta-genre incorporating at once all domains of ideology and all other literary genres. Finally, we must emphasize that Bakhtin's model of genre rests upon his insistence that literary evolution is not the result of device reacting against device, as Viktor Shklovsky believed, but rather of ideological, and ultimately socioeconomic, changes.

We see, then, that Bakhtin's work, in its radical rejection of abstraction, system, and the ideology of bourgeois individualism, forms an arena for a powerful struggle between linguistics and speech, theory and history. His theories' capacities for negation and critique are apparent whether we contrast them to the linguistic theories of his time or of ours. Moreover, this capacity for dialogue, contradiction, and complexity also exists in his work's inner speech—in its allusions to, or silences in the presence of, its own social context. In *The Formal Method*, at the culmination of Bakhtin's presentation of multivalence, we find as a dominant motif an insistence not only on meaning but also on meaningful*ness*. Bakhtin cannot accept the futurist model of perpetual and content-less motion: he continually rejects the futurists, and their influence on formalism, as nihilistic, even hedonistic, perhaps reminding us of Trotsky's position in *Literature and Revolution*. In *Rabelais and His World*, Bakhtin describes a historical period in which the language of the body was transformed by the rise of capitalism into an alien form of discourse. Bakhtin himself lived in a period when a similar drama was being enacted in the transformations of the peasantry by the industrial state. And yet we never find in his work a discussion of the effects of industrial practice or mechanical reproduction on ideological thought. If we look for a pattern of absences in these texts, we may gradually limn the image of the futurist machine and its totalitarian capacity for the negation of dialogue.

1. See Gary Saul Morson, "The Heresiarch of *Meta*," *PTL* 3 (Oct. 1978): 407–27.

2. Mikhail Bakhtin, *Problems of Dostoevsky's Poetics*, trans. R. W. Rotsel (Ann Arbor, Mich., 1973), pp. 150–51; all further references to this work, abbreviated *PDP*, will be included parenthetically in the text. In the text, I follow the current practice of attributing the works of the Bakhtin school to Bakhtin himself; in the notes, I list works by their published authors.

3. See M. A. K. Halliday, "Anti-Languages," *American Anthropologist* 78 (Sept. 1976): 170–83.

4. See V. N. Vološinov, *Marxism and the Philosophy of Language*, trans. Ladislav Matejka and I. R. Titunik, Studies in Language, vol. 1 (New York, 1973), p. 77; all further references to this work, abbreviated *MPL*, will be included parenthetically in the text. See also Vološinov, *Freudianism: A Marxist Critique*, ed. in collaboration with Neal H. Bruss, trans. Titunik (New York, 1976); all further references to this work, abbreviated *Fr*, will be included parenthetically in the text.

5. Ferdinand de Saussure, *Course in General Linguistics*, ed. Charles Bally and Albert Sechehaye, in collaboration with Albert Riedlinger, trans. Wade Baskin (New York, 1966), p. 14.

6. Bakhtin, "Discourse in the Novel," *The Dialogic Imagination: Four Essays*, ed. Michael Holquist, trans. Caryl Emerson and Holquist, University of Texas Press Slavic Series, no. 1 (Austin, Tex., 1981), p. 281; all further references to this work, abbreviated *DI*, will be included parenthetically in the text.

7. For an attempt to link syntactic to larger social transformations, see Rosalind Coward and John Ellis, *Language and Materialism: Developments in Semiology and the Theory of the Subject* (London, 1977), pp. 127–30. This attempt seems at best metaphorical and at worst strangely skewed: without a corresponding theory of language use in context, the linkage involves a confusion of levels of analysis.

8. P. N. Medvedev/Bakhtin, *The Formal Method in Literary Scholarship: A Critical Introduction to Sociological Poetics*, trans. Albert J. Wehrle, Goucher College Series (Baltimore, 1978), p. 132; all further references to this work, abbreviated *FM*, will be included parenthetically in the text.

9. It is thus puzzling when Krystyna Pomorska, in her foreword to Bakhtin's *Rabelais and His World*, insists repeatedly that Bakhtin is a structuralist. Although Roman Jakobson and Jurij Tynjanov wrote in their "Problems in the Study of Literature and Language" that "every system necessarily exists as an evolution while, on the other hand, evolution is inescapably of a systematic nature" (quoted in Titunik, "The Formal Method and the Sociological Method [M. M. Baxtin, P. N. Medvedev, V. N. Vološinov] in Russian Theory and Study of Literature," appendix 2, *MPL*, p. 187), this is hardly a mirror of Bakhtin's rejection of the distinction between synchrony and diachrony. In a later essay, "Mixail Baxtin [Mikhail Bakhtin] and His Verbal Universe," Pomorska writes that Bakhtin is a "real semiotician," and she goes on to explain that, in his rejection of an autonomous function for literature, he prefigures the Tartu school's semiotics. She also writes that, in addition to the Einsteinian revolution and Husserlian philosophy, "the other source," more obvious for Baxtin than, say, for Jakobson or Tynjanov, is classical Marxist dialectics" (*PTL* 3 [Apr. 1978]: 381, 384–85).

10. Noam Chomsky, *Aspects of the Theory of Syntax* (Cambridge, Mass., 1965), p. 8.

11. For a sociolinguistic critique of transformational grammar, see Dell Hymes, *Foundations in Sociolinguistics: An Ethnographic Approach* (Philadelphia, 1974), particularly pp. 119–24, where Herderian and Cartesian linguistics are contrasted; and William Labov, *Sociolinguistic Patterns* (Philadelphia, 1972), p. 200. In a suggestive essay, Henri Gobard has traced some of the sociological functions of abstract languages, particularly the effect of a multinational English upon vernacular French: see Gobard, *L'Alienation linguistique: Analyse tetraglossique* (Paris, 1976).

12. See Stanley E. Fish, "How Ordinary Is Ordinary Language?," *New Literary History* 5 (Autumn 1973): 41–54, and Mary Louise Pratt, "The 'Poetic Language' Fallacy," *Toward a Speech Act Theory of Literary Discourse* (Bloomington, Ind., 1977), pp. 3–37.

13. See Labov, *Sociolinguistic Patterns* and *Language in the Inner City: Studies in the Black English Vernacular* (Philadelphia, 1972).

14. John R. Searle, *Speech Acts: An Essay in the Philosophy of Language* (Cambridge, 1969), p. 37.

15. See, for example, K. H. Basso, " 'To Give Up on Words': Silence in Western Apache Culture," in *Language and Social Context: Selected Readings*, ed. Pier Paolo Giglioli (Harmondsworth, 1972), pp. 67–86.

16. See Matejka, "On the First Russian Prolegomena to Semiotics," appendix 1, *MPL*, pp. 161–74; Viach. Vs. Ivanov, "The Significance of M. M. Bakhtin's Ideas on Sign, Utterance, and Dialogue for Modern Semiotics (1)," *Soviet Studies in Literature* 11 (Spring-Summer 1975): 186–243; and Tzvetan Todorov, *Mikhail Bakhtine et la théorie de l'histoire littéraire*, Centro internazionale di semiotica e di linguistica, Documents de travail, ser. D, no. 87 (Urbino, 1979).

17. Pratt presents a convincing argument regarding the ways in which narrative literary works should not be separated formally from narratives of everyday life. But her assumptions of the linearity and univocality of both types of narrative preclude consideration of the ways in which face-to-face narratives most often are constructed collaboratively and, hence, reveal conflicting social value judgments just as literary works do.

18. Bakhtin, *Rabelais and His World*, trans. Helene Iswolsky (Cambridge, Mass., 1968), p. 34.

19. See Vološinov, *Fr*, pp. 78–79. Cf. Gregory Bateson, "The Message 'This Is Play,' " in *Group Processes: Transactions of the Second Congress of the Josiah Macy, Jr., Foundation*, ed. Bertram Schaffner (Princeton, N.J., 1956), pp. 145–242, and Ray L. Birdwhistell, "Contribution of Linguistic-Kinesic Studies to the Understanding of Schizophrenia," in *Schizophrenia: An Integrated Approach*, ed. Alfred Auerback (New York, 1959), pp. 99–123.

20. Karl Marx and Frederick Engels, *The German Ideology*, ed. C. J. Arthur, trans. Institute of Marxism-Leninism (London, 1970), p. 47.

21. Marx, *Capital: A Critique of Political Economy*, ed. Engels, trans. Samuel Moore and Edward Aveling (New York, 1906), p. 91.

22. In *The Formal Method*, Bakhtin writes:

We think and conceptualize in utterances, complexes complete in themselves. As we know, the utterance cannot be understood as a linguistic whole, and its forms are not syntactic forms. These integral, materially expressed inner acts of man's orientation in reality and the forms of these acts are very important. One might say that human consciousness possesses a series of inner genres for seeing and conceptualizing reality. A given consciousness is richer or poorer in genres, depending on its ideological environment. [*FM*, p. 134]

23. In the recent work of Terry Eagleton we find a similar position, one which sees science, no less than ideology, as the product of concrete social practices. See Eagleton, "Ideology, Fiction, Narrative," *Social Text* 1 (Winter 1979): 62–80.

24. See Coward and Ellis, *Language and Materialism*; Pierre Macherey, *A Theory of Literary Production*, trans. Geoffrey Wall (London, 1978); and Eagleton, *Criticism and Ideology: A Study in Marxist Literary Theory* (London, 1978).

25. For a discussion of the tension between genre and performance, and between tradition and situation, in folkloric performances, see Hymes, "Folklore's Nature and the Sun's Myth," *Journal of American Folklore* 88 (Oct.-Dec. 1975): 345–69.

26. Eagleton, *Criticism and Ideology*, p. 73.

Answering as Authoring: Mikhail Bakhtin's Trans-Linguistics

Michael Holquist

> Men do not understand how a thing which is torn in different directions comes into accord with itself—harmony in contrarity, as in the case of the bow or the lyre.
>
> —HERACLITUS

All of Mikhail Bakhtin's work stands under the sign of plurality, the mystery of the one and the many. Unlike the third eye of Tibetan Buddhism, which gives those who possess it a vision of the secret unity holding creation together, Bakhtin seems to have had a third ear that permitted him to hear differences where others perceived only sameness, especially in the apparent wholeness of the human voice. The obsessive question at the heart of Bakhtin's thought is always "Who is talking?" It was his sense of the world's overwhelming multiplicity that impelled Bakhtin to rethink strategies by which heterogeneity had traditionally been disguised as a unity. In his several attempts to find a single name for the teeming forces which jostled each other within the combat zone of the word— whether the term was "polyphony," "heteroglossia," or "speech com- munion"—Bakhtin was at great pains never to sacrifice the tension between identity and difference that fueled his enterprise. He always sought the minimum degree of homogenization necessary to any conceptual scheme, feeling it was better to preserve the heterogeneity which less patient thinkers found intolerable—and to which they therefore hurried to assign a unitizing label.

Bakhtin's metaphysical contrariness has the effect of making him at times appear to be indiscriminate, as when he refused to recognize the borders between biography and autobiography or, more notoriously, between speaking and writing. But, as I hope to show, these apparently cardinal distinctions are for Bakhtin only local instances of unity that participate in and are controlled by a far more encompassing set of oppositions and differences. All this places an extra burden on those who seek an overarching design in Bakhtin's legacy: the apparently unitizing term "Bakhtin" proves to be as illusory—or more illusory—in its ability to subsume real distinctions as any other, if we submit it to a Bakhtinian analysis.

1

He thought at the edges of several disciplines. Of the many diverse things which might legitimately be subsumed under the rubric "Bakhtin," which shall we single out as most comprehensive in describing the variety of his achievements?

He left books and articles that represent his thinking on a large number of widely differing subjects: Freudianism, axiology, the formalists, Rabelais, Goethe, Dostoevsky, linguistics, vitalism, novel theory, the nature of ideology, and the distinctive features of the humanities. This variety is compounded by the different styles and recurring ideological emphases Bakhtin employed over his long career: in the early twenties (1919–1924) he writes in a style that owes much to German post-Kantian academic philosophy; in the late twenties (1924–1929) he adopts a number of differing styles, all of which are quite noticeably directed at a more popular audience, are simpler and more polemical in their orientation; during the thirties and forties he turns to another style, somewhere between the excesses of the two preceding periods; and in the last decades of his life he becomes increasingly philosophical again.

But there is a common thread running through these heterodox topics and styles that stitches them together into a coherent body of work, the totality of which can be treated as a single text, a unified utterance. This unitizing force is Bakhtin's obsession, early and late, with relations between self and other. Bakhtin's lifetime concern with the interchange between those two poles of human being is why, at the banal but useful level where we speak of -isms, his work may be summed up as dialogism, since the particular way Bakhtin models the relation of self and other is a dialogue of a special kind.

Michael Holquist is professor and chairman in the department of Slavic languages and literatures at Indiana University. With his wife, Katerina Clark, he has just completed *Mikhail Bakhtin*, a study of Bakhtin's life and works, forthcoming in the autumn of 1984. He is currently working in Moscow.

2

Over the years, Bakhtin shed many of the assumptions he had taken in his early work from the German philosophical tradition. But one he never abandoned was the conviction that all existence is divisible into two kinds of being: the almost obligatory post-Kantian distinction between matter, which is simply *there*, given (*das Gegebene, dan*), and consciousness, all that which is created by mind, conceived (*das Aufgegebene, zadan*). Everything is more or less *dan* or *zadan*. A thing is *dan;* a thought, *zadan*. Bakhtin conceives of language as having a peculiar intermediary status between these two extremes: it is both given and created, which is why it can be used to bridge the gap between matter and consciousness, as when mind represents the world. Human being is acted out in a *logosphere*,[1] a space where meaning occurs as a function of the constant struggle between centrifugal forces that seek to keep things apart and in motion, that increase difference and tend toward the extreme of life and consciousness, and centripetal forces that strive to make things cohere, to stay in place, and which tend toward the extreme of death and brute matter.

These forces contend with each other at all levels of existence: in the physical universe, the cells of the body, the processes of mind, as well as in the ideologies of social organization. The constant dialogue between—and among—these partners in the activity of being finds its most comprehensive model in the activity of communication.[2]

At the heart of the Bakhtinian enterprise is a vision of language as constant struggle, movement, *energia*. The logosphere is an ocean of consciousness that floods the world of brute things, a sea whose face is constantly changing and whose depths are torn by the restless flux of discursive striations. Although having patent filiations with ancient Greek and German Romantic ideas about language, this dynamic sense of struggle and exchange sets Bakhtin apart from most modern linguists, especially the school of Geneva. It is not surprising, then, that much of Bakhtin's work is a kind of argumentative dialogue with Saussurian notions and categories.

At first, opposition between Saussure and Bakhtin would appear to be the different way in which each conceives the master distinction between language as system (*langue*) and as performance (*parole*).[3] In Saussure the abstraction and timelessness of the first category, when cut off from the particularity of the second, made great strides in our understanding of grammar, syntax, and phonetics possible. However, a good deal of subsequent linguistic thought has been devoted to putting this conceptual Humpty Dumpty back together again. Linguists such as Roman Jakobson, while themselves continuing to work at a very high level of abstraction, nevertheless felt that Saussure's separation of system from performance was too radical.

Bakhtin, on the contrary, sees it as not radical enough. While Saussure worked almost completely in the sphere of *langue,* it was always implied that the syntactic and grammatical categories he developed there would somehow be applicable as well at the level of *parole.* "Taken as a whole, speech cannot be studied, for it is not homogeneous; but the distinction and subordination proposed here [i.e., the *langue/parole* distinction] clarify the whole issue."[4] What you had was a variant on the theory/praxis relation: the worlds of system and performance were merely different levels for the functioning of the same phenomenon.

Bakhtin makes a more sweeping distinction between these two levels: the cutoff is not merely between linguistic system and speech performance but between mind and matter. Each is so different from the other that categories and practices appropriate to the one will not meet the specific demands of the other. Those aspects of language which Bakhtin calls *langue* are very close to the things of the world; grammar, syntax, lexicon, phonetics are all dead things which should service a living understanding in actual speech situations. The systematic, repeatable aspects of language are to speech as the material world is to mind. Thus they are different from each other but always operate together. The two sets of features are a unity and cannot be separated from each other. The space where they intermingle, the force that binds them and the arena where the strength of each is tested, is the utterance.

The contrast of Saussure and Bakhtin is inevitable, but it carries with it the danger of oversimplification—nowhere more so than in the area of the utterance. Bakhtin is increasingly being hailed as the great champion of performance, who redresses the imbalance created by Saussure's overinvestment in system. However, such an opposition is based on a false analogy: an equation is presumed between what Bakhtin meant by *utterance* and what Saussure intends by *parole* (Bakhtin's term for *parole* is "speech communion" [*rečevoe obščenie*], not *vyskazivanie*). Such an equation is absolutely wrong, not least of all because Saussure still ascribes a great deal of freedom to the individual speaker. The diagram of the speech situation he provides in his *Course in General Linguistics* (the famous drawing of two heads separated by arrows) shows an active speaker sending a message to a passive listener. This diagram is a virtual icon for the age-old suppression of the communicative aspect of the word. For all its schematism, this drawing models a view of language that is still centered on the individual world of the speaker. Saussure had defined *parole* as an "individual act. It is wilful and intellectual. Within the act, we should distinguish between: (1) the combinations by which the speaker uses the language code for expressing his own thought; and (2) a psychophysical mechanism that allows him to exteriorize those combinations."[5]

Performance was at a level that would not lend itself to scientific study. Although the same system that prevailed at the level of *langue* was somehow present in it, too, that presence was hopelessly randomized due to the endless variety of speech situations and the contingency introduced through exercise of the speaker's free will. "We cannot put [*parole*] into any category of human facts, for we cannot discover its unity."[6]

Utterance, as Bakhtin uses it, is *not,* however, unfettered speech, the individual ability to combine *langue* elements into freely chosen combinations. As he says, "Saussure ignores the fact that besides the forms of language there exist as well forms of combinations of these forms."[7] If we take into account the determining role of the other in actual speech communication, it becomes clear that there is not only system in language independent of any particular articulation of it, but there is as well a determining system that governs any actual utterance. We might say the world of *parole*, like the sphere of *langue*, is controlled by laws; but to say so would be to change completely the definition of *parole* as used by Saussure.

This is, of course, precisely what Bakhtin wants to do and why, instead of working with the old dualism of system and performance, he posits *communication* and not language as the subject of his investigations. Language, as conceived by most linguists, would embrace grammar, lexicon, syntax, and phonetics; discussions of word combinations wouldn't include a unit more comprehensive than the sentence. All these features play a role as well in Bakhtin's metalinguistics, but as dynamic elements in constant dialogue with *other* features that come into play only in particular acts of communication. So we would have to add to the list of topics appropriate to the study of language those appropriate to the study of communication as well.

The first such topic would be utterance, the fundamental unit of study in Bakhtin. Utterances provide building blocks for the logosphere just as atoms do for the material world. A second topic in any study of communication would be speech genres, the conventions by which utterances are organized.

"Utterance" is Bakhtin's overall term for a *duality* of roles that previously has been obscured by the assumption that speaking and listening were mutually opposed, unitary activities: a person *did either* one or the other. In fact, of course, we do both simultaneously. Discourse is an action. It is an activity more complicated than that of machines which must, due to mechanical limitations, transmit and receive *sequentially*. When men use language, they do so not as machines sending and then receiving codes but as two consciousnesses engaged in active understanding: the speaker listens and the listener speaks. Any utterance is a link in a very complexly organized *chain* of communication.

Utterances enact "addressivity" [*obraščënnost'*], awareness of the otherness of language in general and the otherness of given dialogic partners in particular. The work of addressivity is constantly to turn a general system of language to the needs of specific experiences: "Language enters life through concrete utterances [which manifest language] and life enters language through concrete utterances as well.[8] Consciousness is the medium and utterance, the specific means by which two otherwise disparate elements—the quickness of experience and the materiality of language—are harnessed in a volatile unity. In a twist on Gottlob Frege's *Sinn/Bedeutung* distinction, Bakhtin argues that words in the realm of language belong to no one, for they have only *significance* (*značenie*), a typical sense, whereas real *meaning* (*smysl*), which is what words acquire in the realm of utterance, involves particular people in actual social and historical situations. We not only know what "joy" signifies, but we can also understand the meaning of locutions such as "Any joy is now a bitterness to me." Moreover, we can also understand further dimensions of the word "joy" as they come up in actual utterances (such as this sentence).

Bakhtin is, of course, not alone in emphasizing the communicative aspect of language. Wilhelm von Humboldt had stated categorically that "man only understands himself when he has experimentally tested the intelligibility of his words on others." And Otto Dittrich, one of the first men to hold a chair in psychology, had said in his *Probleme der Sprachpsychologie* (1900) that "communication is of the essence [of linguistic science]." But no one before Bakhtin had actually thought through the implications of so radical an insistence on dialogue.[9]

We can see some of these implications if we look at what happens when two people actually speak to each other. In an admittedly rough analogy, we might say that such a dialogue is to Bakhtin's system what aphasia is to Jakobson's: a datum from experience that can serve both as an economical paradigm for and a testable proof of a theory encompassing more global dimensions. If we closely analyze exchanges between two speaking subjects, it quickly becomes apparent that what each says to the other is difficult to describe in terms of language alone. The talk is segmented not by words and sentences but by *who is talking*.

Obviously, the different ways in which speakers indicate appropriate points for others to respond are enormously varied, depending on the topic, the speakers, and the particular context of the utterance. But it is important to see from the outset that relations between utterances always presuppose the potential response of an *other*. Thus, these relations cannot be adequately dealt with in terms of the language system alone.

We can see this by comparing the differing roles of sentence (a unit of language) and utterance (a unit of communication). While the sentence is among the most fraught issues in any consideration of language, a definition of "sentence" that would seem to be sanctified at least by consensus is "the articulation of a relatively complete thought." If we assume this to be the case, then, of course the question becomes "What is a complete thought?" and the relation of one sentence to another becomes an issue (as we saw most egregiously in the various attempts that were made, during the late fifties and sixties, to concoct a science of narratology). If a sentence has something to do with a completed thought, what is the force that binds several such thoughts into supra-sentential units? The answer Bakhtin provides is the utterance: it is that greater whole, the governing telos, which determines the subsidiary completeness of sentence.

The sentence, qua sentence (i.e., a unit of language), is itself not *directly* implicated in the experiential context in which it is pronounced, nor is it *directly* correlated with the utterances of other speakers. Its direct connection is to the needs of the utterance of which it is a part and which *is* directly related to the framing situation and other speakers. "A sentence . . . lacks the capability of determining a response; it acquires this capability . . . only in the entirety comprised by an utterance."[10]

If sentence structure does not mark the limits of an utterance, what does? It is, quite simply, the ability to respond to an utterance that guarantees its finalization. And Bakhtin posits three factors that determine an utterance's integrity. These are the semantic exhaustiveness of the theme, the speech plan of the speaker, and the typical generic forms of finalization.

The first is relatively simple to grasp: certain themes are dealt with in highly standardized ways in which the limits of exhaustiveness are rigidly set, such as military orders. Most other subjects have less constricting limits inherent in them, which means in turn that the second aspect, speech plan, always related to the first, plays a more central role in shaping the utterance. In any utterance we perceive or posit or imagine what the speaker wishes to say, a process H. P. Grice has labeled "implicature." Bakhtin wrote:

> According to this speech plan we also measure the finalization of the utterance. This is the subjective aspect of utterance; it is combined into an inseparable unity with its objective aspect, or what is inherently appropriate to the subject of the utterance [i.e., roughly according to the demands of what Grice calls the "Cooperative Principle"], limiting this aspect by relating it to a concrete . . . situation of speech communication, with all its individual circumstances, its personal participants, and with the [particular] utterances that preceded it.[11]

Bakhtin sometimes calls speech plan [*rečevoj zamysel*] speech *will* [*rečevaja volja*]. By doing so he runs the risk of appearing to assign an overabundance of liberty to individual speakers, as had Saussure in his concept of *parole*. In order to meet the danger of being misperceived in this way, Bakhtin goes out of his way to underscore the restraining role played by the third category determining utterance structure, speech genres.

In effect, the will of the speaker can be realized only in his selection of *this* speech genre versus that one in any given instance. These typical forms of utterance come to us as we learn to speak (a process, of course, that does not conclude with the end of infancy but which continues all our conscious lives). In fact, "to learn to speak means to learn to construct utterances. . . . We learn to cast our speech in generic forms and, when we hear others' speech, we deduce its genre from the first words; we anticipate in advance a certain volume (that is, the approximate length of the speech whole) as well as a certain compositional structure. We foresee the end; that is, from the very beginning we have a sense of the speech whole."[12]

The speaker's evaluative attitude toward *what* he is talking about (even attempting to be neutral is to enact certain values), plus his judgment as to *whom* he is talking determine the choice of language units (lexical, grammatical) *and* communication units (the composition of the utterance, the speech genres employed). This evaluative component of speech is what determines the *expressive* aspect of the utterance. Words exist for the speaker in three possible relations that can be enacted toward them: "as a neutral word of the language [i.e., as a word in the dictionary, a word that signifies but does not mean], as an *other's* word [i.e., the word of other persons], and as my word."[13] These last two relations are those in which expressiveness, the individual style of the utterance, comes into play. It is here we see another difference between language and communication: phonemes and syntax have in common with speech genres a tendency to limit the freedom of individual speakers. Not only are words and sentences always already there, but so are the forms for their combination into utterances. The difference between the two is in the *degree* (although the difference is, somewhat paradoxically, absolute) to which each is normative.[14]

The individual style of the utterance can be determined by its expressive side because the forms of communication are more open to play and intervention than the forms of language. Intonation, word choice, selection of speech genre—all these are open to assimilation (*osvoenie*) by individual speakers as means for registering values. Obviously, some genres are more malleable than others: the give and take at the information counter of a railroad station will be maximally codified, whereas the give and take between intimate friends presents possibilities for minimal— but never absent—generic control.

We are touching here on that aspect of utterance which comes closest to explaining why Bakhtin, who began his career with a long philosophical work that used the act of authorship as a means for investigating the play of values, spent most of the rest of his life meditating the social basis of language. For, as denizens of the logosphere we swim in a sea of forms that seek the condition of mere being-there, the givenness of brute nature. In order to invest those forms with life and meaning, so that we may be understood and so that the work of the social world may continue, we must all, perforce, become authors. To use the stuff of signs to represent the world is to use language as an analogue for social relations as the reality of nature. Insofar as we wrest particular meanings out of general systems, we are all creators: a speaker is to his utterance what an author is to his text.

3

That anyone who speaks thereby *creates* is arguably the most radical implication of Bakhtin's thought and the root concern that unifies his trans-linguistics and his literary meta-criticism. The differences between a Rabelais or a Dostoevsky and the rest of us is, of course, very great. But they are not absolute. They are differences of degree and not kind. By studying such paradigms, therefore, we can learn more about an activity in which we are all implicated: Freud studied abnormal patients because he could see the structure of normal behavior writ large in the patterns of hysterics and psychotics—and Bakhtin dedicated himself to exemplary instances of authorship for the same reason.

There is something outrageous in so militantly extended a concept of authorship: it has the effect of abolishing—or at least blurring—the cardinal distinctions between written and spoken texts and aesthetic versus nonaesthetic use of language. In the face of what appears to be a galloping case of hyper-homogenization, it is useful to keep in mind Bakhtin's predilection for difference, for the unique and the particular. Bakhtin batters at the walls between distinctions, which most of us now feel should be even *more* sharply distinguished, because he is convinced such differences are epiphenomena of a more fundamental split: the gap between mind and world that manifests itself as a noncoincidence of the self with itself and with others. The suggestion of Bakhtin's total oeuvre, conceived as a single utterance, is that our ultimate act of authorship results in the text which we call our self.

Of course, what makes Bakhtin interesting is not the abstraction of such a conclusion but rather the idiosyncratic route by which he arrives at it and the particular uses to which he puts it. In what follows, I will attempt to make at least the origin of Bakhtin's theory of authorship more specific. To do this, I'll begin by proposing, as a mediating term between the dialogic aspects of Bakhtin's trans-linguistics and the dialogic basis of his literary meta-criticism, certain ideas he held about the dialogue between stimulus and response in the human body's interchange with the physical world.

Returning to Leningrad in 1924 from the first of his several exiles, Bakhtin met Ivan Ivanovich Kanaev (1893–), a distinguished biologist and historian of science who was particularly interested in Goethe's attempts to overcome the split between literary process and the processes of nature.

Kanaev was to prove a valuable friend to Bakhtin in a number of ways, but perhaps his greatest service was to introduce Bakhtin to the work of the great physiologist Aleksey Alekseevich Ukhtomsky (1875–1942).

In the search for a more concrete and material basis for his metaphysics, Bakhtin in the early twenties had become interested in the work of such leading vitalists as Hans Driesch and, especially, Henri Bergson. Their assumption that the life-force could somehow be isolated, that a substantial entity imparts to a living system powers possessed by no inanimate body, seemed at first to be a scientific corroboration for the Kantian distinction between mind and things. In 1926 Bakhtin actually published (under Kanaev's name) a survey of current vitalist theory, in the popular science journal *Man and Nature*. But it was Ukhtomsky's theory of a cortical *dominanta* that was to prove more decisive in shaping Bakhtin's ideas about utterance and authorship.

Ukhtomsky was a devout Christian who graduated from the Moscow Seminary before going into biology. His dissertation at the Seminary had been a critical survey of changing concepts of space and time in Western metaphysics. Since he began his research on how the human brain orders relations among the various competing stimuli from the exterior world, it was not surprising that he should have focused on the spatial and temporal aspects of such relations. In order to see why the physiologist's work on the "chronotope" should have proved so important for the young Bakhtin, some background on Ukhtomsky's ideas will be necessary.

In the nineteenth century, Ivan Sechenov's *Reflexes of the Human Brain* (1863) had confined itself to a mechanistic, directly cause-and-effect account of the relations between organism and environment. The brain was conceived as a subfunction of the neuromuscular system, constantly responding in preprogrammed fashion to external stimuli. Somewhat later, Nikolai Vvedensky noticed that unlike the relatively unmediated responses of frogs, there was an indirectness in some human responses to stimuli in certain areas. For instance, if the upper laryngeal nerve was irritated, the initial response was not in the larynx itself but in an increase of energy to the breathing center in the brain.

This suggested that there was a seat of control in the cortex which did not automatically respond to local stimuli, but which, upon reception of such a stimulus, surmised its harmful consequences for basic life functions, and *then* translated a response to those functions rather than to the area immediately physically affected. Vvedensky called this process "corroboration," and it was the first suggestion that the organism's responses were monitored and—within a broad range—controlled from inside the organism itself.

Ukhtomsky concentrated his research on such control procedures, the highest level of which he came to call the *dominanta*. He concluded that the central nervous system was in its essence rhythmical: it translated the random, uncoordinated impulses (noise) the body experienced on its surface into a smoothly functioning unity (music) within the various systems of the body itself. To do this, two things are necessary: first, a constant monitoring, a kind of biological "listening," in order to detect any irregularities in the normal sequencing of all the systems' operations; and second, a transfer of electrochemical energy to brake or speed up affected subsystems so that they could be made constant with the rhythm of other systems, a kind of biological "answering."[15]

Both these functions of the *dominanta,* listening and answering, require that it be extraordinarily sensitive to the most minute fluctuations in rhythm. It must, in other words, be extremely sensitive to *time.* A further implication is that the *dominanta* must immediately sense *where,* amidst the miles of fibers and the millions of cells, the need for local adjustment has arisen. In other words, the *dominanta* must be exceedingly sensitive to *place.* And not only is it essentially a clock combined with a range finder, but it performs these gauging operations *simultaneously* in the constantly ongoing work of the body. It is not surprising, then, that Ukhtomsky's work on the *dominanta* should have led him in the summer of 1925 to read a widely attended public lecture on the chronotope at Peterhof. It was this occasion that Bakhtin records as the source of his own speculations on space/time.[16] The theses were never published, and only notes remain, but enough is known to make it clear that the confluence of his own and Ukhtomsky's ideas was to affect far more than Bakhtin's concept of the chronotope, central as that notion was for him.[17]

It first of all became possible to conceive the relation of mind and world as a dialogic continuum rather than as an unbridgeable gap. The body's relation to its physical environment provided a powerful conceptual metaphor for modeling the relation of individual persons to their social environment. In both cases, the emphasis is on ceaseless *activity.* The body is seen as a system by which the individual answers the physical world; in order to do so coherently it must model its environment, track and map it, and then translate its data into a biological representation of it—the body answers the world by authoring it.[18] Analogously, mind can be seen as a system by which the individual answers the social world: responding strongly or weakly to some impulses, screening others out, consciousness constantly tracks its place amidst the axiological hierarchies in which it moves. It responds to social stimuli by authoring its own responses. Homeostasis is the body's mechanism for actively responding to the other, utterance is the mind's. In both cases, authorship is a means for shaping meaning in a long and complex chain of interactions.

4

There are several lessons we might draw from Bakhtin's distinctive concept of utterance and its radical implications for received ideas of authorship. At a time when the humanities are everywhere on the defensive, perhaps the most important aspect of Bakhtin's thought will inevitably appear to be the new significance it assigns the study of the word. In a late, summing-up essay, "Towards a Methodology of the Human Sciences," Bakhtin specifically addresses the need to move from the kind of answerability peculiar to the world of the physical sciences to the complex authorial response that has always been the province of the humanities.[19]

He begins by outlining the first task of any consciousness: to understand the relation between the world of signs and the world of things, "the striving to embody extraverbal, anonymous contexts . . . [where] only I am a creative speaking personality, everything else outside me is only external conditions, causes that evoke . . . my word. I do not converse [with such forces]—I *react* to them mechanically, as a thing reacts to external irritation."[20] At this level, consciousness reacts with its environment much as does the body. But the task of being human consists in causing this "*substantial* environment, which mechanically influences the personality—to begin . . . to reveal potential words and tones, to transform it into a semantic context for the thinking, speaking and acting (including creating) person, to turn it into a word."[21]

Bakhtin, then, reminds us that literature is important not merely because it gives pleasure or leads us to a kind of arcane knowledge we might otherwise lack. No, literature is important because it gives the most rigorous on-the-job training for a work we must all as men do, the work of answering and authoring the text of our social and physical universe. Bakhtin is remarkable for the comprehensiveness of his vision of dialogue and the central role he assigns utterance in shaping the world. His insistence on authorship as the distinctive feature of consciousness is a particularly powerful way of giving meaning to the definition of man that says he is a sign.

1. M. M. Baxtin [Mikhail Bakhtin], *Estetika solvesnogo tvorčestva* (Moscow, 1979), p. 79; all translations are my own.

2. The title of Bakhtin's first book, *The Architectonics of Answerability*, might well serve to subsume his total oeuvre. He worked on this book from 1918 to 1924, although it never saw the light of day. While most of this manuscript is now lost, a portion was published as "Author and Protagonist" in the 1979 collection of Bakhtin's works cited above. This portion will appear in English translation in 1985 in the Texas Slavic Series, together with the 1924 essay, "The Problem of Content."

3. "*Parol'*" in Russian means "password" or "countersign," which creates an irony in some of Bakhtin's work lost in translation. For instance, in 1926 he writes: "Utterance is an objective-social enthymeme, a password [*parol'*], as it were, that is known only to those belonging to the same social milieux" ("Slovo v žizni i slovo v poèzii," *Zvezda* 6 [1926]: 251; my translation). We may say, then, that living speech (Saussure's *parole*) is the countersign (Bakhtin's *parol'*) which enables system (*langue*) to enter experience.

4. Ferdinand de Saussure, *Course in General Linguistics*, ed. Charles Bally and Albert Sechehaye, in collaboration with Albert Riedlinger, trans. Wade Baskin (New York, 1966), p. 19.

5. Ibid., p. 14.

6. Ibid., p. 9.

7. Baxtin [Bakhtin], *Estetika*, p. 240.

8. Ibid., p. 253.

9. Bronislaw Malinowski is another who would seem to come very close to some of Bakhtin's formulations: "Utterance and situation are bound up inextricably with each other and the context of situation is indispensable for the understanding of the words" (Supplement I, "The Problem of Meaning in Primitive Languages" [1923], in C. K. Ogden and I. A. Richards, *The Meaning of Meaning* [New York (1965)], p. 307). But the emphasis on context and function is vitiated by Malinowski's failure to recognize that such features are a universal condition of communication rather than a distinctive feature of the "primitive tongues" found among traditional culture systems. Social rituals are no less elaborate and programmed in the elevators of ninety-story skyscrapers than in the lagoons of Papua New Guinea. And their effect on language is no less binding.

10. Baxtin [Bakhtin], *Estetika*, p. 253.

11. Ibid., p. 256.

12. Ibid., p. 258.

13. Ibid., p. 268.

14. This point is made by Roman Jakobson (with Morris Halle) in "Two Aspects of Language," *Fundamentals of Language* (The Hague, 1956): "In the combination of linguistic units there is an ascending scale of freedom [from distinctive features to phonemes, where] the freedom of the individual speaker is zero [through words, to sentences]." But Jakobson, like Saussure, assumes too great a freedom at the level of utterance, where, he says, "the action of compulsory syntactical rules ceases." He adds that the effect of "numerous stereotyped utterances is not to be overlooked," but by doing so makes it clear he has in mind fixed phrases rather than speech genres (p. 74).

15. We should, incidentally, note the similarity between this conception of a cortical *dominanta* controlling a physiological "system of systems" and the concept of system in the 1928 theses of Jakobson and Jurij Tynjanov—in particular, Jakobson's lectures on "The Dominant" given at Masaryk University in Brno in 1935.

16. Bakhtin wrote: "In the summer of 1925, [I] attended a lecture by A. A. Uxtomskij [Ukhtomsky] on the chronotope in biology" ("Forms of Time and of the Chronotope in the Novel," *The Dialogic Imagination: Four Essays*, ed. Michael Holquist and trans. Caryl Emerson and Holquist, University of Texas Press Slavic Series, no. 1 [Austin, Tex., 1981], p. 84 n. 1). Ukhtomsky and Bakhtin had a common interest in translating their religious concerns into terms that might be convincing to others who did not share their faith. Both men were, from very early on in their careers, preoccupied with questions of free will and the soul. Both translated these terms from theology into subjects that could be pursued within the confines of other disciplines. In Bakhtin, free will is conceived as a category in aesthetics (authority of the author) and philosophy of language (the individual speaker's ability to manifest his intention in utterance). Ukhtomsky took a somewhat different course: free will is studied as the problem of authority over the checks and balances regulating the human body. Both Bakhtin and Ukhtomsky translate the Orthodox fascination with the soul's relation to God into a concern for the self's relation to others.

17. See Akademija nauk, SSSR, Archive Collection 749.

18. Connections between the homeostasis process and communication process will perhaps seem less farfetched if we remember that it is not only scientific autodidacts such as Bakhtin (or the author of the present article) who equate physiology and language. The Nobel Prize-winning biologist (and former president of the University of Chicago) George W. Beadle called the book on genetics which he wrote with his wife Muriel, *The Language of Life* (New York, 1966).

19. See Baxtin [Bakhtin], "Towards a Methodology of the Humanities" [K metodologii gumanitarnyx nauk], *Estetika*, pp. 361–73.

20. Ibid., p. 366.

21. Ibid., p. 367.

A Response to the Forum on Mikhail Bakhtin

Ken Hirschkop

Critical Inquiry's Forum on Mikhail Bakhtin is the latest contribution to the spectacular effort of interpretation and assimilation that is being applied to the work of this recently recovered critic. In such a situation, analysis proceeds with one eye on the work in question and the other on current debates in the field; in the case of Bakhtin, interpretation is at the same time an attempt to come to grips with challenges posed by recent literary theory to certain axiomatic critical assumptions about intentionality, textuality, and the human subject. But the matter is also complicated by the fact that we are dealing here with a critic who was active in the USSR. This brings into play additional ideological pressures, generated by the cold war, which bear on the scholarly assimilation of his work.

The debate on Bakhtin is made yet more difficult by the nature of his writing: immensely varied stylistically and topically but also—and more importantly, I believe—writing which strives for solutions it cannot quite articulate. It moves between alternative and contradictory formulations in a single essay and thus produces a set of concepts whose explanatory importance is matched by an unnerving tendency to slide from one formulation to the next with disturbing ease. Such ambiguities are not the sign of an open and sceptical mind, but neither are they mere inconsistencies which can be safely ignored. These internal contradictions dictate that argument over concepts like "dialogism" and "heteroglossia" cannot be settled by a definitive decision as to what they 'really' mean; instead, we must discuss how to manage these complexities and contradictions, and to what ends. Certain definite strategies of management are emerging, and the articles presented in the forum, while by no means reducible to a single position, share key lines of interpretive strategy that I think ought to be brought out into the open and contested. With the notable exception of Susan Stewart's article ["Shouts on the Street: Bakhtin's Anti-Linguistics," pp. 41–57], the contributions share an ideological drift, the ultimate effect of which is to evade the most radical aspects of Bakhtin's work in favor of an interpretation that renders him useful in the argument against the recent advances of post-structuralism and recent literary theory in general.

Nothing reveals this tactic more starkly than the vision we are offered of what a properly dialogical discourse should look like. The form of Gary Saul Morson's article ["Who Speaks for Bakhtin?" pp. 1–19] is the most vivid illustration: dialogism as a friendly and polite discussion in which a difference of opinion is acknowledged as unresolvable but is nonetheless reconciled to the extent that each speaker 'takes into account' the opinions of the other. For Michael Holquist this dialogism which both recognizes and defuses difference can exist because the speaker is confronted by an otherness made less disturbing by the fact that he is 'aware' of it [see "Answering as Authoring: Mikhail Bakhtin's Trans-Linguistics," pp. 59–71]. Dialogical communication, almost by definition, becomes a give-and-take in which opposing positions find a common ground. And finally, Caryl Emerson aptly describes the dialogical con-frontation as a process of negotiation [see "The Outer Word and Inner Speech: Bakhtin, Vygotsky, and the Internalization of Language," pp. 21–40]. (Michael André Bernstein's vision of the dialogical is different in tone but ultimately relies on the same conceptual coordinates as the others' [see "When the Carnival Turns Bitter: Preliminary Reflections Upon the Abject Hero," pp. 99–121].) What we find in common here is a definition of Bakhtinian otherness in terms of a fundamental uniqueness of the individual that ought to be respected, much as political liberalism in its dominant commonsense form emphasizes respect for the individual as a primary value. At the same time, this vision of dialogism holds out the promise of a coherent and peaceful society in which these individual voices are ultimately reconciled because they 'take into account' each other's opinions. This is a far cry from that condition of fierce social struggle outlined by Bakhtin in "Discourse in the Novel," in which the dialogical forces of language actively contest the social and political cen-tralization of their culture. It is likewise remote from the carnival culture described in the study of François Rabelais, which takes its internally dialogical form from its function as an oppositional and subversive culture.

Ken Hirschkop is a postgraduate student at Saint Antony's College, Oxford University, working on a book about Mikhail Bakhtin.

Indeed, given the conditions of internal social warfare in which Bakhtin was writing in the 1920s and 1930s, it would be extraordinary if he thought of social difference in terms of amicable disagreement. This is not to say that a utopian vision of such a dialogism is not to be found in Bakhtin, but this utopia must be seen as a response to a decidedly nonutopian situation—that is, dialogism itself, as a certain kind of discourse, must be situated dialogically.

What is being negotiated in these interpretations is the double sense of the term "dialogism": it is both the natural state of being of language as such and a valorized category of certain discourses. It has a role both in the theoretical critique of Saussurian linguistics and in the evaluative literary history Bakhtin narrates. When these two senses of the term are conflated, the specific form dialogism takes in the novel is assumed to be the manifestation of the true essence of language, an essence somehow repressed in the monological. In fact, it is the status of monologism which is the most problematic: if dialogism is the nature of all language, then what gives rise to monologism? For monologism is not merely an illusion or an error, it is a form of discourse with real, if mystifying, effects, which must be accounted for in a theory of language. It is this reality, or effectivity, of an illusionary or mystifying language which is evaded when the monological is treated as a theoretical error.

But this repression of a natural dialogism exists as a genuine problem in Bakhtin. His concentration on the transitional moments of cultural history has been often commented upon. The implication of this history is that dialogical forms flourish in those periods located between the deadening effects of a preceding and a following social structure: thus transitional moments are seen as spaces between structures rather than as periods in which the new struggles to supplant the old. That vitalism which Holquist has documented is transplanted into the social realm to produce a distinctly anarchist vision of social change, featuring a natural dialogism again and again repressed by an unnatural monologism. This is not a problem which can be solved by a purely 'interpretive' approach to Bakhtin: if we are going to continue using "dialogism" as a theoretical term denoting a general quality of linguistic practice, then some revision of the term is needed, so that specifically monological cultural forms are understood as *forms* of the dialogical—dialogical in some profound sense— rather than as some inexplicable perversion of the dialogical. But this also means that monologism must itself be recognized as a strategy of response toward another discourse, albeit a strategy which aims to 'ignore' or 'marginalize' the opposite discourse. We are thus led to a very different vision of what Bakhtin means by "dialogue," one which includes not only the liberal exchange of views but also questions of cultural oppression and power.

The assumption that the working of language in the oppositional form of the novel is but the extreme manifestation of the essence of language also leads to the reading of Bakhtin as a champion of some kind of pure and limitless relativism. What this misses is the political meaning of a historicizing and relativizing discourse when it opposes a ruling discourse that presents itself as timeless, natural, and self-evident; dialogism, in its novelistic form, is itself defined by its relation to monologism. Bertolt Brecht's strategy was roughly similar: to dismantle a naturalizing ideology, one opposed it with a discourse which historicized life, revealing it as something produced and therefore changeable, and this was in the service of a definite political project. I entirely agree with Stewart's description of Bakhtin's metalinguistics as a polemic rather than as a transcendence, and I think this places her essay at odds with the rest of the contributions, which each, in one way or another, present novelistic dialogism as something in principle separable from its opposite. The extreme case of this is Holquist's contention that the monological and dialogical actually stand for two different orders of being. The recasting of the opposition in terms of a mind/world dualism preserves the sense of an intimate and necessary relation between the two terms but, crucially, depoliticizes them: an opposition between two competing forms of activity, two opposing linguistic practices, is transformed into a conceptual distinction between two components of all linguistic practice. It may well be that some primordial Kantian split was the starting point from which Bakhtin developed, but by presenting the opposition of linguistic practices described in the 1930s as just another version of this split, Holquist collapses the social struggle implied in the novel/poetic genre distinction into the conceptual distinctions of Bakhtin's critique of Ferdinand de Saussure. For Bakhtin, however, relativizing dialogism is not a theoretical position but a discursive tactic determined by the discourse it opposes.

But the core of the problem is that dialogism is found in Bakhtin's texts as both an oppositional tactic and a theoretical description; the relation of dialogism to monologism is at the same time relational and asymmetrical. While dialogism could not be merely the truth of monologism, it nevertheless contains a utopian element (emphasized in the Rabelais study) lacking in its opposite. The relativist interpretation of Bakhtin avoids this problem and leads to an unfortunate equation: the historicity of discourse equals the relativizing strategy of the novel. The novel (or, more precisely, Bakhtin's novel) seeks to subvert the monological's claim to be timeless, authorless, sacred, and natural; and precisely to the extent that its project is subversive, it will do this by revealing language to be temporal, authored, prosaic, and historical. But the exact meaning of these latter terms should not be construed as the mere converse of their monological antitheses. The form in which the novel brings into consciousness the historicity of discourse is as a relativization, a denaturalization, an uncrowning, but this is not the definition of historicity itself. Discourse is historical; it lacks theological certainty. But this does not mean that its essence is to lack any form of certainty and that therefore every statement is equally, and hence absolutely, provisional. Or, to put it another way, to say that discourse is historical is not to say that its development and movement are random and limitless, in some sense absolutely free. Change need not be random to be genuine change. But this kind of relativism, whose ideological affinities with the commonplaces of Western cold war discourse (the contrast of a liberal openness with a Left 'dogmatism') cannot be missed, crops up again and again when Bakhtin is interpreted. A quotation from Bakhtin's essay "Towards a Methodology of the Human Sciences" is revealing in this regard: "In the case of recollections, we take into account the events that followed (within the limits of the past), that is, we interpret and comprehend what is recollected in the context of an unfinished [nezavershennogo] past."[1] Nezavershennost', the open-endedness or "unfinalizability" of discourse, is not the symptom of an utterly unconstrained future but of the fact of historical change, which can be nonrandom without thereby being nonhistorical. But these two options, a monological denial of history or history as a random mutability pulling the ground out from under our feet, are presented as the available choice in those versions of Bakhtin which celebrate him as a relativist. From this point of view, Bernstein's is the most rigorous contribution, in that he recognizes that a definition of discourse's historicity as infinite and unpredictable self-parody leads to the bitterness and terror of nihilism: this implies that we have not moved far from the Dostoevskian position that, lacking a theological guarantee, "everything is permitted."

If the realm of discourse is being kept free of all finalizing constraints, then it is being kept free for somebody, and that somebody, not surprisingly, is the human subject, whose sovereignty, irreducibility, and originality is never really in doubt throughout the arguments of Holquist, Morson, and Emerson. Although the claim is repeatedly made that Bakhtin offers concepts with which to overcome the opposition of self and society, the formulations we are actually presented with define the social as lacking any determinative power or significance in and of itself; it is never more than the sum of its subjects. Throughout we hear the continual echo of precisely that Saussurian dichotomy of *langue* and *parole* which it was Bakhtin's explicit project to surpass. The social as the ahistorical and systematic, the individual as historical, random, the locus of an unpredictable activity: Bakhtin's purpose was to reintegrate historicity, evaluation, and activity—in short, all that had been excluded as style—into the social reality of language and thereby to develop a concept of linguistic structure which was dynamic rather than ahistorical. Perhaps this objective is best summed up by a provocative phrase from the essay "From the Prehistory of Novelistic Discourse," the idea of *"the style of the language as a totality,"* which proposes the union of value and style, previously subjective phenomena, with the social and structural qualities of language.[2]

But what is proposed by Holquist, Morson, and Emerson is not a reintegration but a critique of Saussurian linguistics that relies on categories derived from Saussure himself. It is true that Saussure's concepts of *langue* and the sign are insufficient for an analysis of the actual practice of language, but the exclusion of certain aspects of language was part and parcel of the Saussurian project itself; an adequate critique of Saussure must question the initial division and not simply come up with an additional theory of what has been excluded. In Bakhtin's view, the struggle among styles and voices was a "struggle among socio-linguistic points of view, not an intra-language struggle between *individual wills or logical contradictions*."[3] But Holquist, Morson, and Emerson attack the 'logical' bias of *langue* by recourse to the other term of the opposition, language as the struggle of individual wills; the abstract linguistic relationships of *langue* are countered by the concrete interpersonal relationships of *parole*. Holquist's characterization of the monological as the realm of dead, inert forms (that is, the realm of *langue*) commits the same error, for the monological is not defined by the exclusion of value and activity but by its location of activity, of life, exclusively in the subject. The division of being into life or force, on one hand, and dead system, on the other, is exactly the division dictated by monologism. Note in this regard that Bakhtin speaks of the centripetal *forces* of language; monologism, like dialogism, is both a particular force and a particular way of conceiving the relationship between force and system.

Because it is based on a conventional liberal opposition of individual and society, the dialogical unit proposed as a radically new unit of analysis is in fact nothing new at all. This version of the dialogical describes exactly the mode of interaction between subjects dictated by a self/society opposition in which society exists as a collection of preconstituted subjects, sharing discourse at the level of logic and reason but individualized at the level of value and desire. Society exists as the space in which individuals encounter each other; to borrow a metaphor from Marx, it is the sack in which the potatoes are kept. Therefore it is no surprise that Holquist can equate the relation of self and other with the relation of self and society, for to enter into the social world as this schema describes it is to encounter other individuals in the form of alien subjectivities. Intention and value are relocated in the social only insofar as the social as been turned into another subject.

The struggle of dialogical discourse then comes to be defined as the struggle of one subject to incorporate another. Telling in this respect is the pair of options implied by Morson: either the expressing subject successfully incorporates its struggle-ridden discursive into its own discourse, in which case dialogism has been reduced to an enrichment of the subject's discourse, or else it fails in this effort and we have the resultant tragedy of expression, in which victory belongs to the other subject. One subject or the other must win the encounter, and this is the form dialogism takes when we start with two preconstituted subjects; the initially given absolute otherness which separates them is, in fact, a consequence of this preconstitution. In such a situation the social can figure only as a gloss on, or a barrier to, the hypothetically original, pure intention of the subject.

In a sense what has happened is that the deconstruction of the self/ society opposition has skipped a crucial stage, that which Jacques Derrida calls "overturning," in which the situation of primacy/marginalization existing within the opposition is reversed. The self/society opposition is one in which the self is original and society is secondary. Holquist, Morson, Emerson, and Bernstein have not given sufficient weight to Bakhtin's claim that "verbal discourse is a social phenomenon," and therefore their efforts to displace the opposition always return to the primacy of the self and its attendant themes.[4] Again, I am at pains to stress that the interpretation I polemicize against has not been pulled out of the air or arrived at by a distortion of the text: there is ample support for it in many of Bakhtin's interpretations. But it has not solved the problems Bakhtin attempted to solve—this is the important thing—and it has not done so because it has blunted the most radical aspects of his thought. The trend in the critical literature on Bakhtin in America and England, which is growing at tremendous pace, is toward an assimilation of Bakhtin into a liberal schema that he opposed, even if he never succeeded in fully transcending it in his theoretical formulations. To say the least, one has to be suspicious of the ideological project enacted in such an assimilation at a time when many critical assumptions based on this schema are under fire.

1. M. M. Bakhtin, *Estetika slovesnogo tvorčhestva* (Moscow, 1979), p. 362; my translation.
2. Bakhtin, "From the Prehistory of Novelistic Discourse," *The Dialogic Imagination: Four Essays,* ed. Michael Holquist, trans. Caryl Emerson and Holquist, University of Texas Press Slavic Series, no. 1 (Austin, Tex., 1981), p. 62.
3. Bakhtin, "Discourse in the Novel," *The Dialogic Imagination,* p. 273; my emphasis.
4. Ibid., p. 259.

Dialogue, Monologue, and the Social: A Reply to Ken Hirschkop

Gary Saul Morson

Ken Hirschkop makes several excellent points in his essay respecting Mikhail Bakhtin and the direction of contemporary literary theory. I express this appreciation at the risk of confirming his description of me as a liberal, as one who believes in seriously considering and, if possible, learning from an opponent's objections.

One particularly interesting aspect of Hirschkop's essay is the repertoire of "double-voiced words" (to use Bakhtin's term for certain rhetorical strategies) it displays. I will enumerate just three of them:

1. *The Misaddressed Word.* Apparently, Hirschkop has been arguing these points with someone else, whose voice has drowned out what was actually said by myself and the other contributors to the Forum on Bakhtin. In a number of cases, Hirschkop objects that we failed to say things that were, in fact, explicitly stated and attributes to us a different, phantom position, which he then cites as evidence of "liberal," individualistic, and "cold war" biases (p. 77; and see p. 74). Likewise, I ostensibly "implied" a number of things, though Hirschkop offers no direct quotations as evidence (p. 78).

2. *The Word That Lies in Ambush* (a special version of what Bakhtin called "the word with a loophole"). In a way that has become increasingly common in theoretical essays, Hirschkop contents himself with stating only what is *not* the case and neglects telling us his conception of the alternative, correct position. For example, Hirschkop says: "Such ambiguities [in Bakhtin] are not the sign of an open and sceptical mind, but

neither are they mere inconsistencies which can be safely ignored" (p. 73). In consequence, respondents who presume to guess at his position, whether they guess rightly or wrongly, are subject to an accusation of total or partial misrepresentation of his position or, perhaps worse, of drawing typically liberal inferences.

3. *The Preemptive Word* (another version of "the word with a loophole"). Using a strategy familiar to most polemicists, Hirschkop attempts to discredit his adversaries by anticipating their objections within his own argument. Unfortunately, he projects responses—that no one has made—as if those responses were inevitable and seeks to dismiss them simply by naming them rather than answering them. Thus, he accuses my fellow contributors and me of a "kind of relativism, whose ideological affinities with the commonplaces of Western cold war discourse (the contrast of a liberal openness with a Left 'dogmatism') cannot be missed" and which "crops up again and again when Bakhtin is interpreted" (p. 77). The phrase in parentheses and the word in quotation marks are an example of preemptive discourse.

In general, Hirschkop seems unable to distinguish his account of Bakhtin's beliefs from a delineation of his own. Perhaps this explains why he attributes a similar confusion to me and the other contributors. In my dialogue, *Elle* accuses *Moi* of just such an error, of equating the phrases "it is true that" and "Bakhtin says" (p. 9). If such a lack of discrimination does not reflect the stance of the hero-worshipper, then it represents the stance of the polemicist, who needs to claim Bakhtin whole and entire as a potentially useful piece of ideological property. For, as we know, some thinkers are not permitted to be wrong, except insofar as they have failed to understand their own theory as well as their putative disciple. Thus, Tony Bennett can argue that Marx's theory of literature is faulty only because it is insufficiently Marxist.[1] (If only Christ had understood his own doctrines as well as Tolstoy did!)[2] If a favored thinker appears to have made some other kind of mistake, then it can only be because he has been systematically misread, because "ideological pressures, generated by the cold war . . . bear on the scholarly assimilation of his work" (p. 73).

Gary Saul Morson is the author of *The Boundaries of Genre: Dostoevsky's "Diary of a Writer" and the Traditions of Literary Utopia* (1981) and the editor of *Literature and History: Theoretical Problems and Russian Case Studies* (forthcoming). He has recently completed *Hazardous Systems: A Study of "War and Peace"* (forthcoming) and, with Caryl Emerson, he is currently writing a book on Bakhtin.

But the most important issues Hirschkop raises concern Bakhtin's conception of dialogue and selfhood.

Dialogue and Monologue

Hirschkop refers to "the double sense of the term 'dialogism' [in Bakhtin's work]: it is both the natural state of being of language as such and a valorized category of certain discourses," a statement with which I entirely agree (p. 75). Quite properly, Hirschkop asks how monologue relates to dialogue in this double sense, an important question to be addressed if confusion is to be avoided.

Bakhtin is often careless in his use of terms, including those of his own coinage. Much of his work reads like "inner speech" (speech in which it is unnecessary to spell out those things one already knows and others are not intended to hear). The understandable, and almost instinctive, desire not to be too explicit in writing for a Soviet audience probably explains some of the obscurities found in Bakhtin and other Russian thinkers, but simple carelessness and the fact that Bakhtin never prepared some of his texts for publication also had an effect.[3]

Let me clarify the two distinct senses of "dialogue" in Bakhtin's work. In the first sense in which Bakhtin uses the word, "dialogue" is a description of all language—in effect, a redefinition of language. Bakhtin understands discourse to be not an individual writer's or speaker's instantiating of a code but, instead, the product of a complex social situation in which real or potential audiences, earlier and possible later utterances, habits and "genres" of speech and writing, and a variety of other complex social factors shape all utterances from the outset. Utterances address an "already-spoken-about" world and arise out of a socially constituted "field of answerability." The only way in which the individual speaker can be sole author of an utterance, according to Bakhtin, is in the purely physiological sense.

This conception of language, which Bakhtin worked out in great detail, still requires a lot more thinking. It offers a fundamental challenge to current alternative models and, especially, to those theories founded on the work of Ferdinand de Saussure, Bakhtin's favorite target. In this sense of the word "dialogue," there can be no "monologue," because language is held to be dialogic universally and by definition.

There is, however, a second sense of the word "dialogue" that does admit—in fact, demands—"monologue" as its opposite. Dialogue in this second sense describes a particular discursive stance of speakers, a stance whose fundamental principle Bakhtin paraphrased in his book on Fyodor Dostoevsky: *"Nothing conclusive has yet taken place in the world, the ultimate word of the world and about the world has not yet been spoken, the world is open and free, everything is still in the future and will always be in the future."*[4] Not every situation does or should provide an occasion for this kind of dialogue, but it is sometimes necessary to create such occasions if a special and specially valuable kind of creativity is to take place. On those occasions, one needs a certain kind of dialogic activity, a certain way of constituting the "field of answerability" in order to favor the *"open and free," "*the unfinalizable," the readiness for something new and original. As Bakhtin outlines the opposition, monologic utterances and situations are constructed so as to restrict or ignore this dialogic possibility. By contrast, dialogue (in the second sense) allows the sort of openness so evident in some of Denis Diderot's dialogues, in Aleksandr Pushkin's *Eugene Onegin,* and in much of Dostoevsky but so clearly absent from catechisms, *Pravda,* and Stalinist fiction. This second kind of dialogue is not—as Hirschkop seems to believe that the contributors and I think—a matter of "negotiation," in which differences are resolved or politely put out of sight; rather, it is an occasion for interaction, in which differences can produce new and unforeseen possibilities (p. 74).

The double sense of dialogue in Bakhtin's work has posed a dilemma for a number of Western, especially British, Marxists and quasi-Marxists who have tried to appropriate Bakhtin. Dialogue in the first sense offers them (and the rest of us) an especially powerful model of language and culture and of how values operate and change; consequently, theorists such as Raymond Williams have made intelligent use of Bakhtinian concepts.[5] Judging from Hirschkop's essay, however, dialogue in the second sense appears to provide some Marxists with a sort of provocation. This is hardly surprising given the dismal record of Marxist societies in fostering dialogic openness and protecting those who think that the ultimate word has not yet been spoken. If "liberals" have not yet appropriated Bakhtin into their ideological arsenal, perhaps it is necessary to claim that they have, in order to prevent them from in fact doing so.

Of course, it should be possible to accept Bakhtin's description of language (dialogue in the first sense) as a starting point for future investigation without committing oneself to an idealization of openness (dialogue in the second sense). This is essentially the option that *Elle* chooses in my dialogue, a choice which leaves her (and me) open to the charge of what Marxists are often pleased to call "bourgeois objectivism." *Moi* leans toward an alternative choice and regards the humanities as the favored place for dialogue in the second sense. His position is, I take it, exemplified by *Critical Inquiry* and by exchanges such as this one.

Self and Society

Hirschkop accuses "Holquist, Morson, and Emerson" of reconstructing Bakhtin's ideas so as to insure the "irreducibility" of "the human subject," to identify the social as "never more than the sum of its subjects," and, thus, to establish once again the "conventional liberal opposition of in-dividual and society," an opposition in which "the self is original and society is secondary" (pp. 77, 78, 79). Of course, in fact, we maintained exactly the opposite position, over and over again. Having written my own essay in the form of a dialogue, in which neither participant speaks directly for me, I suppose I invited misreading—even though neither *Moi* nor *Elle* endorses the view that Hirschkop attributes to me. But Caryl Emerson's essay, "The Outer Word and Inner Speech," provides a direct expository description of the models proposed by Bakhtin and Lev Vy-gotsky to challenge this conceptual opposition of self and society.

We describe Bakhtin and Vygotsky as, at their most basic level, maintaining the social as primary in the sense that selves are constituted and composed of "the social." Selfhood, they argued, derives from an internalization of the voices a person has heard, and each of these voices is saturated with social and ideological values. Thought itself is but "inner speech," and inner speech is outer speech that we have learned to "speak" in our heads while retaining the full register of conflicting social values. Emerson quotes, and the interlocutors of my dialogue allude to, Bakhtin's statement that the psyche "enjoys extraterritorial status . . . [as] a social entity that penetrates inside the organism of the individual person" (p. 25, and see p. 8). And Emerson's article explores at length Vygotsky's efforts to challenge Freud and Piaget by demonstrating that selfhood is a social product. She concludes that, for these Russians, "individual con-sciousness is a socio-ideological fact" (p. 26). Hirschkop's criticism is clearly using a "misaddressed word" and, in the process, misrepresenting us.

A more complex point that we made is that, for Bakhtin and Vygotsky, the very opposition of self and society—as defined in the traditional way by contrast to each other—is untenable. As my interlocutors agree, Bakhtin saw that this opposition of society/individual and its corollary *langue/parole* had left the social sciences and humanities with

> a recurring problem: Which is the fundamental unit, the individual or the group? Whichever you choose, you tend to resolve the other into it. One choice leads to an enormous underestimation of the role of individual action, as with most Marxists; the other, to an insufficient appreciation of the manifold social factors which really make us who we are. Bakhtin's idea was to find a *new* minimal unit . . . from which both the social and the individual, the macro- and the micro-, the systematic and the unsystematic could be derived. [P. 7]

Vygotsky's *Thought and Language* is also quite explicit about the need to find such a "minimal unit," and both men thought they had found it in a particular, "dialogic" conception of language. Most readers of Bakhtin have noticed a recurrent form of argument: first he attacks a reduction of the social to the individual, then he attacks the opposite reduction, and finally he calls for an entirely new reconceptualization that would avoid the opposition altogether.

It follows then that Bakhtin did not reject conceptions of an "original" self in the name of a reified concept of society; rather, he redefines the term "social" so that it no longer stands as the opposite of "individual." As Bakhtin observes:

> The "social" is usually thought of in binary opposition with the "individual," and hence we have the notion that the psyche is individual while ideology is social.
> Notions of that sort are fundamentally false. . . .
> If the content of the individual psyche is just as social as is ideology, then, on the other hand, ideological phenomena are just as individual (in the ideological meaning of the word) as are psychological phenomena. Every ideological product bears the imprint of the individuality of its creator or creators, but even this imprint is just as social as are all the other properties and attributes of ideological phenomena.[6]

Or, as *Moi* paraphrases this and similar passages, "Individual consciousness is social through and through" but the social is no less "individual, bearing the imprint of each person who uses it, thinks it, speaks it, and changes it by dialogic words" (p. 8).

Bakhtin's argument here is a difficult and, at times, a hazy one, and thus there is some disagreement about its meaning among the contributors to the forum. On the one hand, Michael Holquist's article "Answering as Authoring" and his recent biography of Bakhtin stress the theorist's early interest in neo-Kantian philosophy and argue that all of Bakhtin's work "can be treated as a single text, a unified utterance" about "relations between self and other" (p. 60). If I read him correctly, Holquist, like *Moi* in my dialogue, sees Bakhtin as continually reinterpreting and repeating this fundamental split, albeit in remarkably new ways. On the other hand, Emerson and I believe that Bakhtin's most interesting and innovative work occurred precisely because he had largely outgrown his neo-Kantian origins. Where Holquist sees a "single text," we see a decisive break; where he sees dialogue as a way of bridging the gap between self and other, the individual and the social, we see it as a way of doing away with that opposition altogether. "Self" and "other," the "individual" and the "social" are made up of the same "substance," namely dialogic words. The opposition of the individual to the social is at best an occasionally useful fiction but "fundamentally false" when reified or taken as primary.[7]

This view is as different from most versions of Marxism as it is from most versions of "individualism," and so it is not terribly surprising that

Hirschkop should accuse us of not appreciating the social and of viewing it, "to borrow a metaphor from Marx," as "the sack in which the potatoes are kept" (p. 78). Thus, it appears that "Holquist, Morson, Emerson, and Bernstein"—why Bernstein in included in this charge I cannot even guess—have "blunted the most radical aspects of [Bakhtin's] thought." Moreover, we are part of a "trend . . . which is growing at a tremendous pace . . . toward an assimilation of Bakhtin into a liberal schema" (p. 79). Here the words "radical" and "liberal" (like "cold war" elsewhere) are compounds of vagueness and of a misplaced political appeal—the sort of approach that one of my friends labels "lefter than thou." In my view, it is Hirschkop who has "blunted" the truly innovative aspects of Bakhtin's thought. In his attempt to place Bakhtin, and us, on recognized points of his own political spectrum, he has failed to see what those innovations are, to ask whether they are tenable, and, if they are tenable, to inquire how they might be developed into a richer, more adequate, and truer understanding of ourselves and our world.[8]

1. Tony Bennett observes: "It is quite clear, however, that the greater part of Marx's writings on art and literature, although penned by Marx, are in no sense indicative of the position of 'Marxism' on these matters" (*Formalism and Marxism* [London, 1979], p. 101). Current "Marxists" would perhaps do better to call themselves "neo-Marxists."

2. On the peculiar and interesting relation of Tolstoy's Christianity to his use of language, see my "Tolstoy's Absolute Language," pp. 123–43. See also Caryl Emerson, "The Tolstoy Connection in Bakhtin," *PMLA* 100 (Jan. 1985): 68–80.

3. With their remarkable tradition of meticulous scholarship, Soviet editors have published such works exactly (it appears) as Mikhail Bakhtin left them, that is, from notebooks never intended for publication. Emerson observes that the danger facing unwary readers is that they may ascribe an authority to the text that it did not possess for the author. Translators of such texts obviously face special problems, as they must negotiate between fidelity and intelligibility. Notable in this regard is Vadim Liapunov's forthcoming work (for the University of Texas Press Slavic Series) on Bakhtin's "Author and Protagonist in Aesthetic Activity."

4. Bakhtin, *Problems of Dostoevsky's Poetics*, ed. and trans. Emerson, Theory and History of Literature Series, vol. 8 (Minneapolis, 1984), p. 166; italics his. This edition also contains an excellent introduction by Wayne C. Booth and an excellent preface by Emerson.

5. See Raymond Williams, *Marxism and Literature* (Oxford, 1977), esp. pp. 35–42.

6. V. N. Vološinov, *Marxism and the Philosophy of Language*, trans. Ladislav Matejka and I. R. Titunik, Studies in Language, vol. 1 (New York, 1973), p. 34; Bakhtin is at least coauthor of this book, but the precise nature of his collaboration with Vološinov is still a matter for lively discussion. The case for Bakhtin's almost sole authorship appears in Katerina Clark and Michael Holquist, *Mikhail Bakhtin* (Cambridge, Mass., 1984).

7. Emerson and I pursue this argument in the book we are coauthoring, *Problems of Bakhtin's Poetics*.

8. Hirschkop also accuses me of "pure and limitless relativism" and of believing that history is entirely random (p. 76; and see p. 77). What *Elle* and *Moi* say, however, is that, according to Bakhtin, history is not *entirely* systematic and that it contains *elements* of the

random, which interact with more or less stable clusters of received practices and habits. Bakhtin was equally opposed to notions of history as entirely aleatory and to forms of "semiotic totalitarianism" (my phrase)—that is, to theories that presume there is a significance and system behind all events.

Hirschkop believes that "the most vivid illustration" of our liberal "tactic" is the form of my article. The exchange between *Moi* and *Elle*, he observes, is intended to show "what a properly dialogical discourse: should look like . . . : a friendly and polite discussion in which a difference of opinion is acknowledged as unresolvable but is nonetheless reconciled to the extent that each speaker 'takes into account' the opinions of the other" (p. 74). Hirschkop would doubtless avoid such liberal behavior. My intention, however, was quite different. "Dialogue" is generally taken to imply a fundamental disagreement, but in Bakhtin's view, all discourse is dialogic (in the first sense); agreement too is a dialogical relationship, is never simply identity, and always involves a complex process of active and divergent responses—as *Moi* and *Elle*, for different reasons, dialogically agree. I hoped that the form of my dialogue would illustrate this point.

Introduction to Extracts from "The Problem of Speech Genres"

Genre served as a key concept in Bakhtin's analyses of literature, and he formulated several taxonomies. In his often inconsistent writings, the genre of the novel is variously defined in terms of its "chronotope," its specific exploitation of the heteroglot resources of language, the relation ("polyphonic") it establishes between author and protagonist, and its embodiment of extraliterary types of parody ("carnivalization"). The concept of genre was also central to his theories of language, where it signified not primarily classes of literary texts but fundamental units of communication.

As Bakhtin conceived it, genre is necessarily historical and social. For this reason, the concept served as an alternative to timeless or homogenous deep structures, grammatical systems, or sets of conventions. In contrast to those concepts, genre is described as disordered to a great extent. Rather than a system, or anything approaching a system, it is a cluster of habits, which imparts a needed regularity to communication while still remaining open to the shifting pressures of daily life. Genre is an organ of memory, but memories, as we know, alter over time.

Marxism and the Philosophy of Language argues that in order to understand communication one must study "the genres of speech performance in human behavior and ideological creativity as determined by verbal interaction."[1] Laying the groundwork for such a study, "The Problem of Speech Genres" (1952–53) describes the "relatively stable types" of utterances that all speakers and listeners use and acquire. Speech genres temporarily crystallize a network of relations between or among interlocutors—their respective power and status, their presumed purposes in communicating, their characterization of the subject of discourse, and their relation to other conversations. Children learn genres from their earliest experiences with language. Because the social relations that are crystallized in specific genres change, so do the genres themselves.

"Primary" speech genres are combined into complex "secondary" ones, among which are those we call literature. Significantly, Bakhtin refuses to recognize any fundamental distinction between speech and writing and between literary and nonliterary secondary genres. In this respect, he differs from the Russian Formalists, the Prague Structuralists, and numerous others, who have identified one or another specifically "literary" or "aesthetic" quality or function. Perhaps this stance is explained by Bakhtin's desire to treat literature, like the psyche, as essentially social.

1. V. N. Vološinov, *Marxism and the Philosophy of Language,* trans. Ladislav Matejka and I. R. Titunik (New York, 1973), p. 96; the Russian original was first published in 1929.

Extracts from

"The Problem of Speech Genres"

[1–2] . . . Each separate utterance is individual, of course, but each sphere in which language is used develops its own *relatively stable types* of these utterances. These we may call *speech genres.* The wealth and diversity of speech genres are boundless because the various possibilities of human activity are inexhaustible, and because each sphere of activity contains an entire repertoire of speech genres which differentiate and grow as the particular sphere develops and becomes more complex. Special emphasis should be placed on the extreme *heterogeneity* of speech genres (oral and written). . . . It might seem that speech genres are so heterogeneous that they do not have and cannot have a single common level at which they can be studied. For here, on one level of inquiry, appear such heterogeneous phenomena as the single-word everyday rejoinder and the multivolume novel, the military command which is standardized even in its intonation and the profoundly individual lyrical work, and so on. . . . This probably explains why the general problem of speech genres has never been raised. . . .

[3] . . . It is especially important here to draw attention to the very very significant difference between primary (simple) and secondary (complex) speech genres (this is not a functional difference). Secondary (complex) speech genres—novels, dramas, all kinds of scientific research, major genres of commentary and so forth—arise in more complex and comparatively highly developed and organized cultural communication (primarily written) which is artistic, scientific, socio-political and so on. During the process of their formation they absorb and digest various primary (simple) genres that have taken form in the conditions of unmediated speech communion. These primary genres are altered and assume a special character when they enter into complex ones. They lose their immediate relation to actual reality and to the real utterances of

others. For example, rejoinders of everyday dialogue or letters found in a novel retain their form and their everyday significance only on the plane of the novel's content. They enter into reality only via the novel as a whole. . . .

[4] . . . A one-sided orientation toward primary genres inevitably leads to a vulgarization of the entire problem (behaviorist linguistics is an extreme example). The very interrelations between primary and secondary genres and the process of the historical formation of the latter shed light on the nature of the utterance (and above all on the complex problem of the interrelations among language, ideology, and worldview).

[6] . . . The very determination of style in general, and individual style in particular, requires deeper study of both the nature of the utterance and the diversity of speech genres.

[8] It is especially harmful to separate style from genre when elaborating historical problems. Historical changes in language styles are inseparably linked to changes in speech genres. . . . one must develop a special history of speech genres (and not only secondary, but also primary ones) which reflects more directly, clearly, and flexibly all the changes taking place in social life. Utterances and their types, i.e., speech genres, are the drive belts from the history of society to the history of language. There is not a single new phenomenon (phonetic, lexical, or grammatical) that can enter the system of language without having traversed the long and complicated path of generic-stylistic testing and modification.

[9] . . . The transfer of style from one genre to another not only alters the way a style sounds, under conditions of a genre unnatural to it, but also violates or renews the given genre.

[18] Thus all real and integral understanding is actively responsive, and constitutes nothing other than the initial preparatory stage of a response (in whatever form it may be actualized). And the speaker himself is oriented precisely toward such an actively responding understanding. He does not expect passive understanding which, so to speak, only duplicates his own idea in someone else's mind. Rather he expects response, agreement, sympathy, objection, execution and so forth (various speech genres presuppose various integral orientations and speech plans on the part of the speakers or writers). The desire to make one's speech understood is only an abstract aspect of the speaker's concrete and total speech plan. Moreover, any speaker is himself a respondent to a greater or lesser degree. He is not, after all, the first speaker, the one who disturbs the eternal silence of the universe. And he presupposes not only the existence of the language system he is using, but also the existence of preceding utterances—his own and others'—with which his given utterance enters into one or another kind of relation (builds on them, polemicizes with them, or simply presumes that they are already known to the listener). Any utterance is a link in a very complexly organized chain of other utterances.

[19] Thus the listener who understands passively, who is depicted as the speaker's partner in the schematic diagrams of general linguistics, does not correspond to the real participant in speech communication. . . .

[24] The boundaries of each concrete utterance as a unit of speech communication are determined by a *change of speaking subjects,* i.e., a change of speakers. Any utterance—from a short (single-word) rejoinder in everyday dialogue to the large novel or scientific treatise—has, so to speak, an absolute beginning and an absolute end; its beginning is preceded by the utterances of others, and its end is followed by others' responsive utterances (or, although it may be silent, others' actively responding understanding, or, finally, a responsive action based on this understanding). The speaker ends his utterance in order to relinquish the floor to the other or to make room for the other's active responsive understanding. The utterance is not a conventional unit, but a real unit, clearly delimited by the change of speaking subjects, which ends by relinquishing the floor to the other, as if with a silent "dixi," perceived by the listeners (as a sign) that the speaker has finished.

[25] . . . And the sort of relations that exist among rejoinders of a dialogue—relations between question and answer, assertion and objection, assertion and agreement, suggestion and acceptance, order and execution, and so forth—are impossible among units of language (words and sentences) or within the utterance (on the horizontal plane). These specific relations among rejoinders in a dialogue are only subcategories of specific relations among whole utterances in the process of speech communication. . . . The relations among whole utterances cannot be treated grammatically since, we repeat, such relations are impossible among units of language, and not only in the system of language, but within the utterance as well.

[27] . . . the problem of the *sentence* as a *unit of language,* as distinct from the *utterance* as a unit of speech communication.

[29] Here we shall simply note that the boundaries of the sentence as a unit of language are never determined by a change of speaking subjects. Such a change, framing the sentence on both sides, transforms the sentence into an entire utterance. Such a sentence assumes new qualities and is perceived quite differently from the way it would be if it were framed by other sentences within the single utterance of one and the same speaker. The sentence is a relatively complete thought, directly correlated with the other thoughts of a single speaker within his utterance as a whole. The speaker pauses at the end of a sentence in order then to move on to his own next thought, continuing, supplementing, and substantiating the preceding one. The context of the sentence is the speech of one speaking subject (speaker). The sentence itself is not correlated directly or personally with the extraverbal context or reality (situation, setting, prehistory) or with the utterances of other speakers; this takes place only indirectly, through its entire surrounding context, i.e.,

through the utterance as a whole. And if the sentence is not surrounded by a context of the speech of the same speaker, i.e., if it constitutes an entire completed utterance (a rejoinder in dialogue), then it (itself) directly confronts reality (the extraverbal context of the speech) and the different utterances of *others*. It is not followed by a pause which the speaker himself designates and interprets. (Any pause that is grammatical, calculated, or interpreted is possible only within the speech of a single speaker, i.e., within a single utterance. Pauses between utterances are, of course, not grammatical but real. Such real pauses—psychological, or prompted by some external circumstance—can also interrupt a single utterance. In secondary artistic genres such pauses are calculated by the artist, director, or actor. But these pauses differ essentially from both grammatical and stylistic pauses—for example, among syntagmas—within the utterance.) One expects them to be followed by a response or a responsive understanding on the part of another speaker. Such a sentence, having become an entire utterance, acquires a special semantic fullness of value. One can assume a responsive position with respect to it; one can agree or disagree with it, execute it, evaluate it, and so on. But a sentence in context cannot elicit a response. It acquires this capability (or, rather, assimilates to it) only in the entirety of the whole utterance.

[30] All these completely new qualities and peculiarities belong not to the sentence that has become a whole utterance, but precisely to the utterance itself. . . . When the sentence figures as a whole utterance, it is as though it has been placed in a frame made of quite a different material. When one forgets this in analyzing a sentence, one distorts the nature of the sentence (and simultaneously the nature of the utterance as well, by treating it grammatically). . . . One does not exchange sentences any more than one exchanges words (in the strict linguistic sense) or phrases. One exchanges utterances which are constructed from language units: words, phrases, and sentences. And an utterance can be constructed both from one sentence and from one word, so to speak, from one speech unit (mainly a rejoinder in dialogue), but this does not transform a language unit into a unit of speech communication.

[37] This finalized wholeness of the utterance, guaranteeing the possibility of a response (or of responsive understanding), is determined by three aspects (or factors) that are inseparably linked in the organic whole of the utterance: (1) semantic exhaustiveness of the theme; (2) the speaker's intent or speech will; (3) typical compositional and generic forms of finalization.

[38] The first aspect—the referentially semantic exhaustiveness of the theme of the utterance—differs profoundly in various spheres of communication. This exhaustiveness can be almost complete in certain spheres of everyday life (questions that are purely factual and similarly factual responses to them, requests, orders, and so forth), in certain business circles, in the sphere of military and industrial commands and

orders, i.e., in those spheres where speech genres are maximally standard and where the creative aspect is almost completely lacking. Conversely, in creative spheres (especially, of course, in scientific ones), the semantic exhaustiveness of the theme may be only relative. Here one can speak only of a certain minimum of finalization making it possible to occupy a responsive position. . . .

[39] In each utterance—from the single-word, everyday rejoinder to large, complex works of science or literature—we embrace, understand, and sense the speaker's *speech plan* or *speech will*, which determines the entire utterance, its length and boundaries. We imagine to ourselves what the speaker *wishes* to say. And we also use this speech plan, this speech will (as we understand it) to measure the finalization of the utterance. . . .

[40] Let us turn to the third and, for us, most important aspect: the stable *generic* forms of the utterance. The speaker's speech will is manifested primarily in the *choice of a particular speech genre*. This choice is determined by the specific nature of the given sphere of speech communication, semantic (thematic) considerations, the concrete situation of the speech communication, the personal composition of its participants, and so on. And when the speaker's speech plan with all its individuality and subjectivity is applied and adapted to a chosen genre, it is shaped and developed within a certain generic form. Such genres exist above all in the great and multifarious sphere of everyday oral communication, including the most familiar and most intimate.

[41] We speak only in definite speech genres, that is, all our utterances have definite and relatively stable typical *forms of construction of the whole*. . . . We are given these speech genres in almost the same way that we are given our native language, which we master fluently long before we begin to study grammar. We know our native language—its lexical composition and grammatical structure—not from dictionaries and grammars but from concrete utterances which we hear and which we ourselves reproduce in live speech communication with people around us. We assimilate forms of language only in forms of utterances and in conjunction with these forms. The forms of language and the typical forms of utterances, i.e., speech genres, enter our experience and consciousness together in close connection with one another. To learn to speak means to learn to construct utterances (because we speak in utterances and not in individual sentences, and, of course, not in individual words). . . . If speech genres did not exist and we had not mastered them, if we had to originate them during the speech process and construct each utterance at will for the first time, speech communication would be almost impossible.

[42] The generic forms in which we cast our speech, of course, differ essentially from language forms. The latter are stable and compulsory (normative) for the speaker, while generic forms are much more flexible, plastic and free. . . .

[43] . . . But to use a genre freely and creatively is not the same as to create a genre from the beginning; genres must be fully mastered in order to be manipulated freely.

[44] Many people who have an excellent command of a language often feel quite helpless in certain spheres of communication precisely because they do not have a practical command of the generic forms used in given spheres. Frequently a person who has an excellent command of speech in some areas of cultural communication, who is able to read a scholarly paper or engage in a scholarly discussion, who speaks very well on social questions, is silent or very awkward in social conversation. Here it is not a matter of an impoverished vocabulary or style, taken abstractly; this is entirely a matter of the inability to command a repertoire of genres. . . .

[46] . . . the single utterance, with all its individuality and creativity, can in no way be regarded as a completely free combination of forms of language, as is supposed, for example, by Saussure (and by many other linguists after him), who juxtaposed the utterance (*la parole*), as a purely individual act, to the system of language as a phenomenon that is purely social and mandatory for the individuum. . . .

[48] When we select a particular type of sentence we do not do so for the sentence itself, but out of consideration for what we wish to express with one given sentence. We select the given sentence from the standpoint of the *whole* utterance, which is transmitted in advance to our speech imagination and which determines our choice. . . .

[57] . . . The sentence as a unit of language, like the word, has no author. Like the word, it belongs to *nobody*. . . .

[60] Can the expressive aspect of speech be regarded as a phenomenon of *language* as a system? Can one speak of the expressive aspect of language units, i.e., words and sentences? The answer to these questions must be a categorical "no." . . . The word "darling"—which is affectionate both in the meaning of its root and its suffix—is in itself, as a language unit, just as neutral as the word "distance." . . .

[62] One of the means of expressing the speaker's emotionally evaluative attitude toward the subject of his speech is expressive intonation, which resounds clearly in oral speech. Expressive intonation is a constitutive marker of the utterance. It does not exist in the system of language as such, i.e., outside the utterance. . . . If an individual word is pronounced with expressive intonation it is no longer a word, but a complete utterance expressed by one word. . . . Words that acquire special weight under particular conditions of socio-political life become expressive exclamatory utterances: "Peace!", "Freedom!", and so forth. (These constitute a special socio-political speech genre.) In a particular situation a word can acquire a profoundly expressive meaning in the form of an exclamatory utterance: "The sea! The sea!" (exclaimed by ten thousand Greeks in Xenophon).

[66] . . . we choose words according to their generic specifications. A speech genre is not a form of language, but a typical form of utterance; as such the genre also includes a certain typical kind of expression that inheres in it. In the genre the word acquires a particular typical expression. Genres correspond to typical situations of speech communication, typical themes, and consequently also to particular contacts between the *meanings* of words and actual concrete utterances under typical circumstances. Hence also the possibility of typical expressions which seem to adhere to words. . . .

[67] This typical (generic) expression can be regarded as the word's "stylistic aura," but this aura belongs not to the word of language as such but to that genre in which the given word usually functions. It is an echo of the generic whole that resounds in the word.

[73] Thus the expressiveness of individual words is not inherent in the words themselves as units of language, nor does it issue directly from the meaning of these words: it is either typical generic expression or it is an echo of another's individual expression, which makes the word, as it were, representative of another's whole utterance from a particular evaluative position.

[79] . . . any utterance when it is studied in greater depth under the concrete conditions of speech communication, reveals to us many half-concealed or completely concealed words of others with varying degrees of foreignness. Therefore the utterance appears to be furrowed with distant and barely audible echoes of changes of speech subjects and dialogic overtones, greatly weakened utterance boundaries which are completely permeable to the author's expression. . . .

[87] This question of the concept of the speech addressee (how the speaker or writer senses and imagines him) is of immense significance in literary history. Each person, each literary trend and literary-artistic style, each literary genre within an epoch or trend, is typified by its own special concepts of the addressee of the literary work, a special sense and understanding of its reader, listener, public, or people. A historical study of changes in these concepts would be an interesting and important task. . . .

When the Carnival Turns Bitter: Preliminary Reflections Upon the Abject Hero

Michael André Bernstein

> Until the subject of a tyrant's will
> Became, worse fate, the abject of his own
> —PERCY BYSSHE SHELLEY, *Prometheus Unbound*

1

A master and his slave, a monarch and his fool, a philosopher and a madman: even as the particulars of the roles change with the epoch and social milieu, the underlying configuration seems to remain the same. Irrespective of the specific work in which such pairings occur, we respond, long before the details of the argument clearly emerge, to a convention whose power rests upon its promise to subvert our notion of power and convention and to a fixed set of characters whose dialogue will undermine our trust in stable identities and fixed character traits. At the center of the *agon* there is always a moment of absolute reversal, an exchange of positions when it is the slave, like Horace's Davus, who calls his master "o totiens servus [o you slave many times over],"[1] or Denis Diderot's failed parasite, Jean-François Rameau, who proves the *philosophe* no better than the fool of a fool.

It is largely from the writings of Mikhail Bakhtin that we have learned to apply terms like "carnivalization" to the collapse of hierarchic distinctions

Preparation of this essay was assisted greatly by a grant from the American Council of Learned Societies and the National Endowment for the Humanities. I would also like to thank my colleague, Thomas G. Rosenmeyer, for his valuable criticisms on an early draft of this paper.

upon which all such dialogues depend, and it is a major part of Bakhtin's legacy to have taught us better how to value the liberating energy of the carnivalesque. In the last section of this essay, I will return to Davus, Jean-François Rameau, and to their literary progeny, to see in more detail just how the convention becomes increasingly more problematic, the dialogues more shrill and unnerving; but precisely because Bakhtin's analyses are at once so wide-ranging in their choice of *exempla* and so concentrated in their essential thrust, I want to begin my own questioning more obliquely, locating not so much a counter-tradition as a negative and bitter strand at the core of the Saturnalia itself. And although it appears clear to me that Diderot's *Le Neveu de Rameau* represents a crucial turning point in the history of the Saturnalian dialogue, a moment of precarious equipoise after which the destructive forces inherent in the convention begin to dominate over the essentially predictable, and thus optimistic, reversals cherished by Bakhtin, I am less concerned with tracing an exclusively literary genealogy than with locating the family resemblance among a set of diverse but interrelated problems. In each of my instances, however, what emerges is the image of a carnivalization of values during which it is no longer a question of breaking down ossified hierarchies and stale judgments but rather of being denied *any* vantage point from which a value can still be affirmed.

Bakhtin's description of the carnivalesque is, undeniably, a largely *post festum* recollection, a celebration of a tradition whose full realization he finds in the works of François Rabelais. But by his trust in the transcendent power of carnival laughter, Bakhtin himself participates in a critical rhetoric eager to respond to the cathartic energy of the Saturnalia wherever it appears, a rhetoric in whose elaboration Friedrich Nietzsche played a decisive role. Indeed, there are numerous fragments in Nietzsche uncannily similar, except for the temporal perspective, to some of Bakhtin's own formulations. In *Beyond Good and Evil*, for example, Nietzsche claims for his own age a unique preparedness

> for a carnival in the grand style, for the laughter and high spirits of the most spiritual revelry, for the transcendental heights of the highest nonsense and Aristophanean derision of the world. Perhaps this is where we shall still discover the realm of our *invention*, that realm in which we, too, can still be original, say, as parodists of world history and God's buffoons—perhaps, even if nothing else today has any future, our *laughter* may yet have a future.[2]

Michael André Bernstein, associate professor of English and comparative literature at the University of California, Berkeley, is the author of *The Tale of the Tribe: Ezra Pound and the Modern Verse Epic* and *Prima della Rivoluzione*, a volume of verse. He is currently at work on a book about the Abject Hero and literary genealogy.

Perhaps the most immediate way to crystallize the issues at stake in my own darker reading of the Saturnalian carnival is to start with the case of a quite different author, himself a master ironist, for whom the prospect of suddenly finding himself the buffoon of God's buffoon is no mere rhetorical trope or occasion for a Saturnalian laughter but rather an open chasm in which all of his own writings and beliefs risk being engulfed.

2

"I am perfectly willing to be abject, but not under duress."
—DENIS DIDEROT, *Le Neveu de Rameau*

"And to be contemporary with the decisive Christian fact is the decisive thing. This contemporaneousness, however, is to be understood as having the same significance that it had for people who lived at the same time that Christ was living."[3] For Søren Kierkegaard the issue here, as in countless similar passages throughout his writing, is the immediate supra-historical claim of the Christian revelation upon the believer. This claim is addressed, always and only, to the individual in his absolute inwardness. For Kierkegaard, all traditional appeals to the two millennia of Christian cultural and ethical hegemony only succeed in confusing mutually exclusive categories, conflating, in an almost demonic canonization of worldly success, two spheres upon whose radical disjuncture the very possibility of faith depends. The Scriptures are not documents to be deciphered but a permanent summons whose effect is to reveal an abyss no interpretation can bridge and in response to which questions of sequence and chronology, presence and belatedness, become irrelevant. Kierkegaard repeatedly stresses that "he who understands in general that a man might receive a revelation, must after all understand it quite as well whether it happened six thousand years ago, or will happen six thousand years hence, or has happened today."[4] And much of his polemical irony is devoted to satirizing the false terms by which "orthodox Christendom" has defended its authority.

Yet no position is as inherently unstable as that of an ironist confronted, not with a direct attack (for that fate every ironist conscious of the Socratic model is at least in principle prepared) but with a parodic doubling of his own position. Hence Kierkegaard's confusion when, in 1843, the Reverend Adolph Peter Adler (1812–1869) published his *Several Sermons* with a preface announcing that he had received a direct revelation from Jesus Christ. The "case of Adler" vexed the Danish religious authorities for a number of years, and Adler himself was first suspended on account of "derangement" (1844) and then deposed with a pension (1845). But for Kierkegaard the parallels between Adler's claims to divine inspiration and Kierkegaard's own arguments for a direct, existential relationship to God proved more permanently unsettling. In a sense, Adler was the distorted mirror image of Kierkegaard's deepest beliefs, a kind of Smerdyakov to the master ironist's Ivan, and the countless revisions of Kierkegaard's *Book on Adler* (it was never published in its entirety during his lifetime) testify to how disturbing the encounter with his "deranged" double had been.

Even beyond the theological confusion Adler represented, his career contained uncanny parallels with Kierkegaard's own, including family background, education, and publication history.[5] For example, on 16 October 1843, the same year Adler's *Sermons* appeared, Kierkegaard simultaneously published three major books: *Fear and Trembling, Repetition,* and *Three Edifying Discourses,* the last of which he dedicated to his father. This gesture was duplicated by Adler three years later, only with four books, one of which, in turn, was also inscribed to the author's father. Throughout the *Book on Adler,* Kierkegaard nervously confesses his unease with the parallels, admitting that "I as least had not expected to find the memory of this [his own multiple publications of 1843] so quickly refreshed—and so much by way of parody."[6] Adler himself was quite aware of the links between the two men and managed to reinterpret them in his characteristic manner, announcing, on the occasion of their encounter, that Kierkegaard was a sort of John the Baptist to his own role as the new Messiah.

Trivial, or even blasphemous, as Adler's last assertion may appear, it is through his capacity to undermine, by parodic imitation, Kierkegaard's complex "dialectic of faith" that he initiates a singularly disconcerting version of the Saturnalian dialogue discussed in the opening pages.[7] For Adler's claims not only echo, in the form of mimicry, the evolving structure of Kierkegaard's thinking, but they seem, even in their very articulation, like a series of direct, but hopelessly vulgarized, quotations from Kierkegaard's own writings. To Kierkegaard, the author of *Several Sermons* appeared as a mad version of the "knight of faith" celebrated in *Fear and Trembling,* and Adler's famous "Preface" seemed a realization, in the form of buffoonery, of *Fear and Trembling*'s dictum: "The conclusions of passion are the only reliable ones, that is, the only convincing conclusions."[8] Increasingly, Kierkegaard came to regard the whole "case of Adler" as almost that of one of his characters not in search but rather in malicious mockery of the author. After all, Kierkegaard often maintained that he longed "to be better understood, or at least to be more passionately misunderstood," and what more gripping instance of a "passionate misunderstanding" could be imagined than Adler's declaration of a sacred mission?[9] Put more generally, Kierkegaard's anxiety exemplifies the situation of any ironist confronted by an opponent able to marshal the identical structures and tropes of irony on his own behalf, an antagonist whose principal weapon is no more than the literal enactment of the very paradoxes upon which the ironist's discourse depends. And, once set into play, what is to prevent the subversive effects of that irony from striking not only the debased versions of a positive model but also the very ideal the irony was dialectically meant to affirm?

3

> The purpose of asking a question may be twofold. One may ask a question for the purpose of obtaining an answer containing the desired content, so that the more one questions, the deeper and more meaningful becomes the answer; or one may ask a question, not .in the interest of obtaining an answer, but to suck out the apparent content with a question and leave only an emptiness remaining.
>
> —SØREN KIERKEGAARD, *The Concept of Irony*

Ulrich von Wilamowitz-Moellendorff's caustic dismissal of Seneca's *Medea*—"This Medea has obviously read the *Medea* of Euripides"[10]—has been echoed, although rarely with such terse wit, by many other readers of Seneca's tragedy, and his epigram derives its force from the confidence that no one could question seriously its implicit notion of literary propriety. That Seneca himself had studied Euripides with great care is indisputable and hardly an occasion for complaint, but that his character should seem to share the benefits of that study is considered ample evidence of an artistic failure. Taken literally such an interpretation would open the possibility of the Latin Medea appearing not as a vitiated, derivative version of her Greek predecessor but rather as her parodic double, reenacting a role she has memorized but adding the surplus of an ironic self-consciousness brought about precisely by her familiarity with an already scripted .part.

It is along just these lines, allowing for the transposition of genres, that Kierkegaard condemned Adler's *Sermons*, judging them primarily as misguided readings-interpretations of his own complex texts. But my illustration is scarcely intended as a perverse argument for a new perspective on Senecan tragedy. I do, however, want to suggest that while literary criticism, from its classical beginnings, has sought to account for the effects of an *author's* debts to his predecessor, the problem of a fictional *character* deliberately repeating the words and actions of an earlier model has remained largely unexplored. Although often elided in theoretical discussions, the differences between the two types of quotation are powerfully registered in our response to any text, and my own juxtaposition of Wilamowitz-Moellendorff's comment on *Medea* with Kierkegaard's reaction to Adler seems so extravagant because it violates our desire to maintain sharp demarcations between a writer's, as opposed to a character's, use of quotation and mimicry. The instinctive objection that Adler was "only" a writer of worthless books, not a character like Emma Bovary, seduced by reading them, and that Wilamowitz-Moellendorff's witticism simply does not lend itself to categorical extension is undoubtedly valid. But its force becomes considerably attenuated when the works in question deliberately conflate fictional and real personnages. Thus, the example of Kierkegaard and Adler itself, although introduced largely to dramatize the distinction between "authorial" and "fictional" mimicry, is more complex than any simple dismissal would suggest, and its complexity arises because both terms of the dichotomy are equally unstable. Of the historical writer Adolph Peter Adler, all that remains of any interest is the character by that name in Kierkegaard's *Book on Adler,* and there his position is, if anything, considerably worse than that of Emma Bovary, since he is driven to delirium by reading what Kierkegaard clearly regards as eminently salutary and important works—that is, the Bible and his own texts. Considered from the other perspective, however, it is equally true that the very books the "real" Adler could have read were largely pseudonymous, with positions presented by fictional narrators deliberately differentiated both from one another and from Kierkegaard himself. Adler was thus parodying not so much Søren Kierkegaard but the fictional Johannes De Silentio, Constantine Constantius, and so forth—a fact that only made Kierkegaard's situation all the more vexed.

The very elusiveness of my examples thus far, their refusal to stay fixed within a neat framework, only indicates, although in an obviously schematic form, both the need for and the inherent problems confronting a critical language that seeks to register the multiple effects of imitation as ironic subversion. And although the remainder of this essay will consider a set of texts that flourish precisely by exploiting the instability of any categories, it is perhaps useful initially to isolate three principal modes of deliberate citation, each of which offers its own potential for ironic elaborations and variations: (1) an author who cites the work of another writer, either relying upon it as a model in toto or using some particular aspect, a recognizable structural or thematic configuration, from the work of a uniquely significant predecessor (at its simplest, the instance of Seneca deriving his *Medea* from Euripides); (2) a character in a work of literature who knowingly quotes the words or imitates the actions of an earlier fictional character (e.g., Stephen Dedalus' self-conscious identification with Hamlet); or (3) an author who draws upon a particular literary tradition or genre rather than upon any one specific *exemplum,* and whose characters, in order to be locatable within that tradition, themselves also consciously quote from the fictional works that have established the genre's conventions. In this paradigm, aspects of the two other models unite; *both* the author and the characters knowingly use citations and imitation as essential elements of their self-representation.[11]

Although the way we respond to a text will obviously depend upon the kind of imitation it enacts, the difficulty of distinguishing among the various possibilities can lead to sharply divergent readings. The well-known homily warning us that the Devil can quote Scriptures to his own ends, neatly illustrates the hermeneutic dilemma, since we are alerted to Satan's malicious impersonation only because we know that the speaker is really the Devil. And yet it is just his misappropriation of the sacred texts which should identify him as diabolical.

In less lurid terms, we could generalize the predicaments by noting how slight are the cues separating a respectful "identification" with a model from either a parodic "imitation" or a sinister "impersonation."[12] It is only in the last of my three modes that the full resources of citation as identification, imitation, and impersonation can be marshaled *against one another* to undermine the reader's confidence in deciding among the mutually exclusive interpretive options. And it is this mode, as well, which creates the structure required for a new character type, an Abject Hero, in whom the subversive possibilities of manipulating a literary tradition find their most concentrated expression.

4

"Vertumnis, quotquot sunt, natus iniquis"
—HORACE, *Satires*

Le Neveu de Rameau opens with a citation from Horace's seventh satire and describes Priscus, "a man born when every single Vertumnus [the god who presided over the changing of the year and assumed any shape he pleased] was out of sorts." But since these lines are spoken neither by *Moi* nor *Lui,* they do not actually enter into the dialogue proper of Diderot's dialogue; rather, they serve as an index of the text's affiliation with the satiric tradition of a Saturnalian encounter between a master and his slave, during which, as Bakhtin emphasizes, a fundamental transformation of conventional roles, proprieties, and hierarchies is celebrated:

> The literary and artistic consciousness of the Romans could not imagine a serious form without its comic equivalent. The serious, straightforward form was perceived as only a fragment, only half of a whole; the fullness of the whole was achieved only upon adding the comic *contre-partie* of this form. Everything serious had to have, and indeed did have, its comic double. As in the Saturnalia the clown was the double of the ruler and the slave the double of the master, so such comic doubles were created in all forms of culture and literature.[13]

For Bakhtin, the carnival laughter is both the form and vehicle of popular liberation. He sees in the festive license of the Saturnalia, in its carnivalization of all normally inflexible distinctions, the embodiment of a permanent utopian longing, a glimpse of a prelapsarian world free from cast and cant, "opposed to all that was ready-made and completed, to all pretense at immutability."[14] Corresponding to this social freedom is a loosening of the codes of linguistic decorum and a new readiness to mingle forms of address and speech otherwise kept strictly apart:

> This temporary suspension, both ideal and real, of hierarchical rank created during carnival time a special type of communication impossible in everyday life. This led to the creation of special forms of marketplace speech and gesture, frank and free, permitting no distance between those who came in contact with each other and liberating from norms of etiquette and decency imposed at other times. [P. 10]

But in Horace, as later in Diderot, such license is granted only once a year, and although Davus is allowed to chastise and mock his master, both know that their normal roles are only temporarily suspended, not permanently dissolved. During the Saturnalia, each of the characters, master and slave, wise man and fool, speaks with a freedom whose operative condition is a precisely defined temporal span, since, although the golden age of Saturn is of potentially limitless duration, the actual festival of that name has already been marked by the very structuration its activities and language seem to overthrow. What is striking in the literary tradition of the Saturnalian dialogue, from its classical origins until long after the Renaissance, is how rarely the laughter ("festive," "universal," and "ambivalent" in Bakhtin's triad [p. 11]) actually challenges the audience's own sense of judgment and values. In part, no doubt, this is due to the formally authorized nature of the festival, suggesting, in fact, that the ruling conventions permit themselves to be mocked, due to a full confidence in their own power to emerge still more firmly entrenched the following morning.

But this sense of a "licensed"—and thus essentially harmless—liberty is felt at a deeper level in the actual unfolding of the various wise man and fool dialogues. Although the frank speech of his fool may compel the master to acknowledge his own eccentricities and weaknesses, to recognize that the fool may be wiser than he, there is no moment during which a reader or spectator would be unable to judge the justice of each participant's speech. Horace and Davus may each be a mixture of wisdom and folly, insight and self-indulgence, but we, the readers of Horace's satire, have little reason to doubt our ability to decide when one man is telling the truth, or merely deceiving himself or his interlocutor. Even in English Renaissance drama where the "wise fool" attached to a court enjoys the liberty to speak freely to his master on a permanent, if precarious, basis, the audience learns very quickly when the fool's words contain a truth which the master ignores only at his own peril and when the quips are merely witty repartee. Lear's fool, for example, seeks, too often in vain, to instruct his vain king. But he only confirms what the audience already knows from its privileged position outside the drama, and much of the pathos in the Fool's role is due to our independently confirmed awareness of how right his warnings are. Even in Rabelais, Bakhtin's paramount example of the fruitful power of mockery, the reader may be greatly amused by the humor, but he can hardly be unsettled by a text in which praiseworthy and despicable attitudes are depicted on so gigantic a scale that any confusion between them is impossible. To misidentify positive and negative qualities, and thus to risk becoming oneself a target of Rabelaisian laughter, is a possibility that the book's own exuberant language largely precludes. In each case, we are free to second Davus' mockery of Horace, to share the Fool's distress at Lear's folly, or to rage with Panurge at the narrow-souled "agelasts," but only because in a fictional, as opposed to an experientially lived Saturnalian reversal of all values, the stability of the reader's position is already guaranteed, serving as a kind of ultimate court of appeal within whose jurisdiction all questions of folly and wisdom are clearly adjudicated. (In this sense the position of the reader is akin to the function of the next day in a "real" Saturnalia, the instant when everyone resumes his conventional roles, with the important distinction, however, that the reader's position represents a *continuously* present source of authority which even the most anarchic moments of the festival day do not succeed in suspending.)

Thus, although Bakhtin can describe the Saturnalian laughter as ambiguous, the scope of that ambiguity is strictly limited, as indeed it must be to answer his own need for an unmistakably productive agent of liberation. But let us now return to consider a possibility raised earlier— what of a character who has himself studied the Saturnalian tradition, a "wise fool" who has read both the classical satirists and Rabelais and Molière, their modern descendants, a character who cynically exploits the resources of an affirmative buffoonery, not out of any anarchic and unconscious freedom but as a vehicle for self-aggrandizement and as an expression of lacerating *ressentiment?*

5

> CLOV: What is there to keep me here?
> HAMM: The dialogue.
> —SAMUEL BECKETT, *Endgame*

Since Ernst Robert Curtius first called attention to the importance of the Horatian epigraph for *Le Neveu de Rameau,* critics have found themselves in the curious position of recognizing an unmistakable generic affiliation while in fundamental disagreement about how its literary genealogy should govern the interpretation of Diderot's satire.[15] The character of Jean-François Rameau clearly shares numerous traits with Priscus, a man whose fickleness of temperament was matched only by the constant reversals in his fortunes: "Passing from a stately mansion, he would bury himself in a den, from which a decent freedman could scarcely emerge without shame. Now he would choose to live in Rome as a rake, now as a sage in Athens—a man born when every single Vertumnus was out of sorts."[16] Indeed, *Le Neveu* is full of echoes, not only of Horace's poem "Iamdudum ausculto" but of numerous other Horatian satires, including the third satire of book 1, with its description of the singer Tigellius ("no one could be more different from him than himself"; my translation here), the fourth satire of book 1, with its mockery of the parasite in search of a free meal, and so forth.[17] But although scholarship continues to find ever more instances of Diderot's debt to Horace and to the entire tradition of Roman satire, there has been a remarkable lack of consensus about the thematic consequences of these debts. For Curtius, the parallels of form and imagery lead unmistakably to an equivalence of argument; "the basic theme—contrast between the fool, enslaved by want, necessities, lust, and passions, and the self-sufficient and therefore only free man, the sage—is identical in the two works."[18] Yet, in an antithetical reading, represented most succinctly by Herbert Dieckmann, it is the differences between Horace-Davus and *Moi-Lui* which are reckoned decisive: "The *Moi* cannot possibly be identified with the stoic conception of the sage. The nephew, on the other hand, is undoubtedly the victim of desires, passions, and vices, but he has many redeeming features, not only thanks to Diderot's art, but also in Diderot's opinion. He is not a fool in the Stoic sense, but in a modern sense, which presupposes the Renaissance."[19] Essentially, judgments of the meaning of *Le Neveu* keep taking up, with suitable elaborations, one or another of these two fundamental positions, while at the same time each is forced to acknowledge the absence of any conclusive evidence that would prove the opposing point of view untenable.

Rather than continuing to ask how closely the ethical and aesthetic arguments in the two satires correspond or diverge, it seems more profitable to inquire why Diderot's text should have given rise to such mutually exclusive readings and why the character of Jean-François Rameau, although resembling figures like Priscus, Tigellius, and so forth, in numerous specific traits, should leave us, quite unlike the targets of Horatian satire, with such contradictory responses.

Although, as I have said, the epigraph linking *Le Neveu* to "Iamdudum ausculto" serves as a dialogue's frame and not as one of its components, it is also true that both *Moi* and *Lui* themselves regularly cite or paraphrase celebrated lines from the Latin and French satiric-comic tradition (e.g., Horace on page 32, Juvenal on pages 38 and 44, Horace again on page 60, Lucian on page 67, Molière on page 76). Thus there are two distinct orders of quotation, the first, a single keynote sounded by an author who is not a participant in the dialogue, and the second, the multiple references spoken by both participants in the course of their disputes. A number of curious consequences arise out of this doubling, not the least strange of which is the necessary conclusion that *Moi* and *Lui,* as well as the author citing the epigraph, have read the same canonic satires.

The quotation from Molière offers a striking example of the multiple resonances that can emanate from a single "tag" when both the author and his characters draw upon it simultaneously. *Lui* directly cites Molière only once in the dialogue (see p. 76), but when he does so it is to one of the playwright's rare Latin verses that he refers: "Vivat Mascurillius, fourbum Imperator." The line itself, "Long live Mascurillius, Emperor of cheats," from act 2, scene 1 of *L'Etourdi,* adds little to Jean-François' speech, beyond demonstrating his familiarity with France's greatest comic dramatist. But I think that its presence is also *Diderot's* indirect way of establishing a clear structural and linguistic link between Molière and the Latin tradition, his suggestion that the best French comedies (including, by implication, his own dialogue) are the direct descendants of the classical satirists.[20] But the relationship between the two orders of quotation can rarely be resolved quite so neatly, since even if, for example, the writer quoting "Vertumnis, quotquot sunt, natus iniquis" might want to suggest a simple link between Horace and the ensuing French text, *Moi* and *Lui* are able to use the same models for their own—and especially in their ethical interpretations, far from identical—ends.

> *Lui.*—Now what I do is gather there [from the works of the great satirists] a compendium of what I ought to do and what I should not acknowledge. Thus, when I read the *Miser,* I tell myself "Be a miser if you wish but make sure not to talk like one." When I read *Tartuffe,* I tell myself "Be a hypocrite if you wish, but don't talk like one. Keep those vices which are useful to you but don't acquire the tone and mannerisms which would make you ridiculous." [P. 60][21]

Jean-François knows quite well the ambiguous authority ascribed to a "wise fool" and does not hesitate to draw upon it for support in his quarrel with *Moi:*

> *Lui.*—. . . For a long time the King had an official fool, but at no time did the King have an official wise man. I am Bertin's fool and that of many others—your own possibly at this moment; or perhaps you are mine. A real wise man wouldn't have any fool. Thus, anyone who has a fool isn't really wise, and if he isn't a wise man then he must be a fool. And perhaps if he were a King, he would be the fool of his fool. [P. 61][22]

And, of course, *Moi* himself, for all his intellectual self-assurance, and even as a direct result of the education which nourished that confidence, is equally susceptible to the suspicion that he and Jean-François are reenacting a time-honored Saturnalian ritual in which his role as a "sage" is necessarily open to ridicule.

But this doubling of citations, although adding a particularly modern element of self-consciousness, would not, by itself, effect a radical departure from the Horatian model. But it does establish the conditions necessary for Diderot's more fundamental transformation of the satiric convention: the creation of a "wise fool" who can no longer be judged with any confidence by himself, his interlocutor, or even the dialogue's readers. The debate about Jean-François' character has continued so interminably precisely because, unlike in the classical satiric tradition, there simply are no independent criteria upon which to base a coherent judgment. Often *Moi* is forced to admit that "there is some sense in almost everything you've been saying" (p. 82),[23] only to be met with the scorn of a man who realizes full well wherein his knowledge exceeds that of the *philosophe:*

> *Lui.*—That's typical of your kind. If we say something intelligent it's like madmen or people possessed—purely by accident. It's only people of your kind who know what they're saying. But I tell you, Mister Philosopher, I know what I'm saying and I know it as well as you know your own thoughts. [P. 12][24]

But at the same time, Jean-François' repeated failures in life and art, his (economically) enforced buffoonery and parasitism, and, most tellingly, his regular physical and mental collapses into exhaustion and incoherence convince even him that he is far from possessing the inner equilibrium required by his role as a "wise fool." Jean-François admits that he is unable to distinguish between his moments of folly and wisdom, a conclusion which is shared in almost equal measure by *Moi*—and by the reader:

> *Lui.*—. . . The Devil take me if I know what I'm really like at bottom. In general, my mind is round like a sphere, and my character as sturdy as a willow. I'm never dishonest if I have any gain from being true, never true if there is any gain for me in being dishonest. I say things as they come to me: if they are sensible so much the better. If inappropriate, no one really cares. I take full advantage of my right to speak freely. I have never in my life thought before speaking, nor while speaking, nor after having spoken. [P. 56][25]

Just because Jean-François speaks with a knowledge of what a "wise fool" should be, his inability either to control the mixture of wisdom and folly in his words or to master the social rituals required for worldly success as a licensed fool becomes a source of constant frustration and self-abnegation, combined with a kind of desperate pride at the chance— always formally present—that the next moment's words will strike home with the authority of a genuine insight. Jean-François, in other words, is simultaneously a "wise fool," a cynical parasite, and a madman, and because it is impossible to tell who is speaking at any given moment, his *entire* discourse—the arguments which, in another mouth, we might recognize as plausible, as well as those which seem obviously ludicrous—is infected with a fundamental instability. His "truth," throughout the dialogue, is as compromised by madness as his madness is tempered by the possibility of concealing a deeper truth.

A great deal has been written about how closely Diderot identified with either speaker, and the extreme positions have ranged from a view of *Moi* as a ludicrous, Pangloss-like philistine (see James Doolittle) to seeing him as a clear spokesman for Diderot (see Roland Desné).[26] Because Jean-François spends so much of his time satirizing *Moi*'s most cherished convictions, there is an assumption that deciding how closely *Moi* serves as his author's mouthpiece will resolve the dialogue's ambiguities. But this line of investigation substitutes an infinite regress for any real solution since (1) as the division of critical opinion already demonstrates, the putatively "factual" issue of tracing parallels between Diderot's judgments in his philosophical writings and *Moi*'s opinions in *Le Neveu de Rameau* is not susceptible to any categorical determination and itself raises all of the arguments about tone, context, and so forth, which it was supposed to help settle and (2) even if a significant degree of similarity between Diderot's and *Moi*'s positions could be confirmed, the ambiguities generated by subjecting these positions to the derision of Rameau's nephew would remain, and the problem would only be displaced from the level of a literary dialogue to that of an authorial psychology (i.e., How capable was Diderot of such a radical self-mockery, etc.?).

Even the most carefully nuanced attempts to arrest the uncertainties of *Le Neveu* by treating *Moi* as a representative, if diluted, spokesman for Diderot fail by misunderstanding the nature of the relationship between the satiric and the serious in comic literature.[27] As Bakhtin rightly says, "Even the lines which in a different context or taken separately would be completely serious . . . acquire in their context an overtone of laughter; the reflexes of surrounding comic images react on them" (p. 135). If a character in a comic work utters ideas which his author voiced *in propria persona* in another context, the articulation of those ideas in the world of a Saturnalian upheaval of all values decisively changes their resonance. With the addition of the theme of intermittent madness and the burden of an exacerbated self-consciousness, a further turn of the screw in the text's ambiguity is inevitable. Now the question is no longer restricted to the choice between a strictly comic or a serious argument, nor is it resolvable by the sleight of hand of labeling the work as a "comic" presentation of essentially serious themes (e.g., Rabelais' attack upon scholastic pedantry). Instead, all of these modes coexist in the discourse of a character who is himself at a loss to know which response is appropriate, a figure whose speech lacks all of the customary contextual cues separating an articulation according to its degree of truth, folly, or humor, but whose own familiarity with the expectations of the satiric genre makes him long in vain for some stable reference point against which to measure his outbursts.

Thus, to extend Bakhtin's formulation in a direction he would have viewed only with distress, it is equally true that the "serious" lines which in a strictly comic work would acquire an overtone of laughter, take on, in the mouth of an Abject Hero, a far more unsettling quality: the strain of hysteria, perhaps already discernible in the position of even a classical "wise fool," now emerges in its own right as an essential feature of the Abject Hero's speech, infecting the comic as much as the socially "corrective" thrust of his utterances. It is as though, to return to my earlier distinctions, both the Abject Hero himself, as well as his interlocutor, can no longer be certain whether he is really identifiable as a "wise fool," whether he is merely imitating one for his own conscious ends, or whether he is trapped within an impersonation he can neither fully assume nor entirely shake off. As a result, the reader is denied just what Bakhtin most values in the Saturnalian convention—the exuberant joy of witnessing a revolt against petty conventions and the critical pleasure of seeing a "wise fool" instruct his master in a deeper and more democratic truth.

Jean-François Rameau is, I believe, modern literature's first fully realized Abject Hero, the first self-conscious "wise fool" sufficiently versed in the traditional satires to understand the requirements of his role, precariously enough situated in his milieu to feel he has no other social position open to him, and embittered to the extent that he becomes unable as well as intermittently unwilling to fulfill these requirements. It is important, moreover, to stress that *all* of these attributes must be present for a character to be considered an Abject Hero. Thus, for example, a figure like Tristram Shandy, although clearly a self-conscious descendant of the classical "wise fool," is far too exuberant and playful for an Abject Hero. And although there are elements in the Abject Hero's discourse that draw upon the rhetorical tropes and psychological attitudes familiar to us as "romantic irony," both the *ressentiment* and sense of belatedness under which the Abject Hero suffers serve to distinguish him from the typical romantic ironist.[28] It is Jean-François Rameau's painful privilege to have united these diverse ingredients as constituent elements of a new sensibility. His closing line, "He who laughs last laughs best" (p. 109), terminates without in any way resolving Diderot's dialogue, and it opens an equivocal laughter which has continued to trouble literature until today.[29]

6

"What does his penitence amount to? It's just like me saying, 'I am abject, I am abject!' yesterday. You know it's only words."

"So that was only words? I thought you . . ."
"Well, to you, only to you, I will tell the truth, because you see through a man. Words and deeds and lies and truth are all mixed up in me and are perfectly sincere. Deeds and truth come out in my genuine penitence, I swear it, whether you believe it or not; and words and lies in the hellish (and always present) craving to get the better of a man, to make something even out of one's tears of penitence."

—DOSTOYEVSKY, *The Idiot*

For Bakhtin the "gradual narrowing down" of the carnival's regenerative power is directly linked to its separation from "folk culture" and its ensuing domestication as "part of the family's private life." Nonetheless, Bakhtin's faith in the inherent indestructibility of "the carnival spirit" compels him to find it preserved, even if in an interiorized and psychological form, in the post-Renaissance literary tradition, and he specifically names Diderot, along with Molière, Voltaire, and Swift, as authors who kept alive the subversive possibilities of a Saturnalian laughter (pp. 33, 34). But, of course, as Bakhtin himself recognizes, much more has changed in both the nature and the effects of that laughter than merely its locus of action. The crucial difference, according to Bakhtin, is a new sense of terror felt at the heart of the post-Renaissance carnival grotesque:

> The transformation of the principle of laughter which permeates the grotesque, that is the loss of its regenerating power, leads to a series of other essential differences between Romantic grotesque and medieval and Renaissance grotesque. . . . The world of Romantic grotesque is to a certain extent a terrifying world, alien to man. . . . Something frightening is revealed in that which was habitual and secure. [Pp. 38–39]

Directly linked to this burden of terror, of laughter as a response to dread, not exuberance, is a change in the literary function of madness:

> Other specific traits are linked with the disappearance of laughter's regenerating power. . . . The theme of madness is inherent to all grotesque forms, because madness makes men look at the world with different eyes, not dimmed by "normal," that is by commonplace ideas and judgments. In folk grotesque, madness is a gay parody of official reason, of the narrow seriousness of official "truth." It is a "festive" madness. In Romantic grotesque, on the other hand, madness acquires a somber, tragic aspect of individual isolation. [P. 39]

Bakhtin's typology of laughter, for all its richly textured local insights, is haunted, from its inception, by a wistfully nostalgic longing for a realm of pure and ahistorical spontaneity, a rite of universal participation whose essentially affirmative character is guaranteed by its very universality. The most characteristic feature of such a carnival is, in fact, its abolition of all distinctions between participant and viewer:

> Carnival does not know footlights, in the sense that it does not acknowledge any distinction between actors and spectators. Footlights would destroy a carnival, as the absence of footlights would destroy a theatrical performance. Carnival is not a spectacle seen by the people; they live in it, and everyone participates because its very idea embraces all the people. While carnival lasts, there is no other life outside it. . . . It has a universal spirit; it is a special condition of the entire world, of the world's revival and renewal, in which all take part. [P. 7]

Yet as soon as the question of representation arises, whether in Rabelais or in his successors, the "footlights" which separate actor and spectator, reader and character, come into being, introducing the very divisions the work's themes deny. Belatedness, the knowledge of coming after the festival has already been fragmented, is thus not limited to a post-Rabelaisian, bourgeois culture; it is itself a condition of every Saturnalian text, and what has changed is not the inclusiveness of the carnival per se but the literary consequences of acknowledging that belatedness.

In his longing for the all-engulfing vortex of a Saturnalian upheaval, Jean-François Rameau almost begins to sound like an avatar of Bakhtin's own desires. But Jean-François' tortuous motives bring out, in a way Bakhtin was unwilling ever to acknowledge, the potentially vicious and self-serving strand in the position of the carnival "fool," and his failures make clear that even the most skillful attempt to incarnate the anarchic energy of the Saturnalia will be frustrated the moment the "fool" tries to extend his sway beyond the formal limits permitted by the institutions that have determined both the existence and scope of the Saturnalian "license."

There is, however, one way in which *Le Neveu de Rameau*, although not the character whose name it bears, does succeed in enacting a carnivalization of values whose effects escape the normative authority of the Saturnalia-as-a-convention. But it is only because Diderot's dialogue so consistently acknowledges and self-consciously exploits the literariness of the satiric tradition that it is able to turn that acknowledgment against the tradition's own inherently stabilizing tendency. Bakhtin, as we have seen, considers the existence of "footlights," the "distinction between actors and spectators," sufficient to destroy carnival. Yet I have argued that some form of "footlights" is already implicit in the very institution of the carnival as such and doubly so in its literary representation. Diderot's solution, I believe, is not to deny the preexistence of these "footlights" but rather to shake their stability until they begin to occupy the peculiar position of being neither fully within nor external to the turbulence of his dialogue. Diderot, that is, admits the privileged position of the reader but only in order to subvert his confidence as spectator-judge. The reader is drawn into the carnivalesque uncertainty because the entire tradition has schooled him to assume the role of final arbiter, and in the endlessly renewed and perpetually fruitless effort to fulfill the demands of his own expectations, he is compelled to recapitulate the same dilemma confronting all of the dialogue's fictional characters. Thus, paradoxically, it is when the laughter turns bitter, and when, instead of an affirmative celebration, there is a dialogue of frustrated latecomers, imitating models whose naive confidence they can never get quite right, that Bakhtin's paradigm of an all-inclusive ritual comes closest to its realization.

No doubt it is fanciful to speculate that intermittently during his derangement, Adler knew he was only parodying the religious imperatives of his brilliant contemporary, and that his dialogue with Kierkegaard was a particularly disturbing reenactment of the madman and the sage topos, with the Abject Hero as inept theologian and shabby prophet and the sage as author of a university thesis on *The Concept of Irony*. But the literature of the past two centuries offers numerous examples of a "wise fool" who understands clearly the terms—and latent authority—of his archetypal role and yet who, because he is also genuinely mad, can only manage to enact that role in a hysterical mode (e.g., Dostoyevsky, Antonin Artaud, Louis-Ferdinand Céline, William Burroughs, etc.).

Like Jean-François Rameau, these later Abject Heroes are both self-abasing and sneering. Their essential trait is somehow to maintain both qualities at the same instant: figures like Lebedyev in *The Idiot*, the Underground Man, or the Célinian narrator are not pretending to despise themselves while groveling before the representatives of conventional wisdom and power, but neither are they lying when their *ressentiment* erupts in a violent affirmation of superiority; indeed, both their "genius" and their "folly" consists in living simultaneously the antithetical impulses that their interlocutors know only *seriatim*. As Dostoyevsky's Underground Man keeps affirming, in a harangue to the "gentlemen"-readers, who take up, in his imagination, much the same function *Moi* serves for Rameau's nephew,

> I want now to tell you, gentlemen, whether you care to hear it or not, why I could not even become an insect. I tell you solemnly, that I have many times tried to become an insect. But I was not equal even to that.

> You will say that it is vulgar and contemptible to drag all this into public after all the tears and transports which I have myself confessed. But why is it contemptible? Can you imagine that I am ashamed of it all, and that it was stupider than anything in your life, gentlemen? And I can assure you that some of these fancies were by no means badly composed.[30]

And if, as Bakhtin rightly asserts, the language of the novel is inherently "dialogical"—composed as the dramatic confrontation of different utterances, each bearing the imprint of its origin in a specific character's idiolect, point of view, historical circumstances, etc.—then the essential function of the Abject Hero is to foreground, and even to exacerbate, the sense of such a dialogue as an *agon*.[31]

When the Abject Hero is transposed from his origin in Diderot's satire-dialogue into the world of the novel, the dialogic quality of his speech is only intensified by having either a multitude of other characters or, at its most effective, the reader himself, placed in the role of his interlocutor(s). Because the Abject Hero so clearly seeks to sway the opinion of whomever he addresses—even when that "other" is an internalized image to which he can never become equal—his speech is always marked by an awareness, alternately defiant and slyly cunning, of the reactions his words will elicit. It is probably true, to cite Gary Saul Morson's apt formulations, that in all novels, "the reader is implicating as well as implicated," but a novel actually narrated by an Abject Hero will transform the relationship between text and reader from a general, *implicit* precondition into the very basis of its thematic as well as stylistic unfolding.[32] Whatever the specific content of the stories recounted by an Abject Hero, their aim will always be to justify their narrator to the reader and, if possible, to seduce and browbeat him into sharing the Abject Hero's self-estimation. Moreover, the "intertextuality" that critics like Julia Kristeva have posited as the ground bass underlying all literary discourse is heard with remarkable clarity in novels containing an Abject Hero, since a knowledge of the classical satiric conventions is itself part of the Abject Hero's conscious repertoire as well as a crucial element shaping the reader's expectations and responses. But what is unique about novels in which the Abject Hero assumes a central role and what leads to the increasing shrillness of the character in succeeding works is that the possibility for an explicitly thematized dialogical relationship with earlier texts in the same tradition increases in exact proportion to the historical development of the topos. This situation arises because, if Jean-François Rameau has studied the classical *morias encomia* and models himself upon their characters, then his descendants, in turn, can be presumed familiar with, among others, the case of *Le Neveu de Rameau* itself.

Imagine, as a momentary illustration, the following, perhaps familiar, situation: two men meet in a bar or bus station and one begins to tell the other of his woes, introducing numerous details of his well-deserved failures in life, his despair, and so forth, always including, of course, instances of wild self-praise and congratulations. But the listener keeps interrupting, "You know, I've already read that in Diderot and Dostoyevsky. Aren't you only imitating Jean-François Rameau and the Underground Man? Can't you find a more original problem or at least a new story?"

And if, indeed, the first speaker is not only familiar with these authors but quite aware that no matter how he tries his narrative can never emerge except as a variation on their literary paradigms, then, presumably, the last possible claim for his own dignity will have been proved derisive. Jean-François Rameau knew, at least, that he was not an *espèce*, that he had added something decisively new to the tradition of the "wise fool":

> *Lui.*—A hundred fools like me! Look Mr. Philosopher, they're not so easy to find. Ordinary fools, yes. But people are more demanding when it comes to folly than either talent or virtue. I'm a rare example of my kind, yes, very rare. [P. 65][33]

But this consolation, precisely because it was already drawn upon by Rameau's nephew, is no longer available, as he realizes to his own chagrin, for Artaud or for the narrator of Céline's war trilogy. In *Le Neveu de Rameau* the audience and the *philosophe* are rendered as uncertain of their criteria for judgment as is the cynical buffoon, but the confusion is limited to a once-a-year encounter on the safe stage of the Café de la Régence. By the time of *D'un château l'autre*, even the need for a *Moi* has vanished, as the Abject Hero-Narrator directly assaults every value—ethical, aesthetic, and political—which his reader is presumed to hold.

In Céline's trilogy, *D'un château l'autre, Nord,* and *Rigodon,* the reader is cajoled, insulted, complained to, scorned, and solicited for both material and moral support, until all three novels enact an extreme version of a Saturnalian dialogue in which the reader occupies a far more vulnerable position than Horace endured with Davus or *Moi* with Jean-François Rameau. Now, instead of the annual ritual of licensed excess endured by the master in classical satires, history itself provides the Célinian Abject Hero with a global setting of pure destruction, one seemingly without temporal limits or effective restraints. The floor of the Café de la Régence has expanded to encompass a Europe brutalized by war and a France of collaborators, cowards, and toadying profiteers. Céline's narrator is, I believe, the Abject Hero's most demonic incarnation, still trying, against all odds and without the slightest expectation of success, to make something out of his own tears of frustration.

In Rabelais it seems to me that we never respond to all the killings, maimings, humiliations, and catastrophes as if they happened to human beings, and it is a deliberate aspect of Rabelais' art to present Gargantua and Pantagruel, as well as their enemies, in sufficiently caricatured and schematic a fashion so that their fate never troubles us. The excesses are so clearly verbal in nature that no real consequences can be expected to ensue from what strikes us as a celebration of language itself rather than an inventory of possible human actions. Bakhtin's love for Rabelais and for what he sees as the redemptive energy of the Saturnalia, at times blinds him to the fact that it is only because Rabelais' novels are manifestly nonmimetic that he is able to assimilate them to anthropological and folkloristic records of actual carnivals, many of which, as recent studies have shown, ended in a violence that proved devastating both to the innocent victims and to the community as a whole.[34] Although I know that my own hesitations will be attributed to the methodological blinkers of a "naive reader," I think it only just to confess that there are moments when Rabelais' glee in depicting the various torments inflicted upon the novels' villains leaves me considerably more nervous than Bakhtin's account would suggest possible. Indeed, my sense of the energy released by Rabelais' laughter depends in no small measure upon both the nervousness he elicits and his skill in assuaging it. René Girard's *Violence and the Sacred* offers a diametrically opposed view of the Saturnalia than the one endorsed by Bakhtin, and although I am far from sharing all of Girard's conclusions, his vision of the "mimetic violence" underlying the carnival rite and his description of the revellers' Dionysus as a "god of homicidal fury" contains a salutary counterbalance to Bakhtin's optimistic affirmations.[35]

In a sense Bakhtin and Girard, like Diderot's *Moi* and *Lui*, are themselves engaged in an unresolvable dialogue, one in which their positions are already determined by the dialogues they have decided to overhear. And what makes this meta-dialogue so curious is that although each participant selects his primary model from a different literature (Rabelais and the Greek tragedians), both men also draw heavily upon the same texts for additional support (Diderot and especially Dostoyevsky). Yet each critic takes up, although with different degrees of subtlety, essentially only one of the contradictory positions contained in their examples—as indeed they must for a dialogue to be possible. Thus, it seems that dialogues inevitably give rise only to further dialogues and that the critic is no more immune than the fictional characters from the dialogic refusal of closure. This situation, moreover, is precisely what makes *Le Neveu de Rameau* so exemplary a turning point for modern literature, since after Diderot it is increasingly the reader-critic who is thrust directly into the text as the principal representative of social norms, the spokesman for one conception of values and hierarchies against which the Abject Hero's fury is aimed.

From Jean-François Rameau through Lebedyev and the Underground Man to the Célinian narrator, as the Abject Hero's situation becomes progressively more precarious and his belatedness within the satiric tradition an ever greater source of torment, the compensatory violence against his reader-interlocutor is correspondingly intensified:

> "They pocketed everything!" that's all there is to say! I know what
> you're thinking . . . it's only natural! oh, something like that would
> never happen to you! nothing remotely similar will ever happen to
> you! you've taken careful precautions! . . . as good a communist as
> the first new-come millionaire, as good a poujadist as Poujade, as

Russian as all the salads, more American than Buffalo! . . . perfectly
in cahoots with everything that carries weight, Lodge, Cell, Sacristy,
the Law! . . . new *Vrenchmen* like no one else! . . . the movement of
History runs right through your asshole! . . . honorary brother? . . .
sure thing! . . . executioner's underling! . . . we'll see! . . . licker of
the guillotine blade? . . . he! he![36]

Where Jean-François Rameau exposes a sordid beggar's pantomime ["la
pantomime des suppliants"] beneath the Enlightenment's confidence in
the ameliorative power of education and taste, the Célinian narrator
extends a similar leveling to the culture of Europe as a whole. He produces,
as the laborious revisions of the manuscripts make clear, a kind of
carefully orchestrated "delirium effect" in which the traditional satiric
trope, a Lucianesque dialogue of the dead, is taken "seriously" again—
but only as a kind of curtain raiser to the hallucination of modern history
as an apocalyptic dance of death:

> I don't let on . . . I listen to my friends . . . Yeah, sure! me too, poor
> devil, I'm waiting for them to croak. them! them first! they all eat
> much more than me! just let one little artery burst open! what a
> hope! . . . what a hope! . . . then I will meet them all in Charon's
> boat, enemies, friends, all of them with their guts around their
> neck! . . . Charon smashing in their faces! . . . great! . . . [. . .] when
> they come to see me, my old friends, to check if I'm going to kick
> the bucket soon, I tell myself, laughing, that I see them at the Styx,
> with Charon carressing them! *braoum!* . . . *vrang!*[37]

1. Horace *Satires* (trans. H. Rushton Fairclough) 2. 7. 70.

2. Friedrich Nietzsche, *Beyond Good and Evil*, trans. Walter Kaufmann (New York,
1966), sec. 223, p. 150. Nietzsche, however, was not always so sympathetic to the idea of
a Saturnalian carnival. In the first book of *Human, All Too Human*, for example, he refers
scornfully to the "Freude der Sklaven am Saturnalianfeste [the joy of the slaves at the
Saturnalia]" (sec. 213; my translation). Unless otherwise noted, all further translations in
this paper are my own.

3. Søren Kierkegaard, *On Authority and Revelation; or, The Book on Adler, or a Cycle of
Ethico-Religious Essays*, trans. Walter Lowrie (Princeton, N.J., 1955), p. 63.

4. Ibid., p. 64.

5. My information on Adolph Peter Adler's life is derived from Lowrie's introduction
to the *Book on Adler*.

6. Kierkegaard, *Book on Adler*, p. 95.

7. Kierkegaard, *"Fear and Trembling" and "The Sickness Unto Death,"* trans. Lowrie
(Princeton, N.J., 1954), p. 47.

8. Ibid., p. 109.

9. Kierkegaard, *Book on Adler*, p. xx.

10. Ulrich von Wilamowitz-Moellendorff, *Griechische Tragoedien*, vol. 3 (Berlin, 1906),
p. 162. "Diese Medea hat offenbar die *Medea* des Euripides gelesen."

11. For an excellent discussion of the notion of genres, anti-genres, and parodic
genres, see Gary Saul Morson, *The Boundaries of Genre: Dostoevsky's "Diary of a Writer" and
the Traditions of Literary Utopia* (Austin, Tex., 1981).

12. For a psychoanalytic discussion of this problem, see John A. Rajchman, "Lacan's Theory of Language" (forthcoming).

13. Mikhail Bakhtin, "From the Prehistory of Novelistic Discourse," *The Dialogic Imagination: Four Essays,* ed. Michael Holquist and trans. Caryl Emerson and Holquist, University of Texas Press Slavic Series, no. 1 (Austin, Tex., 1981), p. 58.

14. Bakhtin, *Rabelais and His World,* trans. Helene Iswolsky (Cambridge, Mass., 1968), p. 11; all further references to this work will be included parenthetically in the text.

15. See Ernst Robert Curtius, *European Literature and the Latin Middle Ages,* trans. Willard R. Trask (Princeton, N.J., 1967), pp. 573–83.

16. Horace *Satires* 2. 7. 8–14.

> "saepe notatus
> cum tribus anellis, modo laeva Priscus inani,
> vixit inaequalis, clavum ut mutaret in horas,
> aedibus ex magnis subito se conderet, unde
> mundior exiret vix libertinus honeste;
> iam moechus Romae, iam mallet doctus Athenis
> vivere, Vertumnis, quotquot sunt, natus iniquis."

17. Horace *Satires* 1. 3. 18–19 ("nil fuit umquam / sic impar sibi"); and see 1. 4. 86–89. "Rien ne dissemble plus de lui que lui meme" (Denis Diderot, *Le Neveu de Rameau,* ed. Jean Fabre [Geneva, 1963]; p. 4). Diderot's "paraphrase" is actually closer to the Latin text than is Fairclough's standard translation ("Never was a creature so inconsistent") which loses the sense of *sibi.* The French stresses that Rameau, like Tigellius, is inconsistent with himself ("de lui").

All subsequent quotations from Diderot's text are taken from Fabre's edition and will be included parenthetically in the text. The peculiarities of spelling and accentuation in the French are those of Diderot himself as established by Fabre: "Je veux bien etre abject, mais je veux que ce soit sans contrainte."

18. Curtius, *European Literature,* p. 582.

19. Herbert Dieckmann, "The Relationship between Diderot's *Satire I* and *Satire II,*" *Romanic Review* 43 (1952): 25.

20. This last argument is derived from discussions with my friend and former teacher, Robert Hollander of Princeton University.

21.   Moi, j'y recueille tout ce qu'il faut faire, et tout ce qu'il ne faut pas dire. Ainsi quand je lis l'*Avare,* je me dis: Sois avare, si tu veux; mais garde toi de parler comme l'avare. Quand je lis le *Tartuffe,* je me dis: Sois hypocrite, si tu veux; mais ne parle pas comme l'hypocrite. Garde des vices qui te sont utiles; mais n'en aie . . . ni le ton ni les apparences qui te rendroient ridicule.

22.   Long tems il y a eu le fou du roi en titre, en aucun, il n'y a eu en titre le sage du Roi. Moi je suis le fou de Bertin et de beaucoup d'autres, le votre peut etre dans ce moment; ou peut etre vous le mien. Celui qui seroit sage n'auroit point de fou. Celui donc qui a un fou n'est pas sage; s'il n'est pas sage il est fou; et peut etre, fut-il roi, le fou de son fou.

23. "Il y a de la raison, a peu près, dans tout ce que vous venez de dire."

24.   Oh! vous voilà, vous autres! Si nous disons quelque chose de bien, c'est comme des fous, ou des inspirés; par hasard. Il n'y a que vous autres qui vous entendiez. Oui, monsieur le philosophe. Je m'entends; et je m'entends ainsi que vous vous entendez.

25.   Que le diable m'emporte si je scais au fond ce que je suis. En general, j'ai l'esprit rond comme une boule, et le caractere franc comme l'osier; jamais faux, pour peu que j'aie interet d'etre vrai; jamais vrai pour peu que j'aie interet d'etre faux. Je dis les choses comme elles me viennent; sensées, tant mieux; impertinentes, on n'y prend pas garde. J'use en plein de mon franc-parler. Je n'ai pensé de ma vie ni avant que le dire . . . , ni en disant, ni apres avoir dit.

26. See James Doolittle, *Rameau's Nephew: A Study of Diderot's "Second Satire."* (Geneva, 1960); and Roland Desné, *Diderot et "Le Neveu de Rameau"* (Paris, n.d.), "*Le Neveu de Rameau*

dans l'ombre et la lumière du dix-huitième siècle," *Studies on Voltaire and the Eighteenth Century* 25 (1963): 493–507, and "Monsieur le Philosophe et le Fieffé Truand," *Europe* 405–6 (Jan.-Feb. 1963): 182–98.

27. See Donal O'Gorman, *Diderot the Satirist* (Toronto, 1971).

28. Specialized studies on romantic and modernist irony help to confirm my sense of the difference in the position of an Abject Hero. See, e.g., Wayne C. Booth, *A Rhetoric of Irony* (Chicago, 1974); D. C. Muecke, *The Compass of Irony* (London, 1969); Peter Conrad, *Shandyism: The Character of Romantic Irony* (Oxford, 1978); David Simpson, *Irony and Authority in Romantic Poetry* (Totowa, N.J., 1979); and Alan Wilde, *Horizons of Assent: Modernism, Postmodernism, and the Ironic Imagination* (Baltimore, 1981). On irony in Diderot, see Jack Undank, *Diderot: Inside, Outside, and In-Between* (Madison, Wis., 1979).

29. "Rira bien qui rira le dernier."

30. Fyodor Dostoyevsky, *Notes from Underground*, trans. Constance Garnett (New York, 1960), pt. 1, chap. 1, p. 28; pt. 2, chap. 2, p. 74. But for a different reading of *Le Neveu de Rameau*, one which explicitly denies any link between Jean-François Rameau and Dostoyevsky's Underground Man, see Lionel Trilling, *Sincerity and Authenticity* (Cambridge, Mass., 1971), esp. pp. 26–52.

31. See esp. Bakhtin, "Discourse in the Novel," *The Dialogic Imagination*, pp. 259–422. I do not believe it has ever been pointed out how closely Bakhtin's notion of language as a historically changing crystallization of an individual's circumstances comes to the arguments in Diderot's "Satire Première: Sur les caractères et les mots de caractère, de profession, etc."

32. Gary Saul Morson, "The Heresiarch of *Meta*," *PTL* 3 (Oct. 1978): 411.

33.   Cent fous comme moi! Monsieur le philosophe, ils ne sont pas si communs.
       Oui, des plats fous. On est plus difficile en sottise qu'en talent ou en vertu.
       Je suis rare dans mon espece, oui, tres rare.

34. See, e.g., Emmanuel Le Roy Ladurie, *Carnival in Romans*, trans. Mary Feeney (New York, 1979); Kenelm Burridge, *New Heaven, New Earth: A Study of Millenarian Activities* (Oxford, 1969); and Sylvia L. Thrupp, ed., *Millennial Dreams in Action* (New York, 1970).

35. See René Girard, *Violence and the Sacred*, trans. Patrick Gregory (Baltimore, 1977), esp. pp. 118–42.

36. Louis-Ferdinand Destouches [Céline], *D'un château l'autre* (Paris, 1974), p. 4.

"Pochetée!" tout est dit! votre réflexion! je vous entends! . . . bien naturelle! oh, que ça vous arrivera pas! rien de semblable vous arrivera! que vos précautions sont bien prises! . . . aussi communiste que le premier milliardaire venu, aussi poujadiste que Poujade, aussi russe que toutes les salades, plus américain que Buffalo! . . . parfaitement en cheville avec tout ce qui compte, Loge, Cellule, Sacristie, Parquet! . . . nouveau *Vrounzais* comme personne! . . . le sens de l'Histoire vous passe par le mi des fesses! . . . frère d'honneur? . . . sûr! . . . valet de bourreau? on verra! . . . lécheur de couperet? . . . hé! hé!

37. Ibid., p. 15.

Je dis rien . . . j'écoute les amis . . . ouai! ouai! moi aussi diable j'attends qu'ils crèvent! eux! eux, d'abord! ils bouffent tous beaucoup plus que moi! qu'une petite artériole leur pète! espoir! espoir! . . . que je les retrouve tous chez Caron, ennemis, amis, toutes leurs boyasses autour du cou! . . . Caron leur défonçant la gueule! . . . bien! . . . [. . .] quand ils viennent un peu m'observer, les vieux amis, si je vais bientôt casser ma pipe, je me dis, je rigole, je les vois au Styx, comment Caron les caressera! *braoum!* . . . *vrang!*

Tolstoy's Absolute Language

Gary Saul Morson

1. Tolstoy's Dialogue with the Novel

In the kingdom of words, there are two kinds of subjects: one speaks to other words, the other does not. The first answers what has been spoken before and itself anticipates an answer. Aware of its audience, it knows that it is heard against its social and historical background and evaluated in terms of its speaker's personality. It knows it can be paraphrased, for it paraphrases others constantly. The second kind of word refuses to be paraphrased. It does not say; it is a saying. Admitting no authorship, it condescends to no dialogue. It can only be cited, and recited. When spoken, it belongs to no one; when written, it is Scripture.

I paraphrase here Mikhail Bakhtin's distinction between "dialogic" and absolute utterances—or "words," as he puts it—which serves as the basis for his most systematic theory of the novel.[1] Bakhtin suggests that the identifying characteristic of the novel as a genre is its representation of "the concrete life of the [dialogic] word," which is to say, the exchange of utterances in their social and historical context. The novel, he argues, represents the drama of speech reacting to speech, of words struggling

For the Russian texts of Tolstoy, I have used the ninety-volume (Jubilee) edition of his works: *Polnoe sobranie sočinenij* (Moscow, 1929–58). I have modified translations cited in the text for accuracy when necessary.

1. Bakhtin develops this theory of the novel in "Slovo v romane," *Voprosy literatury i èstetiki: Issledovanija raznyx let* (Moscow, 1975), pp. 72–233; a translation of this essay, "Discourse in the Novel," appears in Bakhtin, *The Dialogic Imagination*, trans. Caryl Emerson and Michael Holquist (Austin, Tex., 1981). I discuss Bakhtin's theories of language and the novel in "The Heresiarch of *Meta*," *PTL* 3 (1978): 407–27.

to answer, paraphrase, or even deliberately ignore each other—and of words anticipating how they themselves will be answered, paraphrased, or ignored. Bakhtin holds, in short, that language is not only the medium through which the novelist represents the world, it is also the world he represents. "For the novelistic genre," Bakhtin observes, "what is characteristic is not the image of man himself, but precisely the image of language. But language, in order to become an artistic image, must be the utterance of speaking lips, joined to the image of a speaking person" (p. 149).

This purely linguistic description of the novel, according to which characters exist so that words can be spoken, might at first seem a typical example of bloodless formalism; but the very opposite is the case. Bakhtin's theory was designed in part as a response to what he considered the primary shortcoming of his formalist predecessors, namely, their failure to pay sufficient attention to history and sociology. Bakhtin instead contends that the novel is the most sociological of genres, the genre most responsive to the flux of social history, because the dialogic language that the novel represents is itself the most immediate and sensitive register of changing social attitudes. For in the novel as in life, Bakhtin argues, every utterance is necessarily spoken in some "dialect," "jargon," or "speech" (language, according to Bakhtin, is always language*s*) that carries and implies the attitudes of those who characteristically speak in that way, at that time, and in that particular "extraverbal and verbal (i.e., made up of other utterances) milieu."[2] The novelist's art, in Bakhtin's view, is the orchestration of a verbal "polyphony"—or cacophony—that represents the conflict of linguistic subgroups, a conflict that is itself an index to social and ideological conflict.

It follows for Bakhtin that language in a novel can never be ideologically neutral or free of values: it is always someone's language and bears the mark of its speaker's and anticipated listener's unspoken attitudes. Even the seemingly neutral language of a narrator who resembles the author (as in Turgenev) may be used to carry the attitudes of the literate class to which both author and reader belong. Moreover,

2. V. N. Vološinov, *Marxism and the Philosophy of Language*, trans. Ladislav Matejka and I. R. Titunik (New York, 1973), p. 96. Vološinov's study, originally published in 1929, was probably written in conjunction with Bakhtin; there is some question as to whether Bakhtin himself wrote Vološinov's works.

Gary Saul Morson is an associate professor of Russian literature at the University of Pennsylvania. The author of *The Boundaries of Genre: Dostoevsky's "Diary of a Writer" and the Traditions of Literary Utopia,* he is presently at work on *The Broken Frame: The Anti-tradition of Russian Literature.* The present article is drawn from his work in progress, a theoretical study of literary creativity and the biography of authors.

once placed in a novel, the literary language necessarily enters into complex dialogic relations with the speech of the characters it reports, paraphrases, and selects. In Bakhtin's view, the essence of the novel is to dialogize.

Bakhtin concludes that the novel cannot contain the type of absolute word I described at the outset, inasmuch as absolute words cannot be dialogized. Bakhtin's paradigm of this kind of word is the biblical command: insofar as the command is assumed to have no human author, it bears the imprint of no class and stands above the social and historical flux that novels depict. Inscribed in stone and written in an archaic or foreign language, it precludes dialogue and paraphrase. Placed in a novel, the command inevitably remains inert; it follows for Bakhtin that to the extent that a novel relies on a biblical quotation, it must fail.

As it happens, however, Bakhtin's reasoning on this point implicitly contradicts another of his descriptions of the novel as a genre, according to which the novel differs from all other genres because they are governed by rules and canons while it is anticanonic.[3] The novel's essence, he maintains, is to be anomalous, to violate and, indeed, systematically to invert all rules. For Bakhtin, the novel is not a genre but the antigenre; it follows that no sooner do novels begin to develop rules than other novels parody those rules, just as they parody all other literary and social conventions. The novel knows that it participates in the very historical flux it dramatizes, in that its own conventions are historically given and therefore subject to historical change. Thus the history of the novel includes the history of parodies of the novel.

Bakhtin's second description of the novel suggests the possibility that a novel can successfully violate his first description. For if the essence of the novel is to parody its own rules, then it may also deliberately violate the rule prohibiting unconditional and nondialogic language. That norm could itself become subject to systematic inversion; indeed, it must if we are to take seriously Bakhtin's argument that novels are essentially antigeneric. If Bakhtin's second description is accurate, we may expect some novelists to employ nondialogic language in the midst of a supposedly all-dialogizing context and to take advantage of readers' expectations of novelistic language to shock them with an unexpected contrast. In that case, nondialogic speech could become more effective than it is in contexts where we do expect it: skillfully used, brief sermons in novels may command more attention than long sermons in churches. Considerable literary power could be achieved if, in a context of qualified words reacting to qualified words, of speech struggling to anticipate the objections of future speech, there appeared a sentence that stands above all such petty struggles and pronounces not one man's truth but the

3. See Bakhtin, "Epos i roman (O metodologii issledovanija romana)," *Voprosy*, pp. 447–83. For an English translation, see "Epic and Novel," *The Dialogic Imagination*.

Truth. Indeed, this sentence would not only seem to stand above the language of the particular novel in which it appears; it would also seem to stand outside the genre of the novel as a whole. Its absolute, out-of-frame assertions would be read in contrast not only to the particular speech acts that surround it but also to the entire order of limited, purely historical language as such. The novel would be invaded by the non-novelistic, its diction interdicted.

It is important to emphasize that by including nonnovelistic language, an author would not be ignoring novelistic conventions but deliberately violating them. That is, the effectiveness of his strategy would depend on those conventions and would, therefore, bear tacit witness that they are in force. If readers ever stopped assuming those conventions, or if a writer violated them too frequently, the power of nondialogic speech in a novel would begin to fail. The novelist would not be able to violate his readers' expectations, for those expectations would have changed.

One writer did in fact effectively exploit this strategy: Leo Tolstoy. An examination of Tolstoy's use of "nonnovelistic" language can help to clarify our understanding of the novel in general and the didactic novel in particular. After looking at some of his novels, I will then consider Tolstoy's use of "absolute language" in his nonliterary writings and examine some of the problems which Tolstoy's attempt to speak absolutely and nonhistorically raises for his biography.

Readers of Tolstoy's fiction are usually aware of interesting encounters with an "eternal Truth" in the middle of a fictional context where the surrounding statements are novelistic—that is, ironic or qualified. The examples below include some of the best-known sentences in Tolstoy's literary works:[4]

All happy families are alike; each unhappy family is unhappy in its own way. [*Anna Karenina*]

Ivan Ilych's life was the most simple and the most ordinary, and therefore the most terrible. [*The Death of Ivan Ilych*, p. 255]

He . . . immediately dismissed from his mind this, the sole solution of all the riddles of life and death, as something quite impossible. [*The Death of Ivan Ilych*, p. 295]

And indeed, if Eugene Irtenev was mentally deranged, then everyone is similarly insane. The most mentally deranged people are certainly those who see in others indications of insanity they do not

---

4. These citations are from the following editions of Tolstoy's works: (1) *Anna Karenina;* my translation; (2) *The Death of Ivan Ilych* and *The Devil, Great Short Works of Leo Tolstoy,* ed. John Bayley, trans. Louise and Aylmer Maude (New York, 1967); and (3) *War and Peace,* trans. Ann Dunnigan (New York, 1968).

see in themselves. [*The Devil,* pp. 348–49 (first version); p. 351 (second version)]

On the twelfth of June the forces of Western Europe crossed the Russian border and war began, that is, an event took place counter to human reason and to all of human nature. [*War and Peace,* p. 729]

If we concede that human life can be governed by reason, the possibility of life is destroyed. [*War and Peace,* p. 1354]

There is, and can be, no cause of an historical event save the one cause of all causes. [*War and Peace,* p. 1179]

The higher a man stands in the social scale, the more connections he has with people and the more power he has over them, the more manifest is the predetermination and inevitability of his every act.
"The hearts of kings are in the hands of God."
A king is the slave of history. [*War and Peace,* p. 732]

Tolstoy himself explicitly states the essential difference between unconditional and conditional language in yet another unconditional passage in *War and Peace:*

If the Deity gives a command, expresses his will, the expression of that will is independent of time and is not evoked by anything, for the Deity is not controlled by an event. But when we speak of commands that are the expression of the will of men, acting in time and related to one another, we must, if we are to understand the connection of commands with events, restore (1) the conditions of all that takes place: the continuity of movement in time both of the events and of the person who commands, and (2) the condition of the indispensable connection between the person who issues the commands and those who execute them. [Pp. 1430–31]

That is, the language of God is absolute and unconditional in the sense that, unlike any utterance of a man, it is not a function of the circumstances that evoked it, and its meaning is not qualified by an audience whose potential reactions have had to be taken into account. A biblical command can be disobeyed, but it cannot be answered.[5] Divine speech does not defend itself or allow itself to be limited by particular historical circumstances. No shadow of objectification must fall on it; even when

---

5. Job, for instance, understands well the impossibility of dialogue with God when he challenges God to grant him an audience and to answer his charges against Him like a defendant in court—a challenge he does not expect God to accept: "He is not a man as I am that I can answer Him, or that we can confront one another in court" (Job 9:32). "Then summon me and I will answer; or I will speak first, and do thou answer me" (Job 13:22).

it speaks about history, and even when a particular historical group hears its words, it nevertheless speaks from outside of history.

Proverbs are another kind of absolute language. Like biblical commands, they can be attributed to no particular human author; indeed, it is precisely because they are author*less* that they are authori*tative*.[6] Proverbs are never spoken, they are only cited; and to cite a proverb is to make its nonhistorical statement applicable to, but in no sense conditioned by, a particular historical situation. It is, rather, the historical situation that reveals its conformity to the timeless pattern described by the proverb. It follows that the proverb loses its unconditionality and authority as we imagine or project a personal source for it.[7]

Among Tolstoy's absolute statements are those that exhibit characteristics of both biblical commands and proverbs—and of other types of absolute statements as well. He also draws, for example, on logical propositions, mathematical deductions, laws of nature and human nature, dictionary definitions, and metaphysical assertions. The language of all of these forms is timeless, anonymous, and above all categorical. Their stylistic features imply that they are not falsifiable and that they are not open to qualification: they characteristically include words like "all," "each," "every," "only," and "certainly" and phrases like "there neither is nor can be," "the human mind cannot grasp," and "it is impossible that." Even in sentences that omit such phrases, the very refusal to use a qualifier of any kind can assert unqualifiability. When Tolstoy's absolute statements take the form of syllogisms, the use of the word "therefore" or some explicit or implicit equivalent carries the force of logical inevitability. It carries the same force with Tolstoy's enthymemes, which omit the major premise for the reader to reconstruct. The first of the two examples from *The Death of Ivan Ilych* cited above, for instance, contains a minor premise and a conclusion of a syllogism; the reader himself must supply the major premise, which would be: "The simpler and more ordinary a life is, the more terrible it is."

In a sense, the entire story of Ivan Ilych's life can be regarded as the minor premise of Tolstoy's syllogism, and the experience of reading the entire novel as the discovery of the timeless truth of which the story's plot is an instance. It is indeed characteristic of Tolstoy to frame his stories in this way. These absolute principles, either strongly implied or explicitly stated, are not conditioned by the events in the narrative; rather, they pronounce a timeless judgment on those events. Although

6. I am indebted in this discussion of proverbs to Barbara Herrnstein Smith, "On the Margins of Discourse," *On the Margins of Discourse: The Relation of Literature to Language* (Chicago, 1978); see esp. "Saying and Sayings," pp. 69–75.

7. When we identify it as a German or Russian proverb, for instance, we tacitly admit the possibility that its wisdom may be the product of the particular experience of a single people and could, therefore, be partial and limited. History and contingency are what conditionalize.

part of the work, they are part neither of the story nor of its narration; they seem instead to be *cited* from an extranovelistic source and not to be *spoken* by any novelistic narrator. Indeed, Tolstoy does at times cite well-known proverbs and juxtapose them with proverblike sentences of his own, as in the final example from *War and Peace*.

It is perhaps because these sentences seem both to belong to and to lie outside of the fiction that they frequently occur on the margins of Tolstoy's works—in titles, epigraphs, or opening and closing sentences. This may explain Tolstoy's unusual technique of using complete statements as the titles of his stories, for example: "God Sees the Truth, but Waits to Tell"; "A Spark Neglected Burns the House"; and "Evil Allures but Good Endures." These statements are all proverbs, that is, timeless judgments which may offer a key to a set of events but have not first been uttered in response to them. Tolstoy uses them, as he told Gorky, because they could not be current coinage.[8] The late tales often use their endings instead of their titles to pronounce an unconditional truth. In some cases, the ending will take the form of a moral and in others (for example, "Three Questions") the form of a solution to riddles posed by the narrative.

The absolute statements in Tolstoy's novels (unlike those in his fairy tales) need not occur in a privileged position like the ending. Although the novels do sometimes exploit their margins in this way, Tolstoy will also interrupt the narration in the middle to include statements from outside the novelistic universe. When statements of this sort occur unexpectedly, as they often do, they command the considerable power of surprise. For example, the absolute statement may form the second clause of a sentence whose first clause is narrative in nature: "On the twelfth of June the forces of Western Europe crossed the Russian border and war began, that is, an event took place counter to human reason and to all of human nature." Such a statement functions quite differently from seemingly similar ones uttered by characters in the same novel. The "truths" discovered by Levin and Pierre are qualified by the reader's knowledge of the process of their discovery, and what Pierre and Levin believe to be absolutes are sure to prove limited as the narrative progresses. Such limited truths exhibit what we might call an *irony of origins*. No such irony qualifies or limits the truth of judgments cited from outside the narrative. Their anonymous speech center is as "independent of time and . . . not controlled by an event" in the world of the novel as is God in the world of the novel's author and readers.

---

8. The difference between proverbs and aphorisms according to Tolstoy, that proverbs "are not of today's manufacture," is reported in Maxim Gorky, *Reminiscences of Tolstoy, Chekhov, and Andreyev* (1920; New York, 1959), pp. 9–10; all further references to this book will be included in the text.

It is probable that all novels are framed by an implicit "for instance."[9] What is characteristic of Tolstoy is that the "for instance" is so often close to explicit. Consider the already "proverbial" beginning of *Anna Karenina:* "All happy families are alike; each unhappy family is unhappy in its own way." This is not a statement *in* the story, it is a statement *about* the story, a statement spoken by an anonymous voice securely outside the story. It is a fabular moral displaced from the end to the beginning; everything that follows illustrates it but cannot qualify it. Unlike the rest of the novel, this sentence is not conditional and is not the object of any irony: no perspective exists in the novel from which it could be ironic. The effect would have been entirely different and conventionally novelistic if Tolstoy had instead begun: "Anna thought that all happy families were alike, but that each unhappy family was unhappy in its own way" or "It is common knowledge in all of Petersburg that all happy families are alike and that each unhappy family is unhappy in its own way." Then this common belief about the nature of family happiness would have represented the necessarily limited wisdom of some person or social group and would have become the object of increasing irony as the novel progressed. Whether believed by Anna or the society that condemned her, it would have been deeply qualified by the irony of origins, that is, our knowledge that it was spoken or thought by someone at some time to some real or imagined audience. Its very proverbial quality might, for instance, have become the sign of its naiveté and, as the sign of naiveté, the foreshadowing of tragedy. The novel would then have commented on the statement instead of, as it does, exemplifying it.

It is instructive to contrast the first sentence of *Anna Karenina* with the apparently similar first sentence of *Pride and Prejudice:* "It is a truth universally acknowledged, that a single man in possession of a good fortune must be in want of a wife." Although Jane Austen's opening is also aphoristic, its function is not the same as that of Tolstoy's. Austen's sentence is indirect discourse, and there is clearly a difference in point of view between the paraphrase and the writer who paraphrases. This sentence does not make an assertion, it reports one; and reported speech is already the beginning of dialogue. Considerable irony is implicitly directed at the group that might make such an assertion and identify itself with the universe. The second sentence of the novel, moreover, points to the interests of those who acknowledge the "truth" and to their motives for acknowledging it: we are told it is the neighboring families with marriageable daughters who find this truth most incontestable. The opening of *Pride and Prejudice* is just the sort of sentence that Bakhtin says is conventional for novels; the opening sentence of *Anna Karenina,* a sentence that is unironic and spoken from outside the world of the novel, is not. *Anna Karenina* enters the conventional world of novels only with its second sentence: "All was confusion at the Oblonskys'."

9. On the idea of fictive exemplification, see Smith, "Margins of Discourse."

Let me clarify what is, and what is not, happening when this kind of judgment interrupts the narrative. Tolstoy's novelistic commentary and lectures on narratology function quite differently from, let us say, the commentary and lectures on plot in *Tristram Shandy* and *Eugene Onegin*. In those novels, the commentary is itself clearly fictive and takes place within the novelistic universe. Few readers, I imagine, doubt that Tristram is himself the fictive, not the actual, author. *Tristram Shandy* and *Eugene Onegin* could be novels about the conventions of novel writing, and they violate those conventions in a way that is both conventional and novelistic (Pushkin, in fact, cites Sterne as his novelistic predecessor, as Sterne cites Rabelais). *Tristram Shandy* and *Eugene Onegin* contain fictions within their fiction, and it is only the boundaries of the inner fictions that are seriously in question.

Something quite different takes place in Tolstoy's novels. The first sentence of *Anna Karenina* and the lectures on history in *War and Peace* are not spoken by a novelistic narrator at all, not even by a "reliable" or authoritative one. Their absolute source lies outside the fictive universe altogether. They are governed, it seems to me, by a set of conventions different from those that govern the rest of the novel, namely, those of nonfictive speech. Inserted in a novel, absolute language remains undialogized and—because dialogization is the mark of fictive speech in a novel—nonnovelistic as well as nonfictive. Unlike the rest of the novel in which they appear, Tolstoy's absolute statements claim literal, not literary, truth. The reader is asked to accept them referentially as statements about his own universe, not merely as components of an artistic structure. The reader is expected either to believe or to disbelieve them; he is asked not to suspend his disbelief but to suspend his suspension of disbelief. In the midst of a novel, which insofar as it is a novel renders all of its language conditional, Tolstoy attempts to make statements that are completely nonnovelistic, that is, both nonfictive and undialogized.

That attempt ultimately fails, as I believe it must. For in the final analysis there is no way to speak completely noncontextually in a novel. The reason for Tolstoy's failure is that, inasmuch as his absolute language derives its rhetorical power from defying novelistic conventions, it implicitly relies on them and therefore honors them in the breach. His absolute statements *polemically* assert their unconditionality and so necessarily enter into dialogue with the genre whose speech they reject. In a sense, Tolstoy's attempt to speak nonnovelistically in a novel resembles Dostoevsky's underground man's attempt to show his friends that he is ignoring them: "I tried to my very utmost to show what I could do without them, and yet I purposely stomped with my boots, thumping with my heels. But it was all in vain."[10] Tolstoy's absolute statements are involved in a similar self-contradiction. The contradiction lies in the fact

10. Fyodor Dostoevsky, *Notes from Underground* (with *The Grand Inquisitor*), ed. and trans. Ralph E. Matlaw (New York, 1960), pt. 2, p. 69.

that they are implicitly framed by an assertion of their nonconditionality, and yet this very assertion is conditional and conscious of its audience. In short, the very refusal to enter into dialogue is itself both dialogic and dialogizing.

Although Tolstoy cannot make his language nondialogic, he nevertheless does succeed in changing the nature of the dialogue. The kind of context that conditionalizes Tolstoy's absolute statements differs from the kind of context that conventionally conditionalizes sentences in novels. What dialogizes Tolstoy's absolutes is not the surrounding language of the particular novel but the genre of the novel as a whole. It is the reader's knowledge of the novelistic tradition that forces Tolstoy's statements into proclaiming their nondialogicality. There is no immediate contextualization, but there is a metacontextualization.

The distinction between contextualization and metacontextualization is an important one. To fail to make it would be to mistake not only the way absolute statements function in Tolstoy's novels but also the relation that particular works bear to their genre. For any linguistic structure in a literary work participates in two contexts: the context of the particular work in which it appears and the context of the genre to which that work belongs.[11] Whereas statements in most novels are dialogized by both contexts, Tolstoy's absolute statements are dialogized only by the second context. Dialogicality is ultimately unavoidable in Tolstoy's novels because—and only so long as—they are read as novels.

2. Tolstoy's Life and Lives

Two of the most common critical genres, the "life and works" of a writer and, its close relative, the chronological analysis of "major works," raise troublesome methodological problems that have been largely ignored. In each of these types of criticism, a claim is being made about the connection between a literary work and the world—whether literary or nonliterary—outside it, but it is not clear how or what connections can legitimately be made between the necessarily indeterminate meanings of fictional works and the historically determinate facts of an author's life or between the meanings of one work and the meanings of another. Formalist theory has taught us to beware of making facile connections, but the positive task, the specification of what a sound connection would be, remains to be done. A host of questions presents itself. We might ask, for instance, whether connections between the works of an author's oeuvre should be made prior to, and on different grounds from, connections between the oeuvre and his life. It is not clear just

11. Linguistic structures in literary works participate, of course, in other contexts as well, for example, in the broader contexts of literature or of fiction.

what role the concept of an oeuvre does or might play in literary biography. What is the relation between the author as creator and as reader of his own works, and what do his works mean for him at a later date, especially when he is in the process of new creation: how, so to speak, does he influence, or perhaps even parody, himself? I suspect that to answer these questions it will be necessary to develop a theory of the creative process, that is, of how man makes work, in order to understand the possible relations of man *to* work.

A special set of problems arises in the case of writers who deliberately made their lives into "literary facts." As Boris Tomashevsky observed, there are periods in which writers try "to create for themselves an artificial legendary biography composed of intentionally selected real and imaginary events."[12] A biographer of such an author would be wise to ask what happens to the status of "external" evidence when the life is itself made literary. Does not a life of this sort render the concept of intention, even outside of literary works, problematic? Should we have a tripartite hierarchy in which the fiction is the least reliable biographical evidence, the literized biography next, and the "real" life the most reliable? Or, on the contrary, might it not be the case with writers that what is left over after literature and literized biography is precisely what is least informative? Can a writer's literary biography be, as Yury Tynianov suggests, essentially parodic, either of his "real" self or of other literary lives? To answer these questions it would be necessary to know what the goals of literary biography might be or whether different kinds of literary biographies have different goals. I am not sure, in other words, that we are even clear not only about what kinds of claims can be made but about what kinds of claims we would like to make.

Because these questions remain unanswered and the goal of literary biography remains unclear, I see three reasons why a "life and works" of Tolstoy is an especially perilous undertaking, reasons whose importance biographers have generally underestimated. First, Tolstoy blurred the boundaries between living and telling with remarkable thoroughness. He seems to have taken to pathological extremes the observation of an early Dostoevsky narrator that "to live means to make a work of art of oneself." A biographer looking for some uncontaminated part of the late Tolstoy's life—something that was left out of a deliberately literized biography—is likely to be if not naive, then disappointed. He may even

---

12. Boris Tomashevsky, "Literature and Biography," in *Reading in Russian Poetics: Formalist and Structuralist Views*, ed. Ladislav Matejka and Krystyna Pomorska (Cambridge, Mass., 1971), p. 49. Tomashevsky continues: "A biography of a Romantic poet was more than a biography of an author and public figure. The Romantic poet *was* his own hero. His *life* was poetry, and soon there developed a canonical set of actions to be carried out by the poet. . . . The readers cried: 'Author! Author!'—but they were actually calling for the slender youth in a cloak, with a lyre in his hands and an enigmatic expression on his face" (p. 51).

begin to suspect, as Tolstoy did, the viability and presuppositions of notions like authenticity and sincerity. Second, the thoroughness with which Tolstoy, like Roquentin in Sartre's *Nausea*, "lived his life as if he were telling a story" compromises every piece of documentary evidence. It is hard to see how "private" diaries that were given to scribes and disciples to copy and preserve could be more reliable evidence than a work of fiction. They could, in fact, be less reliable, inasmuch as fiction, precisely because it is conventionally framed as a story, could serve as the best, because protected, place for something like self-revelation. *Father Sergius* may be a more reliable, or less unreliable, source for Tolstoy's biography than his diaries or letters.[13]

The third stumbling block for a biographer of Tolstoy has particularly complex consequences: his aspiration to be a prophet. To be a prophet, as Tolstoy well understood, means to have a special relation to one's biography and to language. For in order to utter timeless or absolute truths—statements which, though about history, morality, and culture, are not compromised by their origin in a particular historical and cultural milieu—it is necessary to speak in what I have called absolute language. Or to put it somewhat differently, absolute truths must issue from a speech center which can be regarded as privileged in that it is limited neither by the contingencies of the moment nor by the anticipation of a response.

It seems clear that Tolstoy was deeply concerned with the possibility of transhistorical truth and with the forms of utterance in which such truth might be expressed. Tolstoy's later life could be seen as a complex series of attempts to speak impersonally and categorically and to liberate his "word" from the irony of origins. In effect, Tolstoy wanted to escape from history and his own biography; his attempts were both futile and heroic. I will not in the space of this essay present a detailed picture of Tolstoy's biography as an attempt to escape his biography, but it would be instructive to describe the three kinds of strategies he used to insure his word against the irony of origins and to suggest why, as Tolstoy knew, those strategies had to fail.

Tolstoy's failure to speak nonhistorically in history is analogous to the reason for his inability to speak nonnovelistically in a novel. No man in history can utter a nonhistorical word, since the very uttering of it is a historical event. So long as the speaker of the utterance can be historically identified, and so long as the circumstances that provoked him to speak to particular people at a particular moment of his life can be at

---

13. I question the distinction R. F. Christian's recent edition of the correspondence (*Tolstoy's Letters*, 2 vols. [New York, 1978]) makes between open and personal letters; it might have been wiser to distinguish instead between avowedly and surreptitiously open letters. I think it is fair to say that Tolstoy lived his life in anticipation of his biographers and planted lives for them to discover. The "life" narrated by Maude was Tolstoy's decoy, by Troyat, his taunt.

least theoretically ascertained, his utterance has an inferable context—or, rather, manifold contexts—that limits it. The aspiring prophet may devise strategies to conceal the circumstances of his utterance and to free it from the taint of contextuality, but those strategies will bear tacit witness to the need for them and, however ingenious they may be, will themselves be referable to the particular man who devised them for particular reasons. There is simply no way to author an authorless word.

The strategy Tolstoy used most frequently was to present his assertions as cited or derived from a nonhistorical source and to define his own role as a simple transmitter of timeless truths—as of course prophets traditionally do. For Tolstoy, however, this strategy was particularly difficult inasmuch as he explicitly denied the possibility of miraculous or divine revelations. He therefore turned to secular versions of the strategy, claiming, for instance, to have done no more than draw logically necessary conclusions from premises that even his enemies accepted. He often explained that his conclusions were his only in the sense that he had published, not authored, them. The nonfiction sequel to *The Kreutzer Sonata*, for instance, makes especially frequent use of this argument. In this essay, Tolstoy presents each of his increasingly outrageous conclusions as a "deduction which seems to me to follow naturally from the above" and which no reasonable and disinterested person could doubt. "These propositions," he repeats so often that the repetition creates its own rhetorical kind of inevitability, "are nothing more than inevitable deductions from the teaching of the Gospels, which we profess, or at least . . . acknowledge to be the basis of our conceptions of morality."[14] Moreover, Tolstoy offers the very outrageousness of some of his propositions—that sex is immoral even within marriage, for instance—as evidence for the logical rigor of their deduction and for the disinterestedness of the deducer. If acceptance of such conclusions would lead to the end of humanity, Tolstoy argues, then logic demands no less. For Tolstoy, logic is not merely nonhistorical: it positively dictates the end of history!

Tolstoyan logic applied to biblical texts produces Tolstoyan textology. Just as Tolstoy sometimes claims to be no more than the transmitter of conclusions logically derived from universally accepted premises, so, at other times, he claims to be simply a meticulous and philologically rigorous editor of the Gospels. He declares that his translation of the New Testament is his only in the sense that he has restored the Gospels to their pristine form and message, the form and message they had before historical men with historical motives corrupted them. "I do not wish to interpret Christ's teaching," he writes, "but should only wish to prevent artificial interpretations of it."[15] If the Church refuses to accept the orig-

14. Tolstoy, *The Kreutzer Sonata*, in *The Works of Lyof N. Tolstoi: Master and Man, The Kreutzer Sonata, Dramas* (New York, 1929), pp. 156, 159.

15. Tolstoy, *What I Believe* (with *A Confession* and *The Gospel in Brief*), trans. Aylmer Maude (London, 1940), p. 307.

inal New Testament and his "uninterpreted" summary of it, Tolstoy argues, then it could only be because their beliefs, not his, are compromised by historical causes and motives.

The rhetorical force of Tolstoy's deductions depends on the impersonality of the process of deduction and on the impossibility of drawing any other conclusion. However, the polemical tone with which Tolstoy utters those conclusions and, indeed, the very uttering of them indicate that this is not the case. Tolstoy's awareness of the implicit contradiction between his argument and its expression is perhaps the reason he sometimes explains why he is stating what he believes to be obvious. One reason he gives is that, although he intended to remain silent, the Church's deliberate falsification of his position forced him to state what he did not say.[16] Nevertheless, Tolstoy's conclusions are obviously not indisputable or he would not have anticipated dispute. Once again, the denial of dialogue is itself both dialogic and dialogizing. As Tolstoy himself observes in the preface to his edition of *The Gospel in Brief:*

> Never, since the time of Arius, has the affirmation of any dogma arisen from any other cause than the desire to condemn a contrary belief as false. It is a supreme degree of pride and ill will to others to assert that a particular dogma is a divine revelation proceeding from the Holy Ghost: the highest presumption because nothing more arrogant can be said than that the words spoken by me are uttered through me by God; and the greatest ill will because the avowal of oneself as in possession of the sole indubitable truth implies an assertion of the falsity of all who disagree.[17]

As Tolstoy must have been aware, however, this reasoning applies to his own arrogant claim to know the truth and to his own dogmatic rejection of dogma. Indeed, his very attempts to speak impersonally have become the mark of his personality.

Tolstoy's second strategy was to exploit speech centers that are traditionally regarded as privileged, as somehow outside of the interests of everyday life and as protected from dialogue. The deathbed was one such tribune that he used frequently in his last years when he was near death several times and when his illnesses were reported in detail by the press. During his illness of 1902, for instance, the seventy-four-year-old author addressed a letter on Christian government to Nicholas II, which he sent via his acquaintance the Grand Duke Nicholas Mikhailovich with instructions that it be shown only to the tsar himself (and so safeguarded from the vicissitudes of merely political life). Sent through this extraordinary channel, the letter began by affirming the privileged context—

16. This argument is made, for instance, in his "Reply to the Synod's Edict of Excommunication," *Selected Essays*, trans. Aylmer Maude (New York, 1964).

17. Tolstoy, *The Gospel in Brief*, p. 127.

or, rather, freedom from context—of its utterance. "Dear Brother," Tolstoy began with astonishing presumptuousness, "I consider this form of address most suitable, because in this letter I address you as a brother-man rather than as a Tsar, and also because, awaiting the approach of death, I write as it were from the other world."[18]

The tsar's only answer was that Tolstoy "should not worry for he would not show it to anybody" (p. 325). Nicholas responded, in other words, not to the message but to the machinery of its utterance and transmission. He perhaps understood both the claim to rhetorical privilege and the would-be prophet's unspoken wish that his private letter should be made public "against his will." Nicholas may also have meant to imply that the premeditated strategy of a deathbed letter resembled Tolstoy's other complex but equally futile attempts to insulate his speech from any ordinary human context. We may add that Tolstoy's subsequent deathbed scenes seem increasingly rehearsed. The claim to nonhistoricity developed a history, and the denial of context became its own context.

If pronouncements made "from the other world" are rhetorically powerful, then, as Tolstoy seems to have reasoned, posthumous speech is even more so. Such a speech center would necessarily be privileged because its utterances could not be explained in terms of the speaker's anticipation of possible responses or personal consequences. Tolstoy's suicide note—he did not attempt suicide but he did attempt a suicide note—constitutes one attempt at posthumous communication;[19] a second was the letter (actually two letters) about his doctrine and his marriage "to be opened fifty years after my death" (p. 265).

Tolstoy's many wills constitute a still more complex attempt at posthumous communication. As he was well aware, a last testament is a privileged one, its privilege marked by the ceremony of its reading and derived in part from its closure to response or qualification. Like biblical commands, wills can be disregarded but they cannot be answered. (It is because wills and suicide notes are usually closed to dialogue that Dostoevsky's novels can derive humor from dialogizing them.)

Because a will's rhetorical privilege depends on its issuance from a posthumous speech center, that privilege will be lost to the extent that the will is identified with the moment of its composition rather than with the moment of its reading. (Those who wish to contest a will may therefore discredit it as a response to particular, therefore potentially "uncharacteristic," circumstances.) Once we are aware of the motives and circumstances that occasioned Tolstoy's attempts to exploit posthumous speech, such a qualifying identification becomes almost unavoidable. The controversy between Tolstoy's wife and disciples over the terms and

18. Cited in Ernest J. Simmons, *Leo Tolstoy*, 2 vols. (New York, 1960), 2:324; all further references to vol. 2 of Simmons' book will be included in the text.

19. The circumstances that occasioned this note and its discovery are described in Simmons, 2:264.

possession of his will became a central fact of his day-to-day life during his last ten or fifteen years. One could narrate Tolstoy's biography for this period as the story of successive revisions, or plans for revisions, of his will. Completely grounded in the circumstances of their composition, these documents became thoroughly dialogized. As each will or draft of a will was abandoned or amended under someone's pressure, and as each "last" testament became a penultimate one, the testament that replaced it necessarily took on the character of a response to objections raised against its predecessor and, implicitly, of an anticipation of future objections that might be raised against it. In fact, the very text of one such will has survived with a written response attached to it. Having discovered the will that Tolstoy had secretly asked his daughter to revise and copy, his wife prevailed upon him to renounce it. She then added the following postscript: "This is not a *will*, and my husband never asked my daughter Masha to copy it; she did it at her own discretion and kept it secret from the whole family, and today my husband gave it to me to destroy at my desire. Sofya Tolstoy" (p. 313).

One of the arguments Tolstoy's wife often used to persuade him not to make a will was that to make one was to contradict his own teachings; for those teachings were anarchic, and wills, as Tolstoy himself conceded, rely on the power of the state to enforce their terms. Moreover, Tolstoy reasoned, the very act of insuring the dissemination of one's writing through legal renunciation of copyright in a will—a provision to which his wife objected especially strenuously—implicitly admitted doubt of their unqualified or absolute truth. As his friend Nicholas Fedorov had argued when they met in the first years after Tolstoy's conversion, the truer an idea is, the less need there is to propagate it. Christ, Tolstoy told Strakhov after agreeing to a new will, made no will:

> The whole affair [of making a will] is very painful to me. And it is all unnecessary—to secure the spread of my ideas by such measures. Now Christ—although it is strange that I should compare myself with him—did not trouble about anyone appropriating his ideas as his personal property, nor did he record his ideas in writing, but expressed them courageously and went to the cross for them. His ideas have not been lost. Indeed, no word can be completely lost, if it expressed the truth and if the person uttering it profoundly believes in its truth. But all these external measures for security come only from our non-belief in what we are uttering. [P. 449]

Tolstoy would therefore occasionally decide to leave not a will but a simple request that his heirs dispose of his property and copyright. These requests appeared in his diaries, which would, he knew, be read after his death. His diaries, in fact, constituted another of Tolstoy's posthumous speech centers and were the most complex of his many attempts at privileged speech. A compulsive diarist for most of his adult life—he is, like Boswell, one of the most extensively documented men who ever lived—Tolstoy was deeply interested in the nature of the communicative context of diaries. He discusses that context in his essay on Amiel's journals, and it is, of course, explored in the many fictional works he wrote in diary form. It is also a recurrent topic in Tolstoy's personal diaries themselves.

The privilege of diaries derives from their presumed privacy: when they renounce that presumption, they lose their privilege. Insofar as they are regarded as having been written for no audience except their author, they may appear to be free from the kind of qualification that must necessarily be made when speaking to someone whose knowledge and interests are not coincident with one's own. The basic logic of Tolstoy's abuse of diaries should by this point be clear. Knowing that diaries are traditionally regarded as maximally sincere, he makes use of them to record statements that he would like to be read as maximally sincere. Because private diaries are, so to speak, not heard but overheard, Tolstoy attempted to create an audience of eavesdroppers, who, like all eavesdroppers, believe more readily what they think they were not meant to hear. His diaries, in other words, became a kind of stage whisper, and his private meditations took on the character of a theatrical soliloquy. The logic of his diaries was that of an "open secret," and their strategy was that of a confidence game, with their future readers as victims.

Tolstoy played this game of spy and counterspy with his wife, with whom he used to exchange diaries. He would reveal his most "private" opinions of her in his diaries—opinions that often contradicted what he professed in conversation that very day—knowing that she would read them. She in turn would answer in the same way, thus turning their diaries into a kind of unacknowledged correspondence, a dialogue of soliloquies: " . . . today he has written in his diary that I *recognized my fault* for the first time and that this is joyous! My God! Help me to endure this! Again, before future generations, he must make himself out to be the *martyr* and me the only one who is at fault. But in what way am I to blame?" (p. 269).

Sonya's reference to "future generations" points to the second audience that each kept in mind while recording his case against the other: Tolstoy's biographers. Sonya, indeed, was so concerned that future generations would regard her as a shrew ("Xanthippe" was her word) that she would insist on Tolstoy's censoring or renouncing his diary's descriptions of her. His response to one such demand was a formal letter:

If you are troubled by the thought that certain passages in my diaries that I wrote, under impressions of the moment, about our disagreements and conflicts will be used by future biographers ill-disposed towards you, I want first of all to point out that such transitory expressions of feelings, both mine and those in your diary, can in no sense give a correct understanding of our true relations. If you fear this, then I will gladly take an opportunity to express in my diary or simply in a letter my relations with you and my appreciation of your life. [Pp. 467–68][20]

The problem with this renunciation, however, is that, inasmuch as it may itself be the response to the shrewish behavior already described in the diary, it is hardly more authoritative than the passages it claims to over-rule. On the contrary, its very composition could be interpreted as con-firmation of those passages, just as the reference to "those in your diary" could be taken as a none-too-oblique reminder of Sonya's hypocrisy in insisting on his renunciation. It is, moreover, equally hard to understand how the diary entry Tolstoy proposes to exonerate her could have any more force than the entries it would be designed to cancel. Sonya must have realized all this and therefore demanded possession of the diaries altogether. Since Chertkov and the disciples also demanded them, the same kind of battle was fought over the diaries as over the will. The story of Tolstoy's late diaries thus became a complex tale of secret trans-ferals and a Moscow vault; of Sonya's insisting on erasures and anxious scribes copying endangered passages; of threats of suicide and appeals to a prophet's integrity. It would, in short, be hard to imagine a more thoroughly compromised set of diaries than Tolstoy's.

It was in this atmosphere of intrigue that Tolstoy began keeping two diaries. With his wife reading and his disciples copying and quoting his now thoroughly public diary, Tosltoy began a "secret diary" in order to reestablish the privilege of communication to no audience except him-self. Nevertheless, when he fell ill later that year (1908), he sent the secret diary to Chertkov—as he probably anticipated doing all along.

A few months before his death, Tolstoy once again started keeping double books. The public diary became a sort of decoy as the private "Diary for Myself Alone" recorded his hostility toward his wife, the steps he was taking to keep his will secret from her, and his doubts that any of his private papers—including this very diary—could be kept from her. This secret diary, in other words, became a secret *from her,* and so she, in effect, became its implicit audience. In this context, I think, the statement on the diary's opening page that it was intended for himself alone constituted less of a safeguard than a provocation—just as its de-scription of her spying and eavesdropping may have been designed for her to spy upon. She did, in fact, discover and read this diary as well— he continued it even after this discovery—and the margins of its surviving

20. As Simmons notes, Sonya responded to this too in her own diary: "It is precisely this that I do not fear at all . . . I was simply hurt that the diaries . . . were accessible to Chertkov, an outsider, and not to me, his wife, from whom they have been concealed and are concealed in all sorts of ways" (2:467, n. 7).

first notebook contain her predictable, perhaps predicted, responses. At one point, she refutes him by quoting a contradictory assessment of her from his earlier diaries, thus creating a dialogue of his own diaries. This counterpoint of text and margin in the "Diary for Myself Alone" is emblematic of the dialogization of all of Tolstoy's "private" writings. Each of his attempts to escape dialogue was in fact a response in a dialogue, a response that looked forward to future responses. His quest for privacy became, as he was aware, a form of publicity.

Because Tolstoy knew that he ultimately could not escape his biography, his third strategy was to try to transform that biography into one he would not need to escape. In order to free his statements from attribution to personality and biographical contingencies, he represented that life as impersonal and archetypal, as the standard by which all other, merely historical, lives could be measured. In this sense, Tolstoy's autobiographical writings—especially the *Confession*—aspire not to be autobiographical; that is, they avoid being a description of what is particular to the man Tolstoy. Tolstoy strives rather to present only the pattern that his life embodies, and he identifies that pattern with the pattern embodied by Jesus, Buddha, and Socrates. Like those three, he seems to say, he too can make nonhistorical statements because his life has not been shaped by the historical period in which it has simply unfolded. The late Tolstoy would have us believe that he did not *live* his life, but rather *lived out* his Life.

Here again, however, Tolstoy's quest runs counter to his own teachings for two principal reasons. First, as Father Sergius learns, one cannot make oneself into a saint because "the consciousness of humility" is itself an inescapable source of pride. Second, it is central to Tolstoy that each man's salvation is unique in that it cannot be achieved by repeating a pattern. *Father Sergius* is the story of a man who tries to be a saint by reliving one of the *Lives of the Saints;* what Sergius learns is that the closer his life approaches prescribed models, the farther it departs from true sainthood. Sergius recognizes at last that the actions that mark a saint are never performed deliberately or experienced as they might someday be narrated. When Sergius at last discovers a true saint in Pashenka, she—and everyone else—is unaware of her exceptionality. He draws characteristically Tolstoyan conclusions from Pashenka's unconscious and inimitable saintliness: if one is canonized, then one cannot be a saint.

Father Sergius suggests that Tolstoy was aware of the reasons he could not liberate himself from his biographical prison. I think that Gorky was the most astute of Tolstoy's many memoirists and biographers because he understood not only Tolstoy's contradictions but also his awareness of those contradictions—what Gorky refers to as "the skepticism applied by him to his own preaching and personality." Gorky's reaction to Tolstoy was therefore itself contradictory, a combination of repulsion and awe. "No man was more complicated, contradictory, and great in everything—

yes in everything," Gorky wrote when he heard the news of Tolstoy's flight and death,

> but what always repelled me in him was that stubborn despotic inclination to turn the life of Count Leo Nikolaevich into "the saintly life of our blessed father, boyard Leo."
> As you know, he had for long intended to suffer; he expressed his regret to E. Soloviov, and to Suler, that he had not succeeded; but he wanted to suffer simply, not out of a natural desire to test the resistance of his will, but with the obvious and, I repeat, the despotic intention of increasing the influence of his religious ideas, the weight of his teaching, in order to make his preaching irresistible, to make it holy in the eyes of man through his suffering; to force them to accept it—you understand, to force them. For he realized that preaching is not sufficiently convincing; in his diary you will, some day, read good examples of skepticism applied by him to his own preaching and personality. He knows that "martyrs and sufferers, with rare exceptions, are despots and tyrants"—he knows everything!—and yet he says to himself, "Were I to suffer for my ideas, they would have a greater influence." It was this in him that always repelled me, for I can not help feeling that it was an attempt to use violence upon me, a desire to get hold of my conscience, to dazzle it with the glory of righteous blood, to put upon my neck the yoke of a dogma. [*Reminiscences*, pp. 26–27]

But Gorky also knew what Tolstoy suffered in not believing the poses with which he deceived others, in always being one step ahead of his most labyrinthine strategies for escaping his biography. As Gorky wrote, "He is too rational for that and knows life and people too well. Here are some more of his words: 'The Kaliph Abdurahman had during his life fourteen happy days, but I am sure I have not had so many. And this is because I have never lived—I cannot live—for myself, for my own self; I live for show, for people' " (*Reminiscences*, p. 33). Gorky does not add, however, that this very admission of the thirst for publicity was itself made to a Russian writer—that is, to Gorky—who, Tolstoy had good reason to believe, would publish it. In other words, even the admission that he lived for show was in part made for show. It was in a characteristically Tolstoyan way true, but with a "loophole": the statement itself was true, but the utterance of it was false. As much as Dostoevsky's underground man, as much as Stavrogin, Tolstoy was the master, and the victim, of the logic of the compromised confession.

In his final delirium, the dying Tolstoy whispered, "To seek, always to seek"; his last clearly audible words were, "To escape . . . I must escape" (pp. 504–5). What Tolstoy wanted to escape from was history and his own biography; what he sought was a position from which to perceive and speak the transhistorical truth. I read Tolstoy's novels—and his life—as a series of dialogues about dialogue, of stories about the ultimately futile attempt to make good that escape. The hero of *The Kreutzer Sonata* enunciates one side of that dialogue: "If life has no [timeless] aim," he reasons, "if life has been given us for life's sake, then there is no reason for living" (*Short Works*, p. 377). On the other hand, Pierre Bezukhov learns, after much fruitless searching for a mystical key to history with which to escape time's "labyrinth of lies," that life *is* given for life's sake. Platon Karataev's wisdom, he comes to understand, lies in his ability to see the historical process itself as meaningful and not to seek any other meaning beyond its changing seasons. Karataev "loved and lived on affectionate terms with everything life brought him in contact with, and especially with man—not any particular man, but simply with those he happened to be with. He loved his dog, his comrades, the French, and Pierre, who was his neighbor; but Pierre felt that for all Karataev's affectionate tenderness toward him . . . he would not have suffered a moment's grief at parting from him. And Pierre began to feel the same way toward Karataev" (*War and Peace*, pp. 1162–63). When he tries to abstract a timeless message from Karataev, Pierre learns that there neither is, nor need be, any noncontextual meaning. Karataev, the personification of the spirit of simplicity and truth "did not understand, could not grasp the significance of words apart from their context. Every utterance, every action of his, was the manifestation of a force unknown to him, which was his life. . . . His words and actions flowed from him as smoothly, spontaneously, and inevitably as fragrance emanates from a flower. He could not understand the value or significance of any word or deed taken separately" (*War and Peace*, p. 1163).

I have stated that the central irony of Tolstoy's life was that his quest to speak like God became the mark of his all-too-human personality. But I find something deeply heroic in the persistence, intelligence, and energy with which he tested human limitations and pursued a quest he recognized as impossible. Among Tolstoy's biographers, it is perhaps only Gorky who, while comprehending Tolstoy's weakness and contradictions, understood his extraordinary heroism as well. When Tolstoy once reproached him for his atheism, Gorky recalled, "I, who do not believe in God, looked at him for some reason very cautiously and a little timidly. I looked and I thought: 'This man is godlike' " (*Reminiscences*, p. 57).

Freedom of Interpretation:
Bakhtin and the Challenge of Feminist Criticism

Wayne C. Booth

> My language is the sum total of myself.
> —CHARLES S. PEIRCE

Most critics today would see the "politics of interpretation" as beginning and ending not with freedom but with power. For them, the central task of a conference on the politics of interpretation would be to see how various forms of power, open or covert, enforce various kinds of interpretation or perhaps how a given interpretation serves a given established power. In that view, the search for freedom of interpretation becomes the problem of how to resist power—how to wrest it from those who have it or how to produce a text that will not be co-opted by it. Who has the power—which class, which ruler, which faction, which sex—to impose what can be said and not said? Whose language, because of the power of its users, imposes a given view of reality upon whoever fails to resist that language?

It is always easy to find examples showing that to control a language is to control everyone who uses that language; critics have found that analysis of power turns up astonishing and sometimes even persuasive transformations of our traditional views, both of our cultural history and

Editor's note.—This essay was first presented at the symposium "The Politics of Interpretation" in 1981 and appeared in *Critical Inquiry* 9 (September 1982). All references to essays "in this volume" are to articles in that issue, later reprinted as *The Politics of Interpretation.*

of our picture of how we work together in discourse.[1] I am not interested in arguing that it is a mistake to travel this route. Power is one good starting point in thinking about any human problem. But of course every starting point exacts a price, and when we start with power as our base term we tend to obscure certain distinctions,[2] especially if we do not quickly throw other ingredients into our blender. And we are almost certain to fall into a self-privileging discourse, the kind that provides a special exemption of itself from the analysis. Like B. F. Skinner's theories of conditioned behavior, such languages can explain the production of every text except the text that provides the explanation. Some of us think that we detect such self-privileging not only in the essays here by Edward Said and Hayden White but in the work of Stanley Fish and of—well, I must restrain myself lest I insult the whole world. Self-privileging is indeed an exercise of power, and thus it may fall under the politics of interpretation; still, it should probably be reserved for some other volume.[3]

In turning to the language of freedom, I am not automatically freed from the dangers of reduction and self-privileging. "Freedom" as a term is at least as ambiguous as "power" (or as "politics" or "interpretation"). When I say that for me all questions about the politics of interpretation begin with the question of freedom, I can either be saying a mouthful or saying nothing at all, depending on whether I am willing to complicate my key term, "freedom," by relating it to the language of power. The best way to do that is to get power in from the beginning, by making a distinction taken for granted by many earlier thinkers and too often ignored today: *freedom from* as contrasted with *freedom to; freedom from* external restraints and the power of others to inhibit our actions, and *freedom to* act effectively when restraints disappear.[4]

1. I am thinking most immediately of Michel Foucault and Edward Said, but I am also attempting to rule out in advance the reduction of feminist criticism to questions of power.

2. Said has charged Foucault with this kind of reduction in "Travelling Theory," *Raritan* 1 (Winter 1982): 41–67.

3. One of the best accounts of self-privileging is Jacques Derrida's "Cogito and the History of Madness," a discussion of Foucault's *Folie et déraison: Histoire de la folie à l'âge classique,* in *Writing and Difference* (Chicago, 1978), pp. 31–63. I recommend the essay to anyone tempted to think of deconstructionist criticism as in any simple sense anti-intentionalist.

4. For the best brief modern discussion of the distinction I know, see F. H. Bradley, *Ethical Studies,* 2d ed. (Oxford, 1927), pp. 55–57. As Bradley's discussion suggests, the distinction has consequences both for our thinking about causation in general (can we really get along, as so much of the modern world tries to, thinking only of "efficient causes"?) and our notions of what the person *is* who causes or is caused, who is freed *from*

Wayne C. Booth's most recent work, *Critical Understanding: The Powers and Limits of Pluralism,* won the Laing Prize in 1982. He is working on a book about ethical and political criticism of narrative. A new edition of *The Rhetoric of Fiction* will appear in 1983.

All the *freedom from* in the world will not free me *to* make an intellectual discovery or to paint a picture unless I have somehow freed myself *to* perform certain tasks. Such freedoms are gained only by those who surrender to disciplines and codes invented by others, giving up certain *freedoms from*. Nobody forbids my interpreting the original text of Confucius' *Analects* or the *Principia Mathematica*, yet I am not *free to* do so, lacking the disciplines—having not *been* disciplined—to do so. The distinction can lead to troublesome complexities, but in its simple form here it cuts through some of the problems that arise in power language.

Every critical revolution tends to speak more clearly about what it is against than about what it seeks. The historicists against impressionism, the New Critics against historicism, the new new critics against intentionalism and the authority of canons, the feminists against misogynous art and criticism—clearly one could write a history of modern criticism as a glorious casting off of errors. But it is rightly a commonplace among intellectual historians that all revolutionaries depend on their past far more than they know. Revolutionary critics are enslaved by a nasty law of nature: I can say only what I *can* say, and that will be largely what I have learned to say from the kings I would depose.[5]

Everyone who tries to forge any kind of ideological criticism must struggle with these complexities. Nobody ever knows just what powers have been rejected and what voices heard. But at the moment it seems clear that what follows here, both in its emerging clarities and remaining confusions, results from my somewhat surprised surrender to voices previously alien to me: the "Mikhail Bakhtin" who speaks to me, muffled by my ignorance of Russian, and the "feminist criticism" that in its vigor and diversity and challenge to canonic views has—belatedly, belatedly—forced me to begin listening.

2

My first step must be an attempt at *freeing from,* joining those who have questioned the incompatibility of concern for ideology and concern for art. The powers whose influence I would thus cast off were themselves busy at casting off. In their view, art, or at least the best art, was to

---

or freed *to*. After sending this article to press, I have discovered a feminist discussion that centers on freedom rather than power and that relies on the distinction between *freedom from* and *freedom to* (though in a somewhat different vocabulary): see Janet Radcliffe Richards, "Enquiries for Liberators," *The Skeptical Feminist: A Philosophical Enquiry* (Boston, 1980), esp. pp. 66–67. I cannot endorse every detail of Richards' mode of argument; she still believes, for example, that reason dictates an absolute separation of the "ought" from the "is." But her sorting out of issues faced by every feminist is the best I've seen; as a result of her clarity, she can provide what is to me an unanswerable argument showing why everyone in our time ought to be a feminist, *while* showing that many arguments for and against feminism are absurd.

5. See my " 'Preserving the Exemplar': or, How Not to Dig Our Own Graves," *Critical Inquiry* 3 (Spring 1977): 407–23, and *Critical Understanding: The Powers and Limits of Pluralism* (Chicago, 1979), esp. pp. 219–23, 341–45.

be achieved by rejecting all practical restraints, and the best criticism was to be written in the same spirit. Increasing numbers of modern critics have until recently found the chief enemy of artistic freedom to be any concern for ethical, political, social, religious, or philosophical validity. Faced with all sorts of obvious restraints imposed by the social and political spheres, threatened by political tyrannies on the one hand and by bourgeois pieties on the other, harangued by scientismists who can prove, so they say, that everything we do is "in principle" programmable, they have found that true art is to be found in opposition to *all that*. Art is the one last saving domain, the domain of aesthetics where alone freedom is untrammeled.

It is then but a small step to the assumption that criticism, like the art it feeds on and supports, should ban all efforts to judge the relative political or ethical powers of individual works of art. *Art* as the general domain of pure freedom thus becomes good per se, so long as it maintains its autonomy; whatever compromises that autonomy is bad, and judgments of relative political or ethical value obviously violate that autonomy. Poetry makes nothing happen. A poem should not mean but be. To judge what it means or does is a form of tyranny.

Such views have never gone uncontested. A history of ethical and political criticism of art through this century would include many distinguished names, from wide-ranging theorists like F. R. Leavis, Lionel Trilling, Yvor Winters, and Kenneth Burke to the hundreds of specialists who defend or attack the morality or political value of individual authors or texts or genres: *Ethical Perspective in the Novels of Thomas Hardy; George Gissing: Ideology and Fiction; The Moral Vision of Oscar Wilde; The Moral Imagination of Joseph Conrad.* The list would include a considerable number of Marxists of various persuasions; they were on principle largely untempted by the drive for aesthetic and critical autonomy, which they considered a foreordained bourgeois deflection (but not entirely so: witness Clement Greenberg's famous *Partisan Review* articles of 1939 and 1940, discussed by T. J. Clark in this issue). What is striking is that almost all of these critics have written with a sense of being the opposition. Academic liberals have in general cast them as outlaws, and as outlaws they have often performed their criticism in tones somewhat less than suave.

As an academic liberal myself—I resist the label, but that's what people call me—as a liberal who has reluctantly been driven to give up dogmas of autonomy, I perhaps exaggerate the degree of change in our climate. But I do see signs of a great shift, and not only in the very existence of a conference of the kind that initiated most of the essays in this volume—a conference, be it noted, organized by a journal founded by "Chicago formalists": a bursting open of sealed caskets. If I am right we can now question, without too much anxiety, the "natural" opposition of the aesthetic order and the political order. We can now look at the ethics and politics that were concealed in the professedly anti-ethical and apolitical stances of modern aesthetic movements. We can question the notion, implicit in certain of those movements, that art is more important than people; that artists not only can but should ignore their audiences; that didactic and rhetorical interests are essentially nonaesthetic; that concern with ideologies and with the truth or practical value of art is a sure mark of its enemies; that didactic intent is always a mark of impurity; that any true art work must be above politics. In short, we may soon be freed of that most debilitating of all inhibitions for the critic— the fear that if we find the artist's self-expressions spiritually empty or socially futile or politically destructive or otherwise repugnant, we should not say so, because to say so reveals us as philistines and bourgeois nincompoops.

As we here participate in that movement, we must all be haunted by the fear that I find expressed whenever I have talked about the possibility of a revived ethical and political criticism. "You are opening the door to censorship, to political suppression of artists. Have you forgotten about what happens to artists whenever the political order takes seriously your claim that artworks may be subjected to moral or political judgment?" The anguishing history of atrocities in the name of political authority over artists—the ever-growing accounts of arrest, exile, torture, and assassination—should be enough, we are sometimes told, to warn us away from even talking about such matters. And the dangers are not all external to criticism itself. Every kind of criticism can produce bad examples; but there is a special badness about the naive application of ready-made ideological standards to isolated elements of artworks reduced for the purpose to propositional simplicities. We can be sure that once the floodgates are opened, what flows will not be only pure spring water.

One way for an ideological critic to escape these dangers is to forego judgment and attempt only description, as some neo-Marxists have done. There are signs that some feminist critics, embarrassed by certain excesses and distortions of the sixties and seventies, are turning away from evaluation—especially the negative grading of sexist works. (See, for example, Elizabeth Abel's introduction to *Writing and Sexual Difference,* a special issue of *Critical Inquiry* on feminist criticism [Winter 1981].) But though it is no doubt important to extend ideological criticism far beyond the mere grading of works as sound or unsound, it is a serious mistake to give up the claim that the quality of an artwork's ideology affects its quality *as art.* Indeed when we use the term "ideology" in the general sense I intend here, it is clear that the struggle for an art freed from ideology was itself informed by an ideology. The "dehumanized," ideologically pure art pursued by so many through this century thus becomes subject to our ideological criticism;[6] it is as thoroughly tainted with choices among possible values as is *Paradise Lost*—if having an ideology is a taint.

I am consequently driven to seek some path—or rather paths, because in such matters no one way will ever say all we want to say— between obviously undesirable extremes. Freedom from past dogmas of autonomy can do nothing for me unless I can find a mode of ideological criticism that will avoid the faults of ideologues.[7]

3

No doubt that is why the work of Bakhtin seems so attractive to me now. Bakhtin was dissatisfied both with his formalist mentors of the twenties and with the simpleminded ideological labelings and gradings of too many Marxist colleagues. In a series of books, written often under great political pressure and published, many of them, only late in his life, Bakhtin undertook to develop a dialogue between two truths: our sharing of artworks offers forms and experiences found in no other activity; yet art is inherently, inescapably, loaded with—indeed made of— ideology. Art springs from and in turn influences systems of belief and human practice. It is true that one can, with a little tinkering, find in the great Western ideological critics, from Plato on, useful ways of harmonizing these two truths. Bakhtin seems to me to require less tinkering than most. Discovering a "dialogic imagination" at the heart of human life in all its forms, he can discuss its artistic expressions with no temptation to place isolated, simple ideological propositions into flat opposition. At the same time he provides clear, bold, yet flexible criteria for appraising ideological worth.

6. José Ortega y Gasset's *"The Dehumanization of Art," and Other Writings on Art and Culture* described a modern art that was programmatically against all "human" impurities: "Tears and laughter are, aesthetically, frauds" (trans. Willard R. Trask [Garden City, N.Y., 1956], p. 25). By the time I wrote my own first questioning of such views (in *The Rhetoric of Fiction* [Chicago, 1961]), they had long since been carried beyond anything Ortega could have dreamed of. And in the twenty years since, the effort to remove even the last vestiges of human reference from the words used in literary art has been so widespread that citation would be pointless.

7. In "The 'Second Self' in Novel Criticism" (*British Journal of Aesthetics* 6 [1966]: 272–90), John Killham suggested that *The Rhetoric of Fiction* was a mistaken effort to mediate between doctrines of autonomy and everyone's knowledge that works of fiction do, after all, express their author's commitments. He was wrong about the central thrust of that book; he would be closer to being right about my present project. But I do not see the problem as a simple dilemma, presenting me with the task of grasping or passing between two clearly pointed horns. As the afterword to the new edition of *The Rhetoric of Fiction* makes clear (Chicago, 1983), the question of who does what to whom in writing and reading fiction seems even more complicated to me now than it did in 1961, and the problems for any ideological criticism, ethical, political, religious, psychological, are even more complicated than the formal analysis of telling and listening to stories.

Even if space permitted, it would be a mistake to pretend to summarize Bakhtin's immensely varied and aggressively fluid views; for him all "monologue" is faulty, and flat summary is an especially destructive form of monologue. But for the purpose of thinking about freedom of interpretation, one can extract—somewhat brutally—two elements in the dialogic imagination that he both exemplifies and defends: his view of what people are made of and his view of how fictions are made.[8]

1. He conducts a steady polemic against atomized, narrowly formalist or individualistic views of selves. His targets here—all "monological" views—are shared with other Marxists and with many a social psychologist in the West: he demolishes the notion of the atomic self, authentic in its privacy only, clearly separable from other selves and identified as free to the degree that it has purged itself of "external influences."

For him, as for more orthodox Marxists, what I call my "self" is essentially social. Each of us is constituted not as an individual, private, atomic self but as a collective of the many selves we have taken in from birth. We encounter these selves as what he calls "languages," the "voices" spoken by others. Languages are of course made not only of words; they are whole systems of meaning, each language constituting an interrelated set of beliefs or norms. "Language" is often thus for him roughly synonymous with "ideology." Each person is constituted as a hierarchy of languages, each language being a kind of ideology-brought-into-speech.

In this view ideology cannot be conceived as something to be avoided at all cost; it is inescapable in every moment of human speech. We speak *with* our ideology—our collection of languages, of words-laden-with-values. And the speaking is always thus more or less polyglot—it *is* a collection. Though some speakers may aspire to the condition of monologue, we have all inherited languages from many different sources ("science, art, religion, class, etc."), and to attempt to rule out all voices but "my own" is at best an artificial pretense. We are constituted in polyphony.

8. I am unfortunately having to rely entirely on works in translation: see Bakhtin, *The Dialogic Imagination*, ed. Michael Holquist and trans. Holquist and Caryl Emerson, University of Texas Press Slavic Series, no. 1 (Austin, Tex., 1981); the better-known *Rabelais and His World*, trans. Helene Iswolsky (Cambridge, Mass., 1968); *Problems of Dostoevsky's Poetics*, trans. R. W. Rotsel (n.p., 1973); in manuscript, a new translation of the latter by Emerson (forthcoming from the Univ. of Minn. Press); and the work of disputed authorship, P. N. Medvedev/Bakhtin, *The Formal Method in Literary Scholarship: A Critical Introduction to Sociological Poetics*, trans. Albert J. Wehrle, Goucher College Series (Baltimore, 1978). For assistance in reading Bakhtin through the murk of translation, I am especially indebted to Tzvetan Todorov, *Mikhaïl Bakhtine: Le Principe dialogique* (Paris, 1981); to Julia Kristeva for her *"presentation"* to Bakhtin's *La Poétique de Dostoïevski*, trans. Isabelle Kolitcheff (Paris, 1970); and to Gary Saul Morson, *The Boundaries of Genre: Dostoevsky's "Diary of a Writer" and the Traditions of Literary Utopia* (Austin, Tex., 1981).

Social man [and there is no other kind] is surrounded by ideological phenomena, by objects-signs [*veshch'-znak*] of various types and categories: by words in the multifarious forms of their realization (sounds, writing, and the others), by scientific statements, religious symbols and beliefs, works of art, and so on. All of these things in their totality comprise the ideological environment, which forms a solid ring around man. And man's consciousness lives and develops in this environment. Human consciousness does not come into contact with existence directly, but through the medium of the surrounding ideological world. . . . In fact, the individual consciousness can only become a consciousness by being realized in the forms of the ideological environment proper to it: in language, in conventionalized gesture, in artistic image, in myth, and so on.[9]

2. Such a view of the polyphonic self accords necessarily with a view of artworks as more or less adequate representations of polyphony. Throughout his wide-ranging histories and typologies of literary forms runs a consistent standard: since literary forms are in fact formed ideologies, and since those who make and receive them are in fact plural selves, those works that do most justice to polyphony, or "heteroglossia," are most praiseworthy. The formal critic must be an ideological critic, since ideologies, as embodied in "languages" or "voices," are what forms are made of. The path from this point to the conclusion that "the novel" is the highest literary form, and Dostoevsky the greatest of novelists, is too intricate to be traced here. What is important is his insistence on the supreme value, in art as in life, of resisting monologue: our essence and our value are found in whatever counters the temptation to treat human beings as "objects" reducible to their usefulness to us. People—and this includes the people who inhabit fictions—are essentially, irreducibly "subjects," voices rich beyond anyone's uses, performing in a chorus too grand for any participant's full comprehension.

Bakhtin sometimes makes the list of sources of ideology, whether in selves or in novels, seem deceptively short and simple: "scientific statements, religious symbols and beliefs, works of art, and so on." The "and so on" refers explicitly, in some contexts, only to ethics. But we can find scattered through his work a much longer list of particular languages that for any individual constitute the society of ideologies that will be either "authoritatively persuasive," if left uncriticized, or perhaps

9. Medvedev/Bakhtin, *The Formal Method*, p. 14. Obviously in this view whatever *freedom to* we possess will depend absolutely on the "languages" we have imbibed. I find it interesting—though not surprising in view of common Hegelian origins—that the same Bradley whom I cite for a discussion of *freedom to* versus *freedom from* should provide one of the best nineteenth-century critiques of individualism, in the name of an irreducibly social psyche; see his *Ethical Studies*, esp. "My Station and Its Duties," pp. 160–213.

"internally persuasive," if they survive the winnowing of a conscious critical review.

The list, and the subordination of items on it, will be somewhat different for each of us, even if we live in the same society; each of us has had different parents, read different books, met different people, conversed in different bars or dining rooms or truck stops. But what I—*call* it "I"—can utter will nevertheless always be some sort of complex amalgam of voices derived not only from my patria, as emphasized beautifully in Donald Davie's essay, but more particularly, within any one society, from my economic class; my profession (we at the conference shared certain special dialects, not to say jargons); my particular social circles (gourmet cooking clubs, chamber music societies, bowling leagues); my generation (*I* happen to know what it means to be "cooking with gas" or to "consider joining the CCC until I find a job," yet most younger people today do not); my epoch (no one in the nineteenth century organized a conference anything like "The Politics of Interpretation," and if anybody from that time attended ours, much of what we said would have been unintelligible—not just because of lexical difficulties but because our language places quite different values on the very words we inherit from that time); my political party; the special institutions I have belonged to (my college, my trade school, my church—Bakhtin seems to have been deeply and even "dangerously" religious[10]—my neighborhood ethnic group); my family, with its private jokes and ethnic echoes; even my particular political "day" (the way I talked during Watergate is different from how I talk during Reagan's Revolution).

> At any given moment of its historical existence, language [and of course my own resources of language] is heteroglot from top to bottom: it represents the co-existence of socio-ideological contradictions between the present and the past, between differing epochs of the past, between different socio-ideological groups in the present, between tendencies, schools, circles and so forth, all given a bodily form. These "languages" of heteroglossia intersect each other in a variety of ways, forming new socially typifying "languages."[11]

10. The claim that Bakhtin's own base is finally religious is not accepted by all Bakhtin scholars. It is sometimes said that the claims about his religious beliefs were invented by those who preferred to see him as in opposition to the regime. But there can be no question that he sees the effort to improve the possibilities of genuine critical understanding among undiminished voices as at the heart of all human endeavor. And his ultimate reason for this placement is obviously cosmic, not political or in any sense "merely personal." I am aware that to say that he is clearly religious in this sense gets us nowhere in resolving the debated question of his degree of orthodoxy. That question is touched on by several contributors to the forum on Bakhtin.

11. Bakhtin, "Discourse in the Novel," *The Dialogic Imagination*, p. 291.

I run through all this in some detail to underline the omission that you will have noticed. Is it not remarkable to discover no hint in such a penetrating and exhaustive inquiry into how our various dialects are constituted, no shadow of a suggestion in the lists and the "and so forths" of the influence of sexual differences, no hint that women now talk or have ever talked in ways different from men's? The omission may not seem strange if we view Bakhtin in the light of Western literary criticism, which has seldom acknowledged separate female voices. And it is not strange, in the light of the almost exclusively male criticism in the Soviet Union during Bakhtin's lifetime. But surely it is strange discovered in a Bakhtin. The omission is so glaring that it makes one long for the skill to make up for it. If only we could have the work of a Bakhtin who had, in violation of all history, undergone a full "raising of consciousness" and decided to add one more source of our voices, perhaps the most important of all, to his contrapuntal chorus.[12]

4

Despite the many differences between Bakhtin's situation and our own, I see strong similarities that make his version of dialectical thinking peculiarly useful to us now. Various formalisms and scientific structuralisms offer themselves, each one promising to provide the language of languages, the one right way. In reaction, various antiscientific rebels recently have raided the scientific bastions, insisting on freedom from the restraints of system or the need for proof.[13] And among these we witness the conflict I have described between those who would find their freedom in an autonomous artistic domain (even while sneaking

12. There are obvious parallels between Bakhtin's dialogical enterprise and the work of prominent Western critics of positivism: Kenneth Burke, Michael Polanyi, Richard McKeon, Roland Barthes, John Dewey, George Herbert Mead and other founders of "social psychology," and cultural anthropologists like Clifford Geertz. But Bakhtin's claims seem most forceful about why the drive toward monologism is morally—or even metaphysically—wrong. I like to imagine a dialogue among such pluralizers. Among other topics I would assign them is the question of why, despite their rich underminings, dogmatic monologists still dominate our scene.

13. I'm thinking here not only of the many anti-intentionalists in literary criticism and the many new critics who happily violate the old "affective fallacy" and "didactic heresy" but of a new groundswell of impatience with methodical rigor: the Paul Feyerabends in the physical sciences, the Hayden Whites in history, the Richard Rortys in philosophy. The pragmatic moves that I make in *Critical Understanding* might be considered as part of the same explosion outward from "the text itself" (and its explication) and away from scientific or logical proof. But my pluralism is not "unlimited," and I insist that critical modes and conclusions can be judged as better or worse, tested both by special criteria within a given mode (for example, coherence, correspondence, and comprehensiveness) and by three transmodal values, justice, vitality, and understanding.

ideological judgments into their discourse)[14] and those who proclaim the saving power of this or that ideology.

In attempting to emulate Bakhtin's way of preserving ideological criticism from its characteristic dangers, we might pursue any ideology that any critic has seriously embraced. Every intrusion of "the good" into the domain of "the beautiful" will encounter the same problems and possibilities. But I have chosen the feminist challenge as perhaps the most important, if only because it is the only one that is presented directly to everybody who deals with any literature of any period or culture. As I offer a version of it now, I naturally hope that you will find it recognizably close to what you think about misogyny or androcentrism in literature, in any of their forms, open or disguised. But if you happen to find my version of a feminist standard offensive, then please slot *that* anti-ideology—itself an ideology—into my later argument. Or you may want to make explicit some other code, objecting to works that "feed the complacency of the sleepy bourgeoisie," or that "portray romantic love as the ultimate good," or that "show men as *not* superior to women." It is extremely difficult not to cheat in such matters. An astonishing number of critics have ruled out ideological criticism as always irrelevant—except of course when the ideology in question is one that they care about. If ideological intrusions are critical errors, it is as wrong to condemn a work for being "self-indulgent" or "puritanical" or "jingoist" as to reject it for undermining belief in God, Church, and Country.

Here, then, is my ideology for the day:

1. It is an act of injustice to treat women as members of a class inherently, inescapably inferior to men; it is a manifestation of this act to reduce individual women to objects, not persons, objects to be used or abused for the delectation of men. (On another occasion one could of course reverse the genders, with the happy consequence of decimating the available instances for study.)

2. To *talk* of women unjustly is to act unjustly. Talking in such matters is action. Though the *degree* of an injustice may vary immensely from overt rape to varying kinds of verbal rape to "harmless" jokes about dumb broads, hot chicks, and farmers' daughters, the *kind* of injustice remains for our purposes the same.

3. Therefore works of art that portray women as inherently inferior to men, as objects for use, commit unjust acts—unless, of course, the portrayal is somehow effectively criticized by the work itself. The injustice may be subtle; it may be gross. It can occur in works as sophisticated as *Don Giovanni* or Norman Mailer's *The Deer Park* or as crude as Mickey Spillane's *I, the Jury*. In blatant form it violates the poor fantasy

14. I trace some of these in a paper, "The Language of Praise and Blame in the Arts," delivered at Columbia University's centenary celebration of the founding of the graduate school.

creatures who, for the delectation of the readers of *Penthouse* magazine, find themselves at first frightened and then overjoyed to be gang-raped.

It may seem politically absurd to pick at a possible flaw in a great imaginative author, François Rabelais, as I shall now do, instead of spending my energies on the gross injustices committed daily by the pornographic industry. *Penthouse: The International Magazine for Men* boasts 5,350,000 "average monthly sales," and there are scores of other such magazines, accounting, my neighborhood news vendor tells me, for far more than half of his total business. Yet if Rabelais finds fifty readers in America this month, I'll be surprised. The politics of sexism in America cries out for interpretation, and more of us should be engaged in it. But the consequences for critical theory, and for what we do as teachers, are raised more acutely when we face works that are not so easily dismissed as trashy regardless of ideology.

The question we now face, then, as believers in feminist (or any other) ideology, is this: Am I free, in interpreting and criticizing a work of art, to employ that ideology as one element in my appraisal of the artistic value of that work? Or is my freedom best served by casting off such concerns and letting art works behave in any way they please, so long as they do so "artistically"? To put the challenge at its best, the inquiry would require me to develop here a fully articulated attempt at feminist criticism. Instead I can only sketch a reply to Bakhtin's effort to exonerate Rabelais from the charge of antifeminism.[15]

What might it mean to say, as many have said before me, that Rabelais' great works, *Gargantua* and *Pantagruel,* are flawed by their sexism—or, in the earlier language, their antifeminism? The books were published at a time when the great *querelle des femmes,* begun in medieval times (or one could say in classical times), was still raging;[16] all of the

15. As I reported earlier, it is being said frequently now that the feminist effort to revalue masculinist classics has been outgrown. The movement in its early days, the claim goes, did indeed spend its energies showing how male chauvinism scarred many a work in the official canon, but women have by now gone beyond that rather immature stage—having been caught in unfortunate overstatements and simplified misreadings—and are working at the more mature task of interpreting work *by* women. The new moves are clearly important, as is illustrated throughout the Winter 1981 issue of *Critical Inquiry* on *Writing and Sexual Difference.* The authors provide the best single survey of where feminist criticism now is and a first-class selective bibliography (in footnotes) of where it has been.

16. A good brief summary of the state of the quarrel in Rabelais' time is given by Michael A. Screech in "The Rhetorical Dilemma: the Background to Rabelais's Thought," *The Rabelaisian Marriage* (London, 1958). A bibliography of nearly nine hundred primary Renaissance texts about women, many of them directly concerned with the quarrel, is given in Ruth Kelso's *Doctrine for the Lady of the Renaissance* (Urbana, Ill., 1956). A bibliography of both primary and secondary texts dealing with the question of feminism and Rabelais is given by Julianna Kitty Lerner in "Rabelais and Woman" (Ph.D. diss., The City University of New York, 1976). Every issue of *Etudes Rabelaisiennes* seems to add to the immense

topics of that quarrel receive explicit discussion, showing Rabelais to have been master of every topic of such a debate. From the beginning readers have disagreed about precisely where he stands on the issues: Was he *for* women or *against* them? What critics have not done is to face the immense technical problems raised when we try to ask such questions, or the consequences for criticism if we answer them in this or that way.

The technical problem is primarily that of deciding what it is that we are to judge. A surprising amount of worthless attack and defense has been conducted as if the problem is to determine what Rabelais *says* about women, collecting favorable and unfavorable propositions from the works and balancing them against each other. But surely what we shall want to grapple with is not words or propositions in isolation but the total "act of discourse" that the author commits. Rabelais cannot be blamed for an act of injustice unless we have some reason to believe that his work as a whole—the complete imaginative offering, the experience the work makes possible for us—is vulnerable to the charge.[17] In short, ideological criticism depends on discovering the ideology *of* the form.

Judging isolated parts is particularly pointless in a work as rich as Rabelais', offering as it does a marvelous encyclopedia of every conceivable crazy way of talking. An easy and useless case for the charge of sexism could be made—and indeed it has often been made—simply by listing the immense number of moments in which women are degraded, mocked, humiliated, or explicitly pronounced as inferior to men. One character, Rondibilis, argues for example that a woman is inherently, simply, biologically, a failed or botched man. He describes all of her grotesque flaws and concludes:

> I've thought it all over a hundred and five times, and I am sure I do
> not know what conclusion to come to, unless it is that, in turning
> out woman, Nature had more in mind the social delectation of man
> and the perpetuation of the human species than she did the per-
> fecting of individual womankind.[18]

bibliography. It is no exaggeration to say that by now the literature on this one aspect of Rabelais' work alone is so extensive that no one can pretend to do more than select from it.

17. I deliberately avoid the term that hovers in the background here, "speech act." The connotations of that term, as used by most people, are much too narrowly verbal or propositional for my purposes. Though speech-act theory has to some degree corrected the desiccations of some earlier systems of linguistic analysis, it still tends to do scant justice to the richness of human action performed by any developed literary work. Questions about the rhetorical effectiveness of an interchange tend to be ignored; in the special jargon that has almost become public currency, the connection between the illocutionary and the perlocutionary act is in effect broken—not always, of course, and not programmatically, but see, for example, J. L. Austin, *How to Do Things with Words* (Oxford, 1962), the last half of lecture 9.

18. Rabelais, *Third Book, The Portable Rabelais*, trans. and ed. Samuel Putnam (1929; Harmondsworth, 1977), p. 477; chap. 32 in the original. It should be noted that the *Third*

It is really astonishing to see how many critics from the sixteenth century on have taken such statements as self-evidently coming from Rabelais himself, proving his sexism. Regardless of how offensive any such quotations may be, taken out of context they prove nothing until we can establish either how they are intended or—if we reject concern for intentions—how they are actually taken by sensitive readers. And the fact is that it has been equally easy for defenders of Rabelais to find many quotations showing a much different picture.

Consider the utopian Abbey of Thélème at the end of *Gargantua* (that is, of the *First Book*, written, or, at any rate, published, a couple of years after *Pantagruel*, the *Second Book*). In constructing what seems to be his ideal of a human community, Rabelais shows women in a light totally foreign to the vision of Rondibilis: they are admitted to the abbey equally with men; they are given, so the text directly states, equal rights in the daily conduct of the abbey; they are educated in full equality in the same gracious arts and sciences as the men. And they are given equal rights of free choice about how to spend their days. Obviously, Rondibilis could not have created that abbey.[19] Surely the fact that critical history has been able to compile *double* columns, and not just the sexist column that

---

Book was published many years after the first two; but I cannot discern any difference in tone that fundamentally affects our problem. Because it is the most up-to-date and accessible, I have used Putnam's translation for most quotations that follow, giving in the text, when relevant, first the book and chapter reference to the original and then the page number in Putnam. Unfortunately this edition of Putnam's translation is not complete, and he does not provide the original chapter divisions.

19. Another favorite of the defenders of Rabelais is the highly favorable description of the ideal wife given by Hippothadeus as advice to Panurge to help him avoid becoming a cuckold. The theologian first describes all of the qualities of the wife most to be recommended: "Commendable extraction, descended of honest parents, and instructed in all piety and virtue; . . . one loving and fearing God . . . ; and finally, one who, standing in awe of the divine majesty of the Most High, will be loth to offend Him and lose the favourable kindness of His grace, through any defect of faith or transgression against the ordinances of His holy law, wherein adultery is most rigorously forbidden, and a close adherence to her husband alone most strictly and severely enjoined; yea, in such sort, that she is to cherish, serve and love him above anything next to God, that meriteth to be beloved" (3, 3; the Thomas Urquhart–Peter Antony le Motteux trans., ed. Albert Jay Nock and Catherine Rose Wilson, 2 vols. [New York, 1931], 2:538. Putnam, whose translation is in general more reliable than the livelier Urquhart–le Motteux, does not include this chapter in his edition).

A modern feminist might well bridle at the explicitly submissive role assigned here, but what follows has impressed critics looking for evidence in defense of Rabelais:

"In the interim, for the better schooling of her in these instructions, and that the wholesome doctrine of a matrimonial duty may take the deeper root in her mind, you [Panurge] must needs carry yourself so on your part, and your behavior is to be such, that you are to go before her in a good example, by entertaining her unfeignedly with a conjugal amity, by continually approving yourself, in all your words and actions, a faithful and discreet husband, and by living not only at home and privately with your own household and family, but in the face also of all men and open view of the world, devoutly, virtuously and chastely, as you would have her on

the word "Rabelaisian" connotes, exonerates the author at least from simple charges that can be made based on what is said by his characters.

What's more, if surface attitudes count, we ought to do some counting of the attacks on *males*. Here we find hundreds of satirical pages with no references to women whatever. Indeed, *Gargantua* and *Pantagruel,* the two first books, are in no sense "about" women or even "about" men and women together. It is true that much of the *Third Book,* published fourteen years after *Pantagruel,* is ostensibly about Panurge's attempt to decide whether to marry and how, if he marries, to avoid being cuckolded. But anyone who pays attention to what is being satirized when women are discussed will recognize that the central subject is more often something like "zany reasoning" than "the nobility or baseness of women."

Propositions *about* women can tell us nothing, then, until we ask, Who utters them? In what circumstances? In what tone? With what qualification by other utterances? And, most important of all, What is the quality of our emotional response, point by point and overall? Unless we face such questions, we can at most establish that the *narrator,* Alcofribas, exhibits a leaning toward sexism. For all we yet know, Alcofribas could have been used by Rabelais to exhibit sexism ironically, just as Mark Twain sometimes used Huck Finn and others to expose racist language ironically. "Anybody hurt?" asks Aunt Sally. "No'm," Huck replies. "Killed a nigger."

There is no escape then from the task, difficult as it is, of appraising the quality of the response invited by the whole work: What will it do with or to us if we surrender our imaginations to its paths? It is to Bakhtin's credit that in his discussion of Rabelais he faces this question head-on. Generations of critics have accused Rabelais of a kind of moral fault, that of being "Rabelaisian." Standard critical practice has been to say, "Yes, of course: a great comic (or satiric) genius, but unfortunately he is coarse, gross, base; he asks us to laugh in ways that no civilized reader should laugh, at scenes that no civilized reader can enjoy." Bakhtin refuses to offer the easy reply: "Moral questions about comedy or satire represent an absurd confusion of the aesthetic and practical domains." Instead he accepts the charge: if Rabelais is in fact what is usually meant by Rabelaisian, if he asks us simply to snigger at dirty

---

her side to deport and demean herself towards you. . . . Just so should you be a pattern to your wife, in virtue, goodly zeal and true devotion." [Pp. 538–39]

Panurge dismisses this advice with a twist of his whiskers and a claim that he never saw such a woman: "Without all doubt she is dead, and truly, to my best remembrance, I never saw her—the Lord forgive me!" (p. 539). Does this conclusion mock mocking Panurge for his failure to hear what a man must do to deserve a good woman? Or does it mock the theologian for naive and preachy idealism? Readers have seen it both ways. But in either view the question still remains of how such bits are viewed by the work as a whole.

words scrawled on toilet walls, then the book is not by any means worthy of the praise it has received. But if the quality of the imaginative experience, and particularly of the *center* of that experience, our laughter, can be defended on ideological grounds, then Rabelais is redeemed. Thus, though the ideological test is subtle and complex, it is the final test. It cannot be applied in separation from inquiry into the work as a created form: the ideology is not something separable from the form, and the form is not something separable from our emotional engagement with it. (The question of whether judgments about it can be separated from historical placement is something else again; Bakhtin would seem to answer yes and no.)

If this is ideological or "sociological" criticism (the word Bakhtin himself applies to his work on Dostoevsky), it is also affective and historical and expressive. It is both author-criticism and reader-criticism. The laughter we appraise is not only what we infer in Rabelais himself but also what we find in his society as influencing the work and what we find in ourselves. Thus a great deal is at stake when we ask, with Bakhtin, What is the quality of that laughter? Generalized to include all qualities, the question will become, What is the quality of the imagination that wrought this book? And that will be no different from the question, What is the quality of the effects, in us as readers, of reading this book "in its own terms"?

From the beginning, many readers have been offended by the more extreme bits of scatology and bawdry in the book, especially those that seem to ask us to laugh at women *because* they are women and hence inferior. How are we to respond, for example, to the famous episode that almost everyone would consider as in itself sexist, the trick Panurge plays upon the Lady of Paris who refuses his advances? He sprinkles her gown, you will remember, with the ground-up pieces of the genitals of a bitch in heat and then withdraws to watch the sport, as all of the male dogs of Paris assemble to piss on her, head to toe ("la sentens et pissans. . . . C'estoyt la plus grande villanie du monde. . . . un grand levrier luy pissa sur la teste" [2, 22]). She flees through the streets of Paris, pursued and pissed on by more and more dogs, laughed at by all, her story later laughed at again when Panurge tells Pantagruel about it. And Pantagruel, who by this point is by no means clearly distanced from Rabelais, "trouva [le mystère] fort beau et nouveau."[20] Her offense, remember, is simply that she turned Panurge down and—I suppose—that she is a woman of high degree.[21]

20. The scene is often chosen by illustrators and is used for the cover of the paperback *Rabelais and His World*. The illustrators generally soften the harsh details: the dogs are shown scurrying about the great lady, with at most an occasional lifted leg over a slipper.

21. One friend has suggested that the whole scene is centered not on the lady as representative of her sex but as representative of the haughty upper classes. Another friend, closer to Bakhtin, sees it not as ridiculing women but as a healthy comment on our

Or what shall we say about Panurge's suggestion of how to build an impregnable wall? You should build it of women's "what-you-may-call-thems," he says. "What the devil could knock down a wall like that? There is no metal that is so resistant to blows. And then, when the culverins came to rub up against them, you'd damned soon see the blessed fruit of the old pox distilled in a fine rain." The only drawback he can see is that such a wall would attract flies that would "collect there and do their dung," and all the work would be spoiled. But then that difficulty might be obviated; one must wipe (*esmoucheter;* Putnam translates the verb as "fly-swat") them with "nice foxes' tails or a big ass's prick from Provence [gros vietz d'azes]" (2, 15; p. 301).

Bakhtin recognizes that any full defense of Rabelais must deal with the quality of the laughter sought in such moments. Though his main effort is to refute those who would call Rabelais' laughter base or destructive, he makes quite explicit the claim that though Rabelais was not, as many have claimed, on the side of the feminists in the great *querelle,* his laughter, so often using women as its center, is finally the expression of a healthy counter-ideology, an ideology invaluable in his time as in our own. (It is important to see that Bakhtin's lengthy discussion of Rabelais' *attitude toward* women does not contradict my earlier claim that the *voice* of women does not enter his dialogue.)

Bawdy, scatological laughter is for Bakhtin a great progressive force, the expression of an ideology that opposes the official and authoritarian languages that dominate our surfaces. Bakhtin sees Rabelais' period and his work as the last full expression of a folk wisdom that could enjoy a harmonious dialogue between the "lower" body and the "higher" and more official "spirit": the "voice" of the body transforms monologue into chorus. Carnival laughter, the intrusion of everything forbidden or slanderous or joyfully blasphemous into the purified domains of officialdom, expressed a complex sense that the material body was not unequivocally base: every death contains within it the meaning of rebirth, every birth comes from the same region of the body as does the excremental. And the excremental is itself a source of regeneration—it manures life just as the dogs' urine in Panurge's trick becomes the source of a well-known modern creek.

Rabelais in this view represents a possibility that the world later lost, the possibility for what Bakhtin calls "grotesque realism." When Rabelais and his predecessors made sexual and scatological jokes, they were not serving a sniggering laughter that divorced spirit from body, seeing the latter as merely dirty. References to the lower body were not simply

---

sexuality in general. Perhaps both elements are present; both might be encompassed in Bakhtin's notion of carnival laughter. But both seem to me too easy. The whole episode consists of a relatively sustained wooing by Panurge, with only a hint or two of the possibility that the lady's rejection may be hypocritical. The laughter it invites is surely informed with the feeling: *that's* exactly what those resistant bitches deserve.

naughty or degrading: they were used to produce a regenerative, an affirmative, a healing—finally a politically progressive—laughter. When the natural forces of joyful celebration of the lower body reached their peak, in time of carnival, mankind was healed with a laughter that was lost when, in later centuries, the body, and especially the lower body, came to be viewed as entirely negative and shameful.

Bakhtin distinguishes two strands in the "Gallic tradition" of portrayals of women. The ascetic Christian tradition opposed Platonist idealizing of women by showing them as "the incarnation of sin, the temptation of the flesh."[22] But the "popular comic tradition," he says, was in no way simply hostile to women, though it provides plenty of material that may look sexist when viewed out of context through modern eyes. It viewed women as representing "the material bodily lower stratum; she is the incarnation of this stratum that degrades and regenerates simultaneously. She is ambivalent. She debases, brings down to earth, lends a bodily substance to things, and destroys; but, first of all, she is the principle that gives birth. She is the womb. Such is woman's image in the popular comic tradition" (p. 240). Treating her as such, Bakhtin goes on, is by no means to be guilty of antifeminism. "We must note that the image of the woman in the 'Gallic tradition,' like other images in this tradition, is given on the level of ambivalent laughter, at once mocking, destructive, and joyfully reasserting. Can it be said that this tradition offers a negative, hostile attitude toward woman? Obviously not. The image is ambivalent" (p. 241).

It is the treatment of this ambiguous image in later centuries that for him debases it and trivializes it, turning woman into a merely "wayward, sensual, concupiscent character of falsehood, materialism, and baseness" (p. 240). As "considered by [both] the ascetic tendencies of Christianity and the moralistic abstract thought of modern satirists, the Gallic image loses its positive pole and becomes purely negative" (p. 241). Thus we have a double answer in Bakhtin to the question of whether Rabelais was ideologically defensible on the feminist issue. No, he did not support the feminist cause in the great quarrel—but then the feminist position was itself a simplified debasement of women in the misleading form of idealization. On the other hand, yes, he was essentially defensible on the woman question, when we place him in his true tradition, the tradition of the carnivalesque laughter of grotesque realism, the tradition of a true ambivalence about the destructive and energizing powers of the lower body. If we imagine the world that Rabelais imagined, and laugh as he would have us laugh, we are healed.

The defense is impressive, especially since it is buttressed by an immensely energetic and sympathetic reconstruction of Rabelais' histori-

---

22. Bakhtin, *Rabelais and His World*, p. 240; all further references to this work will be included in the text.

cal situation. Surely it is true that we moderns, freed as we have been from our Victorian prejudices, should be able to revel in Rabelais' comedy in something like the healthy spirit in which 'twas writ?

Unfortunately, "we" have all this while been ignoring a crucial question: Who are "we" who laugh, who are those to whom the defense is being written, who are those who are healed by this laughter? The questions raised with great force at the beginning of Said's essay, "Who writes? For whom is the writing being done?" have all this while gone begging. And as soon as we raise them, we see that just as the original *querelle des femmes* was conducted largely by men, accusers and champions, this exoneration of carnival laughter is conducted by and for men, ignoring or playing down the evidence that the book itself largely excludes women. A man of great genius wrote a book offering a rich imaginative experience to men of sensitive and liberal spirit, and a male critic of great genius wrote a defense of that great book, addressed to other men.

It is in the nature of the case that I cannot really demonstrate my claim. I can look you in the eye and assert that if you go read or reread Rabelais now, you will find both a surviving masterpiece and its serious flaw. I can ask you to question male and female readers and try to discover women who like the book *very* much or who like it as much as the many males who have written about it. Or I could take you through a further sampling of passages. What I cannot do is bring before us the very thing I am trying to talk about: the central imaginative experience offered by Rabelais to readers of his time or of ours. Even if given unlimited time, even if I were to read the whole thing aloud to you here and now, I could not demonstrate my case decisively, because what you imagined as you listened would not be precisely what I imagined as I read. It does seem to me extremely unlikely that you would deny my case at the end, but if you did, saying that you saw nothing flawed in all that, where would we turn?

I would be forced as I am forced now to look closely at fragmentary evidence showing who is included and who excluded. An examination of the actual language of almost any passage, whether it at first appears superficially pro- or anti-feminist, shows quite clearly who are the laughers, and how they laugh.

Consider the opening addresses to the readers of each successive book. Those readers are invariably "lads," "drinking comrades," "syphilitic blades," "gentlemen," "Lords," "paternal worships." The *Second Book* begins: "Most illustrious and most chivalrous champions, gentlemen and others, . . . you have already seen, read, and are familiar with . . . *Gargantua,* and, like true believers, have right gallantly given [it] credence; and more than once you have passed the time with the ladies—God bless 'em—and the young ladies, when you were out of any other conversation, by telling them fine long stories from those chronicles . . ." (p. 224).[23] Quite clearly those "honorables dames et damoyselles" are not invited to pick up the book on their own, though they were expected to enjoy their menfolks' retelling of the juicier narratives.[24]

Alerted by such clues we see immediately that though a great deal of the work is addressed to interests and responses we all might share, there is really no passage that counters the general address to males and implied exclusion of female readers. It is not only that there are no significant female characters;[25] it is that even the passages most favorable to women are spoken by and addressed to men who are the sole arbiters of the question.

23. Rabelais' *Gargantua* is not being referred to here but a popular anonymous story of giants: *Les Grandes et Inestimables Cronicques: Du grant et enorme geant Gargantua . . .* published in 1532, the same year as Rabelais' work.

24. A possible exception is the dedication of the *Third Book* to "the soul of Marguerite, Queen of Navarre," urging it to descend from the ecstatic heights of the queen's recently embraced mysticism in order to read "this third history / Of the joyous deeds of good Pantagruel" (p. 386). Since we know that the queen did in fact read his work (see *Oeuvres*, ed. Abel Lefranc, 6 vols. [Paris, 1931], 5:2, n.9), it seems probable that other educated women of the time did so too. But even if we knew that every literate woman read him cover to cover, the knowledge would not affect our conclusions about our question, any more than discovering that many women of our time read Fitzgerald and Faulkner with pleasure would settle whether Fitzgerald's and Faulkner's works are—as I would claim—often marred by sexism.

Many critics slightly alter their accounts, consciously or unconsciously, to soften the realities of Rabelais' views and procedures. Jean Plattard, perhaps the most respected critic and biographer in the first half of this century, changes the whole direction of the opening address. In his report, Alcofribas addresses *Pantagruel* to the "très chevaleureux champions, gentilshommes, honorables dames et damoiselles" (*La Vie et l'oeuvre de Rabelais* [Paris, 1939], p. 37). But in fact he addresses only the men and assumes that they will have recounted to the women some of the more interesting anecdotes of the *Cronicques*. While judging Rabelais to be antifeminist, Plattard barely mentions the episode of the Parisian lady; she is one victim among many, and he gives his reader little hint of what Panurge actually does. Anatole France retells the pissing anecdote like this: "Le lendemain, à l'église, il s'approche de la dame, lui prend son chapelet et lui fait gâter sa robe par des chiens. Indigne vengeance. Telles sont les amours de Panurge; elles ne sont point honnêtes" (*Rabelais* [1909; Paris, 1928], p. 88). That France, the passionate opponent of hypocrisy and deceit, felt it necessary in his praise for the great Rabelais to change "pissed on her head" to "defiled her dress" surely says something about a need to rescue the classic from what it in fact says.

25. There are only two possible exceptions, the giant mothers Gargamelle and Badebec. Gargantua's grief over the death of his beloved wife is sometimes cited, for example, as a sign that women *are* important in the work. But the whole passage is handled as a source of male laughter, as Gargantua balances the two male emotions, grief over losing a helpful wife and joy over gaining a son. The epitaph Gargantua composes concludes with a joke:

HERE LIES ONE NOT TOO REMISS,
WHO DIED THE DAY THAT SHE PASSED OUT. [P. 241]

CY GIST SON CORPS, LEQUEL VESQUIT SANS VICE,
ET MOURUT L'AN ET JOUR QUE TRESPASSA. [3, 3]

Consider again the Abbey of Thélème (1, 52–57; pp. 196–216), where Gargantua and Friar John set up no rules except one: "Fay ce que vouldras"; Do what thou wouldst. To make the rule work, Gargantua has provided that nobody can enter the convent except handsome healthy people who, because they were "free born and well born, well brought up, and used to decent society," possessed "by nature" the unfailing instinct to do right, that is, a sense of honor (p. 214). He explains that all are to be educated alike, male and female: "They were all so nobly educated that there was not, in their whole number, a single one, man or woman, who was not able to read, write, sing, play musical instruments, and speak five or six languages, composing in these languages both poetry and prose" (p. 215).

So far, so good. But now note the summary of who these people are: "In short, there never were seen knights so bold, so gallant, so clever on horse and on foot, more vigorous, or more adept at handling all kinds of weapons. . . . There never were seen ladies so well groomed, so pretty, less boring, or more skilled at hand and needlework and in every respectable feminine activity" (p. 215). The men bold, gallant, good at riding, hunting, and war; the women well groomed, pretty, not boring (not boring *to whom?*), and skilled in handwork and other respectable feminine activities.

Rabelais goes on to reveal—I confess, with considerable diffidence, that I think the revelation quite unconscious—just how equal the ladies really were. "For this reason [that is, because they were all such paragons], when the time came that any member of this abbey . . . wished to leave, he always took with him one of the ladies, the one who had taken him for her devoted follower, and the two of them were then married." And they "remained as ardent lovers at the end of their days, as they had been on the first day of their honeymoon" (p. 215). One must ask, What happens here to the *lady* who might decide on her own to leave the abbey? She is simply not mentioned, not thought about, and never missed, so far as I can determine, until this moment in 1982, though hundreds of pages have been written praising Rabelais for imagining a society providing total equality. Some may object that "it would have been unthinkable in Rabelais' time to go that far, to allow a *lady* that kind of freedom to leave Utopia and return to the real world, taking with her some anonymous will-less male who was her choice." To which I must answer, "Of course. But isn't that what we are talking about: human ideals, how they are created in art and thus implanted in readers and left uncriticized—even by the subtlest of critics who makes it his business to discover ideologies as revealed by language and to do justice to every genuine human voice?"

The truth is that nowhere in Rabelais does one find any hint of an effort to imagine any woman's point of view or to incorporate women into a dialogue. And nowhere in Bakhtin does one discover any suggestion that he sees the importance of this kind of monologue, not even when he discusses Rabelais' attitude toward women.[26]

5

I am suggesting, then, that Rabelais' work is unjust to women not simply in the superficial ways that the traditions have claimed but, to some degree, in its fundamental imaginative act. But I have not established yet either the degree of his offense or the meaning of that offense in our final view of Rabelais.

To undertake this inquiry requires, of course, that I try to exercise my *freedom from* the restraints of certain contemporary dogmas teaching that I should never attempt such a thing in the name of literary criticism. But my *freedom to,* feeble as it may be, is earned by surrendering to certain other contemporary voices, particularly those of feminist critics I have admired, and to the voice of Bakhtin. Surrendering to these voices, some of them providing ideology and one providing a method, I find their ultimate conclusions in conflict, and I have chosen to speak with the feminists, finding Bakhtin in this one respect entirely unpersuasive. I know in advance, of course, that there must be booby traps along this trail that I haven't even dreamed of yet. And I am aware that I have largely bypassed the question of the source of my freedom to make that choice among voices.

Where then, for me, does this, my first and belated effort at feminist criticism, seem to lead? I can imagine someone answering:

> Nowhere, really, because your exercise could self-evidently be per-
> formed, with the same results, on a great majority of the classics
> written before our time. Rabelais was indeed a male-centered au-
> thor writing primarily for males and reinforcing their views that
> women are at best a delectation for the life of man and at worst a
> threat to it; let us admit as well that Bakhtin, otherwise a subtle
> critic of ideologies and pleader for a dialogic imagination, has
> largely excluded women from the dialogue. Nothing in that is
> either surprising or new. According to Bakhtin's own analysis all
> language is not only tainted with ideology—it actually exists *as*
> ideology. Every statement, every work of art, will be ridden with
> ideologies—which means that even the most polyphonic work must
> exclude, simply by its existence, some languages in order to do
> justice to others. We could not even have *Gargantua* and *Pantagruel*
> without the raucous bawdry that you have judged to be sexist. It
> doesn't matter to a serious criticism that a given work is built upon

26. If it were my purpose to pick at Bakhtin, I could cite many more signs of his casual assumption that women are not present. See, e.g., his *Rabelais and His World,* pp. 420–21.

offenses to this or that group, since all works will commit offenses to *many* groups. Why can't we simply place Rabelais in his time, and Bakhtin in *his,* and accept them for what they are?

One reads many statements of this kind, particularly by male critics, in response to what they consider the excesses of feminist criticism.[27] Often the response is reinforced by reference to the widely accepted belief considered earlier, that ideological criticism is simply forbidden—uncritical, old-fashioned, by definition doctrinaire.

The response simply will not do. For one thing, both Rabelais and Bakhtin would view such neutrality with contempt. As Bakhtin says, "Rabelais has no neutral words; we always hear a mixture of praise and abuse. But this is the praise and abuse of the whole. . . . The point of view of the whole is far from being neutral and indifferent. It is not the dispassionate position of a third party, for there is no place for a third party in the world of becoming. The whole simultaneously praises and abuses" (pp. 415–16). In every part of Bakhtin's work it is clear that he hails Rabelais' simultaneous celebration and comic denigration of the lower body as a mark of an ideological—that is, artistic—superiority to those corrupted divorces of spirit from body that too often followed the move into modernism. He is eager to show, as part of the evidence for Rabelais' greatness, that "in the political conflicts of his time Rabelais took the most advanced and progressive positions" (p. 452). One cannot, in short, do justice to aggressively evaluative novelists and critics without daring to face evaluative questions of one's own.

But in the second place, the defense is itself sexist. It is based on a comfortable acceptance of the open misogyny and covert sexism in other

---

27. But not only male critics. The "apology by historical placement" plays a heavy role in Julianna Kitty Lerner's claim that Rabelais was a feminist: "Rabelais in many ways transcended his contemporaries in his feminist views" ("Rabelais and Woman," p. 217). Lerner is right that many of Rabelais' contemporaries were much harder on women than he. Reading some of their stuff does indeed provide a valid defense for the *man,* Rabelais, and surely that to some degree excuses the books. Since he wrote at a time when no one, meaning in effect no male, seems to have thought more than ten minutes about what equality for women might mean or about what the religious, literary, and political traditions had done to women, he could hardly be expected to leap suddenly into a different order of imagination entirely. Indeed I have already given evidence that with far less historical excuse I accepted without criticism, until well past middle age, something like the perspective he offers. A man who was able to write an entire dissertation on *Tristram Shandy* without once even thinking about, let alone mentioning, so far as I can remember, the problem of its sexism, can hardly feel any moral superiority in his critique of Rabelais. Only now does it occur to me to check such a matter as my youthful bibliography: How many women, do you suppose, had written on *Tristram Shandy,* in nearly two hundred years, with sufficient interest (for me) to include them in my highly selective fifty-item bibliography? Exactly two, both Germans, both writing in the 1930s, about questions of form and technique. I remember that I had *read* Virginia Woolf and others on Sterne, but they are not listed.

classics. The fact that Rabelais is far from unique is the very reason why a feminist critique is important. If Rabelais were alone, if the other classics of our tradition were addressed equally to men and women, portraying both with equality, implanting favorable or unfavorable stereotypes in full impartiality, then the tradition itself would criticize Rabelais for us, and we would have no worries. But of course the reverse is true. Many a classic that seems less offensive on its surface turns out on close reading to be more sexist than Rabelais' masterpiece. Indeed, many later canonic works, like *Tristram Shandy,* borrowed and cheapened Rabelais' materials and effects, as Bakhtin shows.[28] The tradition thus does not, on the whole, criticize his work and mitigate its possible effects in constituting readers' views of women. Rather, insofar as it may excuse Rabelais as one of many, it exacerbates our problems in thinking about this kind of fault, wherever it is found. If our goal is not to arrive at fixed labels but to find better ways of talking about ideological faults, we merely postpone our problem when we blame the absent cronies, not the thief who got caught.

Finally, the answer will not do, just because—and here is a scandal indeed—I find that my pleasure in some parts of this text has now been somewhat diminished by my critical act. This is not a theoretical matter. If it were, I could perhaps reject it or change my theory to fit my reading. The fact is that reading now, try as I may to "suspend my disbelief," reading *now* I don't laugh at this book quite as hard or quite as often as I used to.

When I read, as a young man, the account of how Panurge got his revenge on the Lady of Paris, I was transported with delighted laughter; and when I later read Rabelais aloud to my young wife, as she did the ironing(!), she could easily tell that I expected her to be as fully transported as I was. Of course she did find a lot of it funny; a great deal of it *is* very funny. But now, reading passages like that, when everything I know about the work as a whole suggests that my earlier response was closer to the spirit of the work itself, I draw back and start thinking rather than laughing, taking a different kind of pleasure with a *somewhat* diminished text. And neither Rabelais nor Bakhtin can be given the credit for vexing me out of laughter and into thought: it is feminist criticism that has done it.

It is not hard to predict what some will want to say to *that:* I've lost my sense of humor or I don't know how to read "aesthetically." But if you really want to take a neutralist position on such a matter, you must be ready to imagine, or to conceive of some woman's imagining, an alternative scene in which the lover is a woman, not Panurge, and the dogs are led to piss on a man as the comic butt.[29] If you can imagine

---

28. What I am saying can be said considerably more strongly about the most influential translation in English, that of Urquhart and le Motteux.

29. In an early draft of this paper I attempted to construct such a scene. The construction simply would not work. One woman friend said that it was in "impossibly bad

yourself finding such a scene *as* funny as male readers have traditionally found the actual scene, or if you think the masterpiece undiminished by the substitutions, then perhaps you are that perfect reader we are all advised to emulate: one who is freed of ideological biases, one who reads aesthetically. But of course I won't believe you. Bakhtin is right: none of us can be freed from ideological biases; what we can hope to be freed from is a kind of monologism that turns all ideologies into falsehoods.

6

Any critic, male or female, who tries to break through the hegemony of male voices is going to sound, as I have no doubt sounded here at least to some readers, a bit marginal, perhaps greatly so. Everyone who has attempted feminist criticism can tell you stories of how that kind of marginality feels.

But it is not the marginality that troubles me; what was extremely daring fifteen years ago is now only slightly marginal and tomorrow may be mainstream. What worries me rather are the two violations that I have committed along my way. I have said that Rabelais' work, though to me still a great classic, is flawed by its sexism. I could also have shown that it is flawed by other ideological limitations, such as the author's total obliviousness to the lot of the lower orders—those slaveys whose daily ministrations make possible the freedoms of the Abbey of Thélème.[30] I have spent my time on the ideological fault, not on the greatness, thus doing a disservice to Rabelais, especially for any reader who may come to my discussion without personal knowledge of his full genius. Similarly, I have said that Bakhtin is a great dialectical critic who provides a path we might follow. Yet I have dwelt more on a voice he leaves out than on the power of his achievement.

Two distortions, then, distortions built into my enterprise from the beginning. But if we take Bakhtin seriously in his pursuit of a polyphonic language that is rigorously critical, we find built into the project the proper form of correction. Whatever monologic distortions I have committed cannot be corrected by anything I might say in a parenthesis,

---

taste." That was hardly what was wrong with it, though, because the original is in impossibly bad taste, too.

30. One could wish that all of the modern spirits who have hailed the Abbey of Thélème and its free-spirited motto as a classic of liberalism had read what we might call the fine print about those plentiful servants, the "functionaries" who dress and feed and clean and barber the blessed monks and nuns. They live in houses nearby the abbey: "houses that were well lighted and well equipped, in which dwelt the goldsmiths, lapidaries, embroiderers, tailors, gold-thread-workers, velvet-makers, tapestry-makers, and upholsterers; and there each one labored at his trade and the whole product went for the monks and nuns of the abbey" (1, 52; p. 213).

but they can be corrected by anyone who returns to listen to the two
masters themselves.

Rabelais, first, will survive gloriously, even if I were to strengthen
my statement of feminist reservations. What has been most obviously
missing from my account is the sheer pleasure of *his* text, the exuberance, the subversive, vitalizing laughter that survives the worst that can
be said about its sources. If you do not return to Rabelais for that fun (or
to other accounts like Erich Auerbach's that do it more justice), your
freedom to add an alien voice to Rabelais' dialogue will have been dearly
bought. At the same time, I am convinced, with no possibility of providing evidence, that Rabelais himself would have welcomed my effort at
intruding a new voice into his chorus. As Auerbach says, "The revolutionary thing about his way of thinking is not his opposition to Christianity [or to any other single belief], but the freedom of vision, feeling,
and thought which his perpetual playing with things produces, and
which invites the reader to deal directly with the world and its wealth of
phenomena."[31] The essential artistic drive of Rabelais will thus criticize
both himself *and* me, no doubt with raucous laughter.

Similarly, Bakhtin, if given a chance, will respond triumphantly, and
his response will be, as always, at least double. I hear him saying:

> None of the voices in your troubled dialogue-with-yourself can be
> taken as justified without the correction of other voices. To those
> who, like you, would join the effort to bring the long suppressed
> voices of women into critical dialogue, reviving as you do so an
> ethical and political criticism that risks putting art into some kind of
> subordinate place, I would warn against turning art into a simple
> message. Don't reduce fictions and the criticism of fictions to a
> simple conflict of doctrines or dogmas. Don't assume that an idea
> expressed in a great complex imaginative work is exactly the same
> as that "same" idea when it is extracted and restated in your critical
> work. Art can do what no other human activity can do, and you will
> not find freedom of interpretation by a simple rejection of what
> seemed to be said by it, and by its critics, in the past.
>
> But as for my own failure to invite women into the discussion
> [I hope he might go on], it illustrates perfectly my point about the
> dangers of monologue and the need for a deliberate drive for
> heteroglossia. It had not occurred to me that sexual difference
> might yield a further source of "hybridization." Now that I see the
> possibility, my task is to look more closely at what women writers
> have said and at what they are now saying. If I have committed the
> sin, in my discussion of Rabelais, of treating women not as subjects
> but as objects, objects of male laughter and male-dominated in-

31. Erich Auerbach, *Mimesis: The Representation of Reality in Western Literature*, trans.
Willard Trask (1953; Garden City, N.Y., 1957), p. 242.

tellectual dispute, then their critique might be for me as important as carnival laughter has been for others at other times.

But we need not rely on imagined words. Toward the end of *Rabelais and His World,* Bakhtin offers the words to describe our situation:

> In the sphere of literary and artistic creation it is impossible to overcome through abstract thought alone, within the system of a unique language, that deep dogmatism hidden in all the forms of this system. The completely new, self-criticizing, absolutely sober, fearless, and gay life of the image can start only on linguistic confines [is that to say, perhaps, the borders between an older sexist "language" and a new feminist voice?].
>
> In the system of one language, closed to all others, the image is too strictly imprisoned to allow . . . [a] "truly divine boldness and shamelessness." . . . We repeat, another language means another philosophy and another culture but in their concrete and not fully translatable form. The exceptional freedom and pitiless gaiety of the Rabelaisian image were possible only on the confines of [borders between?] languages. [Pp. 472–73]

7

Even if we could hear Rabelais and Bakhtin brought back into full voice, we would still be left with a multitude of questions, difficulties, and objections. To me, the most troublesome objections are those based on the appeal to historical placement. To wrench Rabelais and Bakhtin out of their moments and then blame them for not seeing the world my way is to risk violating not only their integrity but my own as well. Everything I know about trying to understand someone requires me to suppress my "local" biases and enter as intimately as possible into the alien moment.

The objection seems to me to hold, so long as I am thinking about justice to the *men,* Rabelais and Bakhtin. It would be absurd to blame them for faults that I would almost certainly have exhibited, living in their time and place (see n. 27 above). Even the works themselves, so long as we view them as objects to be understood, must surely be viewed only in the light cast by their own historical setting.

But the objection has its own difficulties, difficulties that perhaps reveal a permanent irreconcilability of a fully historical and a fully critical view. There is first the plain fact that nobody ever manages fully to enter an alien period or culture. We bring ourselves with us wherever we go; we cannot ever deliberately forget the voices that have become "internally persuasive." I must always look skeptically at anyone's claim to have judged authors entirely according to "the standards of their own times." It will be an ideal that I constantly strive for, when I am attempting to discover what any work of art *is* (or, in another critical language, what it is "attempting to do to me"). But it is a permanently elusive ideal, and criticism should always be seeking ways of uncovering our failures to understand and the grounds for such failures.

But there is a more serious problem with the historical objection. Though it is true that Rabelais the man cannot be justly blamed for not being someone else living at another time, it is also true that the "Rabelais" *I* have is here and now. I do not possess Rabelais' works *then;* I possess them, if at all, *now.* I read him as I read anyone: in my own time. Whatever he does to me will be done in my time, not his. There is thus a quite obvious truth to the once famous and often refuted claim by T. S. Eliot in "Tradition and the Individual Talent"—that the whole literary tradition exists simultaneously and is shifted somewhat whenever a new work is added. For me, here and now, the power of any classic to work on me and to reshape me, for good or ill, is in one sense ahistorical. All works I rework speak to me where I am, and they speak, more often than not, conflicting messages. To pretend that they all are equally defensible, because when seen in their own time they are equally explicable, is to dodge my own life with them. The only way I can do justice to their history is to re-create that history in myself. Some of that work is done for me simply by my inevitably imbibing whatever traditions are alive in my time. Some of it can be done by hard work and thought. But even at best, I still have only the Rabelais I have and not the Rabelais that any one of his contemporaries could have enjoyed.

A related problem lies in the selectivity of our ideological attention and thus of our willingness to excuse on historical grounds. Our own interests dictate concern about some ideological deflections and not others. How many faults and of what kinds are we willing to forgive, and why? Why is it that some ideological conflicts between myself and an author seem like faults, and others, like my disagreement with Rabelais about many religious doctrines, or about the casual and grotesque mistreatment of animals, or about the trustworthiness of Italianate lawyers, or about the quality of scholarship at the Sorbonne, seem hardly worth mentioning? And why, among the faulty views, do some seem to affect the quality of the work while others do not matter?

I can only hint at an answer here, considering briefly another act of injustice that on any abstract scale might seem much worse than humiliating women: Rabelais' cruel indifference to the burning of heretics. Michael Screech points to jokes about such burnings and concludes that in *Gargantua* Rabelais "positively incites Francis I to send the Principal of the Collège de Montaigu to the stake, together with his cronies."[32]

---

32. Screech, *Rabelais* (Ithaca, N.Y., 1979), p. 73; all further references to this work will be included in the text.

Screech's defense is a historical placement: "Renaissance Christians were, on the whole, highly selective with their pity," and besides Jean de Caturce (if that is who the Principal was in fact) was a puritan who tried to substitute Christian prayers for the carnival buffoonery of Twelfth Night—"a sectarian extremist whose death would not call forth Rabelais' pity as a matter of course. All the great figures of the time seem impervious to the sufferings of those they fundamentally disagreed with" (pp. 72, 73).

To say that "everybody else was doing it" seems a rather feeble excuse for cruelty to heretics. Yet curiously enough it works better for laughter about heretic burning than for the ridicule of women *as* women. No doubt this is partly because the reasons for the two forms of ridicule are disproportionate: to mock individuals because of something they have done or might do to you and yours is really quite different from laughing at a person because she belongs to the wrong half of the race.

Not only are the reasons of a different kind, but the likely moral effects will trouble me in different ways and degrees. Whatever harm Rabelais might do in reinforcing his contemporaries' willingness to burn heretics or to witness the burning without pity is, viewed from our time and place, scarcely threatening. But there is no modern reader, however up-to-date, who is immune to the effects of reading about how men and women treat each other. The specific ideology on which Rabelais' laughter often depends is in 1982 still a dominant ideology of our culture: women are fair game; they are sillier than men, as nine out of ten television comedies proclaim; it is funnier to set pissing dogs onto their fine gowns than onto male finery. Unlike most other views that we might dispute, this one goes to the very heart of our picture of what it is to be human. And unlike most others, it involves everyone in its threat, not just some minority and not just unsophisticated readers. *If* a work may be harmful, it threatens us all.

The ideological differences that bite, then, are those that present alternatives still tempting in our own time—or in our own souls. For someone like myself, having changed my views, however slightly, about the greatness of a classic, the effect is something like that of losing a brother, or a part of my past, or a part of myself. My need to sharpen my statement of the differences is thus strengthened both by my regret at the loss and by my fear that others, my contemporaries, may still be taken in by what was once for me seductive. If this is so, it is another reason for saying that any ethical criticism we try to develop in a systematic way must take into account an ethics of the reader as well as an ethics of what is written. Works that might be ideologically worrisome for some readers in some times might later be excused. We might very well conclude that the same Homer who was feared and banned by Plato as a bad "core curriculum" for Greek youth should present no ideological problem for modern youth, who are not likely to change their notions of the gods very much as they read the *Iliad*.[33]

A third and even more difficult question concerns the import of all this for our judgments about literary traditions. If Rabelais and Bakhtin have revealed a failure of imagination, a failure that for both is in direct conflict with what they seem most strongly to stand for, we can never again listen to them uncritically. And if we say that of *them,* we are simultaneously saying it of most of the classics. I have heard men say—not often in the presence of women—that the feminist critique is absurd, because if you took it seriously you would have to repudiate almost the whole of Western literature and most of the rest of the world's literature, too. "Repudiate" is no doubt too strong a word, but it is quite true that if what I have been doing here has any legitimacy at all, then most of the world's classics are indeed placed into a controversy that will never be easily resolved. Not thrown out, not censored, not burned, but thrown into controversy. In short, I finally accept what many feminist critics have been saying all along: our various canons have been established by men, reading books written mostly by men for men, with women as eavesdroppers, and now is the time for men to join women in working at the vast project of reeducating our imaginations.

If we choose to listen, we will find no simple direction. As male critics are too fond of pointing out, feminist critics present no unified front; and it is probably at least as easy to write a bad feminist indictment as to write a bad *explication de texte* or historical study. The easy feminist way would be to think only in terms of *freedom from* all those wicked male voices of the past. But as Bakhtin would want to point out, the very language with which one does the casting off will be a collection of inherited languages.

8

In that collection we can always expect to find legitimate male voices asking whether after all feminist perspectives are not as biased as masculine perspectives. And are we then to have many canons, one for each legitimate ideological interest? Or should we hope for a time when all

---

33. My speculation here about the relative degree of offense was stimulated in part by criticism from my colleague, Gregory Colomb. Since the effort to do feminist criticism is entirely new to me, I have sought and received far more advice about this essay than I usually do. In addition to Colomb I wish to thank Elizabeth Abel, Phyllis Booth, James Chandler, Marcel Gutwirth, Robert von Hallberg, David Hanson, Françoise Meltzer, W. J. T. Mitchell, Robert Morrissey, Janel Mueller, Wendy Olmsted, Nancy Rabinowitz, Judith Sensibar, Michael Silverstein, Richard Strier, Frantisek Svejkovsky, Charles Wegener, and James White—not to mention many who offered criticism at the conference and some whose criticism must have been so devastating that memory has repressed the encounter.

readers will exercise imaginations so fully educated that only those works written *for* all will be enjoyed *by* all?

Nobody can answer such questions with much confidence. But my hunch is that we will always have—and need—alternative canons and controversy about our canons. As Hume says, concluding "Of the Standard of Taste," though standards are not merely a matter of individual preference, we cannot expect that all people of taste will on all occasions recognize the merits of all works of high quality. The poems I loved as a young man I may not respond to at all as an old man; the British reader will rightly admire some works that the French cannot even understand. What's more, he goes on, we all find ourselves disagreeing with the "manners" portrayed in some admired works, and each of us will be inclined to respond somewhat differently depending on whether the differences are great or small.

But Hume then makes an important distinction that I think applies directly to our problem here.

> Where any *innocent* peculiarities of manners are represented . . . they ought certainly to be admitted; and a man who is shocked with them, gives an evident proof of false delicacy and refinement. . . . But where the ideas of morality and decency alter from one age to another, and where *vicious* manners are described, without being marked with the proper characters of blame and disapprobation, this must be allowed to disfigure the poem, and to be a real deformity. I cannot, nor is it proper I should, enter into such sentiments; and however I may excuse the poet, on account of the manners of his age, I can never relish the composition. The want of humanity and of decency, so conspicuous in the characters drawn by several of the ancient poets . . . diminishes considerably the merit of their noble performances, and gives modern authors an advantage over them. [My italics]

Though the language of innocence and viciousness is not fashionable, I hope that we could all agree that some ideological faults, like debasement of women, must ever be taken seriously, while others may be merely "innocent peculiarities."

In all of his sensitive discrimination of the sources of prejudice, curable and incurable, Hume gives no hint (shall I say that *of course* Hume gives no hint?) that the "men" who may fail in their taste might suffer from sexual prejudice. The only females mentioned are certain characters in earlier literature who exhibit absurd manners that should not trouble us. But Hume's oversight should not obscure the usefulness of his way of accommodating irreducible differences of perspective. If old "men" and young "men" are different in their "passion," they will always exhibit some differences in responding to literature; to the extent that women and men *really* differ—nobody knows now and perhaps nobody ever will know the extent to which we do—they will respond differently to those works of art that engage with those differences.

   With this concession made to perspectivism, and with many other problems left in the air, a final word about freedom. Can we not say that if there is no freedom of interpretation, there is no significant freedom of any kind? If the critic of a given repressive regime and the *Gauleiter* who arrests and tortures that critic are expressing equally convention-bound preferences, and if, in *interpreting* their interpretations, I am simply playing a game according to unbreakable rules imposed on me by my culture or ideological perspective—if, in other words, there is never any real sense to the question, Which one of these two interpreters has produced a better reading of the dictator's words?—then of course all political questions are reduced to questions of power, and we are back in Thrasymachus' trap: Justice is whatever power says it is, and if you disagree with me, then of course I will seek ways of showing you, by all the means available, that I am right; I will bludgeon you with propaganda, or if that does not work, I'll use truncheons or prisons.
   But no reader of Bakhtin can conclude that we are in Thrasymachus' trap. He shows us that we are not freed merely by learning how to cast off the powers that made us; we are freed by taking in the many voices we have inherited and discovering, in our inescapably choral performance, which voices must be cast out of our choir. Each of the voices within is already itself such a chorus, and thus each voice was always at least partially free even as we took it in.
   Perhaps it remains true that the freedom to make new interpretations by exercising freedom from old methods and assumptions is more important in some epochs than in others. There may even have been past moments when freedom from established interpretations was not even possible, whether desirable or not. One can place oneself, Bakhtin says, "outside one's own language only when an essential historic change of language occurs. Such precisely was the time of Rabelais. And only in such a period was the artistic and ideological radicalism of Rabelaisian images made possible" (p. 471).
   We seem to be living in another such period. What would it mean to make it work for us as something other than a threatening chaos?

Introduction to Extracts from "Notes" (1970–1971)

In these notes, we catch Bakhtin meditating, yet again, on the central concerns of his life: "unfinalizability," responsibility, authorship, the unrepeatability of the utterance, and the genres of silence. His jottings, alternately aphoristic, poetic, and scholarly, reflect the development of his ideas as they were still evolving. The meaning of "unfinalizability" itself remains unfinalized.

He criticizes contemporary literary scholarship for the various ways it has abridged true dialogue by misunderstanding the very nature of understanding. In writing about the past, we fail to portray it as open (as time always is at each moment), as something that possessed undeveloped but existing potentialities. History, he implies, is essentially a matter of potentials.

Contemporary scholars also fail to learn from the past when they reduce it to a mere anticipation of the present. We may infer, for example, that reading works of other ages as essentially modernist in theme (everything is about language), tone (everything is ironic), or technique (everything is self-referential) not only distorts them but also impoverishes us. By making others a version of ourselves, we transform them so that we learn nothing.[1] It is no less impoverishing to empathize with others so much that we silence our own voice. We learn most when we engage in dialogic interaction. Such interaction should not exhaust humanist inquiry, but could be more common than it now is. Marxist dialectics is also but the corpse of dialogue.

Bakhtin calls attention to the reasons, both positive and negative, for his own inconsistencies: on the one hand, his ideas are in the process of development ("internal open-endedness"); on the other hand, there are also genuine shortcomings in terminology and argument ("external open-endedness"). The dialogue of Bakhtin breaks off (as true dialogues must) with possible, though not necessary, continuations and exchanges projected.

---

1. The argument applies to the study not only of other ages but of other cultures as well. See, for instance, Dell Hymes' insistence that "texts fight back" in two articles on native American oral literature: "Language, Memory, and Selective Performance: Cultee's 'Salmon Myth' as Twice-told to Boas," *Journal of American Folklore* 98, no. 390 (1985): 391–434, and "Anthologies and Narrators" (unpublished manuscript).

Extracts from

"Notes" (1970–1971)

[1–2] Irony has penetrated all languages of modern times (especially French); it has penetrated into all words and forms. . . . Irony is everywhere—from the minimal and imperceptible to the loud, which borders on laughter. Modern man does not proclaim; he speaks. That is, he speaks with reservations. . . . The speaking subjects of high, proclamatory genres—of priests, prophets, preachers, judges, leaders, patriarchal fathers, and so forth—have departed this life. They have all been replaced by the writer, simply the writer, who has fallen heir to their styles. . . . The novel, deprived of style and setting, is essentially not a genre; it must imitate (rehearse) some extra-artistic genre: the everyday story, letters, diaries and so forth. . . .

[3] The word removed from dialogue: it can only be cited amid rejoinders; it cannot itself become a rejoinder among equally privileged rejoinders. This word had spread everywhere, limiting, directing, and retarding both thought and live experience. During the process of struggling with this word and expelling it (with the help of parodic antibodies), new languages were also formed. . . .

[5, 7] . . . *Quietude* and *silence* (the absence of the word). The pause and the beginning of the word. The disturbance of quietude by sound is mechanical and physiological (as a condition of perception); the disturbance of silence by the word is personalistic and intelligible: it is an entirely different world. In quietude nothing makes a sound (or something does not make a sound); in silence, nobody *speaks* (or somebody does not speak). Silence is possible only in the human world (and only for man). Of course, both quietude and silence are always relative. . . . Silence— intelligible sound (a word)—and the pause constitute a special logosphere, a unified and continuous structure, an open (unfinalized) totality.

[14] The study of culture (or some area of it) at the level of system and at the higher level of organic unity: open, becoming, unresolved and unpredetermined, capable of death and renewal, transcending itself, i.e., exceeding its own boundaries. . . .

[15] The utterance (speech product) as a whole enters into an entirely new sphere of communication (as a unit of this new sphere), which does not admit of description or definition in the terms and methods of linguistics or—more broadly—semiotics. This sphere is governed by a special law, and its study requires a special methodology and, it should be said outright, a special science (scientific discipline). The utterance as a whole does not admit of definition in terms of linguistics (or semiotics). The term "text" is not at all adequate to the essence of the entire utterance.

[18] The second consciousness and the metalanguage. The metalanguage is not simply a code; it always has a dialogic relationship to that language which it describes and analyzes. . . . The problem of the second consciousness in the humanities. Questions (questionnaires) that change the consciousness of the individual being questioned.

[22, 24] The witness and the judge. When consciousness appeared in the world (in existence) and, perhaps, when biological life appeared (perhaps not only animals, but trees and grass also witness and judge), the world (existence) changed radically. A stone is still stoney and the sun still sunny, but the existence as a whole (unfinalized) becomes completely different because a new and major character in this event appears for the first time on the scene of earthly existence—the witness and the judge. And the sun, while remaining physically the same, has changed because it has begun to be cognized by the witness and the judge. . . . the witness and judge *of the whole* human being, of the whole *I*, is consequently not man, not *I*, but *others*. . . . it can change only the *sense* of existence (to recognize, to justify and so forth); this is the freedom of the witness and the judge. . . .

[32a, 34, 37] The narrow historical horizon of our literary scholarship. Enclosure within the most immediate historical epoch. The lack of definition (methodological) of the very category of the epoch. . . . What we foreground is the *ready-made* and *finalized*. . . . Even in antiquity we single out what is ready-made and finalized, and not what has originated and is developing. . . . Possibility and necessity. It is hardly possible to speak about necessity in the humanities. Here it is scientifically possible only to disclose the *possibilities* and the *realization* of one of them. The repeatable and unrepeatability. . . . We have narrowed it [the past] terribly by selecting and modernizing what has been selected. We impoverish the past and do not enrich ourselves. We are suffering in the captivity of narrow and homogeneous interpretations. . . . One cannot understand understanding as emotional empathy, the placement of the self in the other's position (loss of one's own position). This is required only for peripheral acts of understanding. One cannot understand understanding as a translation from the other's language into one's own language.

[38] Understanding and evaluation. Understanding is impossible without evaluation. . . . they are simultaneous and constitute a unified integral act. The person who understands approaches the work with his own already formed world view, from his own viewpoint, from his own position. These positions determine his evaluation to a certain degree, but they do not themselves always stay the same. They are influenced by the artwork which always introduces something new. Only when the position is dogmatically inert is there nothing new revealed in the work (the dogmatist gains nothing; he cannot be enriched). The person who understands must not reject the possibility of changing or even abandoning his already prepared viewpoints and positions. In the act of understanding a struggle occurs which results in mutual change and enrichment.

[47] Sciences of the spirit; their real field of inquiry is not one but two "spirits" (the studied and the person who studies, which must not be merged into one spirit). The real object of study is the interrelation and interaction of "spirits."

[67] Dialogue and dialectics. Take a dialogue and remove the voices . . . remove the intonations . . . carve out abstract concepts and judgments from living words and responses, cram everything into one abstract consciousness—and that's how you get dialectics.

[68] Context and code. A context is potentially unfinalized; a code must be finalized. . . . A code is a deliberately established, killed context.

[70] Dostoevsky's quests. The journalist. *The Diary of a Writer*. . . . Christ as truth. I ask him. . . .

[71] The problem of the image of the author. The primary (not created) and secondary author (the image of the author created by the primary author). . . . The primary author cannot be an image. . . . When we try to imagine the primary author figuratively, we ourselves are creating his image, i.e., we ourselves become the primary author of the image. The creating image (i.e., the primary author) can never enter into any image he has created. The word of the primary author cannot be *his own* word. . . . Therefore the primary author clothes himself in *silence*. But this silence can assume various forms of expression, various forms of reduced laughter (irony), allegory, and so forth.

[75] Quests for my own word are in fact quests for a word that is not my own, a word which is more than myself; this striving to depart from one's own words, with which nothing essential can be said. I myself can only be a character and not the primary author. The author's quests for his own word are basically quests for genre and style, quests for an authorial position. This is now the most critical problem of modern literature, which leads many to reject the genre of the novel altogether, to replace it with a montage of documents, a description of things, to

bookishness and, to a certain degree, also the literature of the absurd. In some sense all these can be defined as various forms of silence.

[79] In rhetoric there is the unconditionally innocent and the unconditionally guilty; there is a complete victory and destruction of the opponent. In dialogue the destruction of the opponent also destroys that very dialogic sphere in which the word lives. . . . This sphere is very fragile and easily destroyed. . . . Impartiality and *higher* partiality. . . .

[96] Are there genres of pure *self*-expression (without the traditional authorial form)? Do there exist genres without an addressee?

[97] Gogol. The world without names, in which there are only various kinds of sobriquets and nicknames. The names of things are also sobriquets. Not from the thing to the word, but from the word to the thing; the word gives birth to the thing.

[103] Pure denial cannot give birth to an image. In the image (even the most negative one) there is always an aspect of the positive (of love— of admiration). . . .

[105] The unity of the emerging (developing) idea. Hence a certain *internal* open-endedness of many of my ideas. But I do not wish to turn shortcomings into virtues; in these works there is much external open-endedness, that is an open-endedness not of the thought itself but of its expression and exposition. Sometimes it is difficult to separate one open-endedness from another. . . .

Index

Abel, Elizabeth, 149
Abject hero, x, 105, 111–12, 116–19
Absolute language, xi, 123–43
Absolute past, 14, 34
Abstract objectivism, 24, 28, 45, 48
"Addressivity," in utterances, 63–64
Adler, Adolph Peter: and Kierkegaard, 101–4, 115; *Several Sermons,* 101, 102, 103
Aesopian language, 10, 16
Agreement, as a dialogic relationship, 2, 88 n. 8
Allusion: living, 2; non-verbal and verbal, 4
"Already-spoken-about" ("already said"), 50, 83
Althusser, Louis, 52
Amiel, Henri, 139
Anna Karenina (Tolstoy), 15, 126, 129, 130, 131
Anti-languages, 42
Aristotle, 11, 44
"Architectonics of Answerability" (suggested title for unfinished Bakhtin book), 70 n. 2
"Art and Psychoanalysis" (Vygotsky), 36
"Art and Responsibility," x, 17
Artaud, Antonin, 115, 117
Auerbach, Erich, 170
Augustine, Saint, 44
Austen, Jane, 15, 130; *Pride and Prejudice,* 130
Austin, J. L., 46, 157 n. 17
"Author and Protagonist" ("Author and Hero"), x, 70 n. 2
Authorless utterances, 127–28, 135
Authorship, and author, image of, 17–18, 32, 67, 70, 97, 134–35, 177, 181; relation to speaking, 66–67, 83; as response to social world, 69–70; theory of, 17–18, 177. *See also* Creative process, Primary author
Autobiography, non-autobiographical, 141

Bakhtin, Mikhail: absence of feminist voice in theories of, 154, 161; Aesopian language of, 16; and analysis of antifeminism of Rabelais, 156, 159–60, 161–62, 166–67, 171; *"The Architectonics of Answerability,"* 70 n. 2; "Art and Responsibility," x, 17; "Author and Protagonist" ("Author and Hero"), x, 70 n. 2; and Christianity, 11, 15, 17–18, 19, 33, 39 n. 22, 71 n. 16, 153, 153 n. 10, 181; development of theories of, 60, 67–69; *The Dialogic Imagination: Four Essays by M. M. Bakhtin,* vii, 44, 48; "Discourse in Life and Discourse in Art" (Vološinov), 47–48, 51; "Discourse in the Novel," 2, 31, 43, 74; dislike of relativism, ix, x; disputed texts, vii–viii, 16, 37 n. 2, 87 n. 6; diversity of work of, 14–16, 60; and epic, theory of, 14, 34–35; "Epic and Novel," 13, 34–35; ethical concerns, ix–xi; executors of, 15, 16; and Russian Formalism, 9–10, 45, 124; *The Formal Method in Literary Scholarship* (Medvedev), 43, 45, 52, 53–55, 57 n. 22; *Freudianism: A Critical Essay* (Vološinov), vii, xii n. 4, 16, 22, 26–27, 32, 48, 50, 51; "From the Prehistory of Novelistic Discourse," 77; history of works of, vii–ix, 15–16; and the humanities, 1–2, 11–12, 70, 180, 181; and "ideology," 49–55, 150–53; and intentionalism, 17, 154 n. 13; life of, viii, 15–16; and Marxism, xi, 9–11, 15, 84, 86–87, 151; *Marxism and the Philosophy of Language* (Vološinov), vii, ix, xii n. 4, 2, 7, 11, 17, 22, 26, 42–43, 46–47, 49, 50, 52–53, 86, 89; and neo-Kantian philosophy, 60, 61–62, 76, 86; "Notes" (1970–1971), 16–17, 19, 177, (extracts from this article) 179–82; and novel, theory of, 13–15, 34–35, 39 n. 26, 76–77;

21